Praise for *Phenomenal*

"Intricately detailed, impeccably researched, eloquently described stories about the world's most phenomenal places." —*The Oregonian*

"Part travel memoir, part parenting manifesto, and part inquiry into those 'fleeting, extraordinary glimpses of something that left us groping for rational explanations in the quicksand of all-encompassing wonder.'" —Oprah.com

"Henion . . . takes readers around the world in her lovely, lyrical memoir." —*Backpacker*

"Henion pursues her quest with great integrity, and in turn, the reader does too, as we begin to see . . . the true inherent wonder in her world—and in ours." —*Literary Mama*

"What a cool and fascinating ride. Leigh Ann Henion has tackled one of the great questions of contemporary, intelligent, adventurous women: Is it possible to be a wife and mother and still explore the world? Her answer seems to be that this is not only possible, but essential. This story shows how. I think it will open doors for many."
  —Elizabeth Gilbert, author of *The Signature of All Things* and
  Eat, Pray, Love

"A moving and original memoir about the search for transcendence in moments both large and small."
  —Jenny Offill, author of *Dept. of Speculation*

"Leigh Ann Henion's exhilarating book (and life!) is everything the title suggests and more. Reading *Phenomenal* will give you courage—courage to explore the world we live in, and further, courage to explore your self. With moments of breath-stealing beauty, wild intelligence, and unrelenting honesty, *Phenomenal* is a true gift for everyone who's ever been curious."
  —Ruth Ozeki, author of *A Tale for the Time Being*

"Even a cynic reading *Phenomenal* will yearn for a taste of wonder."
  —*Sydney Morning Herald*

ABOUT THE AUTHOR

Leigh Ann Henion has contributed to *The Washington Post Magazine*, *Smithsonian*, *Orion*, and *Oxford American*, among other publications. Henion's debut book, *Phenomenal: A Hesitant Adventurer's Search for Wonder in the Natural World*, was a *New York Times* bestseller. Her work has been cited in three editions of *The Best American Travel Writing*. She lives in the mountains of North Carolina.

Visit the author at leighannhenion.com.

PHENOMENAL

A Hesitant Adventurer's Search for
Wonder in the Natural World

LEIGH ANN HENION

PENGUIN BOOKS

PENGUIN BOOKS
An imprint of Penguin Random House LLC
375 Hudson Street
New York, New York 10014
penguin.com

First published in the United States of America by Penguin Press,
a member of Penguin Group (USA) LLC, 2015
Published in Penguin Books 2016

Portions of the introduction and Chapter One appeared in
different form in *The Washington Post*.

THE LIBRARY OF CONGRESS HAS CATALOGED THE HARDCOVER EDITION AS FOLLOWS:
Henion, Leigh Ann.
Phenomenal : a hesitant adventurer's search for wonder in the natural world / Leigh Ann Henion.
pages cm
ISBN 978-1-59420-471-5 (hc.)
ISBN 978-0-14-310803-0 (pbk.)
1. Henion, Leigh Ann.   2. Spiritual biography.
3. Women shamans—Biography.   I. Title.
BL73.H43A3 2015
910.4092—dc23
[B]
2014036661

Printed in the United States of America
1   3   5   7   9   10   8   6   4   2

DESIGNED BY STEPHANIE HUNTWORK

MAP ILLUSTRATION BY MEIGHAN CAVANAUGH

Penguin is committed to publishing works of quality and integrity.
In that spirit, we are proud to offer this book to our readers; however, the story,
the experiences, and the words are the author's alone.

For Archer
& Matt
& Randall
& Carolyn

Family,
my guiding constellation

The most beautiful thing we can experience is the mysterious.
It is the source of all true art and science.

—EINSTEIN

Don't be satisfied with stories, how things have gone with others.
Unfold your own myth.

—RUMI

CONTENTS

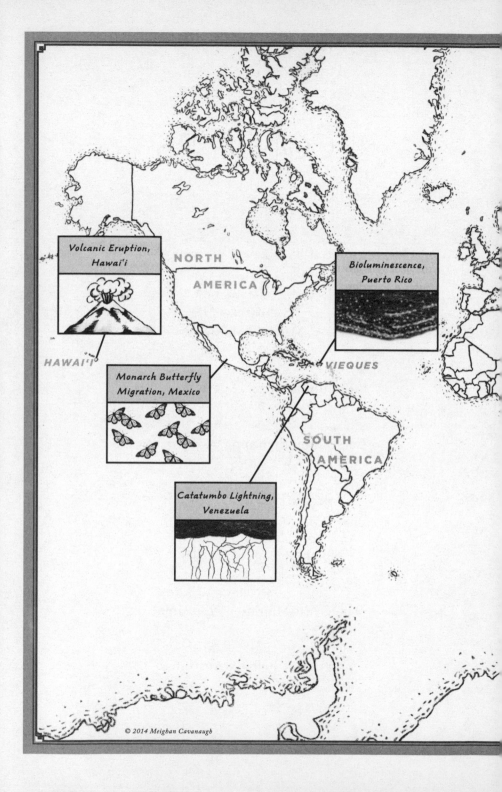

Volcanic Eruption,
Hawaiʻi

Bioluminescence,
Puerto Rico

NORTH
AMERICA

HAWAIʻI

Monarch Butterfly
Migration, Mexico

VIEQUES

SOUTH
AMERICA

Catatumbo Lightning,
Venezuela

© 2014 Meighan Cavanaugh

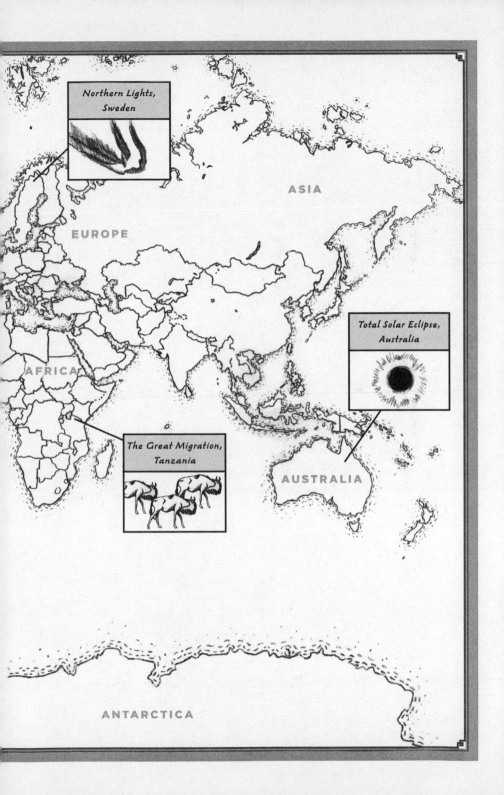

Northern Lights,
Sweden

ASIA

EUROPE

Total Solar Eclipse,
Australia

AFRICA

The Great Migration,
Tanzania

AUSTRALIA

ANTARCTICA

PROLOGUE

A REPORT CAME OVER THE RADIO IN SWAHILI: SOMEONE HAD spotted a cheetah and her cubs.

"We'd have to drive fast to get there. Do you want to go?" my guide David Barisa asked, breathlessly. David was in his thirties, but he had a certain youthful panache given his shaven head, gold-plated sunglasses, and street-savvy nubuck boots. I couldn't tell if his excitement was over the predator sighting or the excuse to speed.

"Sure," I said.

We'd been watching the largest wildebeest herd I'd seen in the Serengeti, roughly 10,000 animals grazing and shuffling their feet in migration. Each year, some 1.3 million wildebeest move full circle through Kenya and Tanzania, following rains. They're joined by zebra and gazelle, as well as a cast of hungry characters that lurk in the fray. And the drama of all this—as it's taught in textbooks—was transpiring before me.

In the distance, thousands of additional wildebeest were clumped on the horizon, moving like silt-colored rivers. Breezes brought the sweet, nostalgic smell of hay. We bounded across rutted roads while David reeled off names of the animal groupings we'd seen over the past few days: clan of hyena, pack of wild dogs, pride of lions, herd of elephants.

"So, what do you call a group of cheetah?" I asked.

"They're usually alone," David said, grinding a gear. "But when I see them together, I just call them a family."

I had to ask because I'm not a scientist. No, I'm a part-time teacher and freelance writer, mother of a young child, wife of a carpenter. So what was I—grader of papers, changer of diapers—doing gallivanting around the Serengeti? Why had I left my husband and two-year-old son back home in the hills of southern Appalachia?

My answer might come across as insane, or—at the very least—overly dramatic.

But here's the truth: I was on an epic quest for wonder.

I'd been chasing phenomena around the world for more than a year when I arrived in the Serengeti, and I still had many miles to go. But my inspiration had been sparked even before I became a mother, when—three years before my son's birth—I visited the overwintering site of the monarch butterfly in central Mexico. Before I accepted the magazine assignment that took me there, I'd never even heard of the monarch migration, during which nearly the entire North American population comes to roost in a small swath of forest. But witnessing millions of butterflies swirling, dipping, and gliding over a single mountaintop gave me an actual glimpse of what I mean when I refer to myself as spiritual but not religious.

And—in difficult times—memories of that experience sustained me.

I don't know that I suffered clinical postpartum depression when my son was born, but I began to empathize with the horror stories the condition can lead to. Inspired by butterflies, I had long ago dreamed up a list of other natural phenomena I'd like to experience. But travel to far-flung lands? Once I had a baby, I considered myself lucky to make it to the grocery store before it was time for bed.

Still, I mused: Children have the capacity to marvel over simple things in nature—leaves, twigs, pebbles. Couldn't exploring just a few of earth's most dazzling natural phenomena—steeped as they are in science and mythology—make the world similarly new again, reawakening that sort of wonder within me? Drudgery, after all, has nothing to do with growing up if we do it right and—beyond tending to the acute physical needs of a child—little to do with what it means to be a good parent.

Right?

Back then, I didn't know that acting out my self-designed pilgrimage would put me in the path of modern-day shamans, reindeer herders, and astrophysicists. I had no idea there were lay people from all over the world, from all walks of life, already going to great lengths to undertake the sorts of phenomena chases I'd dreamed up. Some took odd jobs to stay under the northern lights. Others left white-collar positions to make time for swimming in glowing, bioluminescent bays. These were people who braved pirates to witness everlasting lightning storms, stood on volcanoes, stared into solar eclipses. They trusted their instincts, followed their passions, willfully shaped their days into the lives they most wanted to lead.

And, somewhere along the way, I became one of them.

David pulled into a line of safari vehicles. The cheetah family consisted of a momma and three cubs. We stood in the pop-up roof of our Land Cruiser to see into the heart of their grassy nest. After a few minutes, the mother decided to rise. Her babies followed, in single file, and she crossed the dirt road to approach a wildebeest herd.

When they were still a ways out, the cubs took a seated position. "She's telling them to stay back," David said. The mother moved on.

When she was just beyond the herd, she stopped to watch. "She's teaching them how to stalk," David reported. "How to survive. She's watching for a young wildebeest, the weakest of the herd."

The cubs were dark fuzz balls floating in a sea of grass. The mother cheetah stood taller. All her babies' eyes were on her, watching. The light of day was beginning to fade. A giant elder wildebeest walked five feet in front of her. I gasped. Still, she waited.

"He is too big for her," David said.

Finally, she found a baby wildebeest that had been pushed to the edge of the herd, and she slipped through grass like a fish slicing through a wave. The young wildebeest reacted, going from standing to swerving in seconds flat and, before I could even take a breath, a mother wildebeest appeared. She pushed the baby to the center of the herd, which erupted into honking that rippled across the savanna.

"They're warning each other," David said, like a foreign language interpreter. The cheetah was still, as if she'd forgotten something. "She doesn't like to waste energy chasing something she doesn't think she can catch."

I quietly cheered for the young wildebeest. He was, after all, the main hero of the migratory story. *Wasn't he?* I watched the cheetah turn back toward her babies, who had traced her every move. Her head hung low. She appeared to be sulking. "She's going back to tell them they're going to bed hungry tonight," David said.

There were no clear winners. No easy answers. Only hard questions and survivors. But, because I had, for so long, only seen the pain of the wild on television, I had forgotten that there is also this: Long days of grazing through fields, listening to wind. Whole weeks spent sleeping in trees.

David, who had spent nearly every day of that year cruising the

Serengeti, had seen only four predator kills in his lifetime. But he'd logged thousands of hours of watching animals—prey and predators alike—relaxing. This is the sort of life human bodies were also built for—acute stress and long periods of leisure, not the other way around.

A small group of wildebeest stopped to watch us pass. They were headed to the larger herd. Their life was a process, a cycle, a never-ending circle. But wasn't mine, too? All my life, I'd thought: If I can just get into that college. If I can just make more money. If I can just birth this baby. If I can just get him through those scary first few months. If I can just make it through my first three weeks back at work. If I can just get my son potty trained. If I can just get a book contract. If I can just make it through the next eight nights sleeping alone in a canvas tent. *If I can just. If I can just. If I can just.*

Staring into the field of hooves pounding the earth, it was clear I had been denying myself this: The seasonal migrations of my life, the initiations, would never end. There would always be a proving ground to face. But acknowledging and embracing this was crucial to moving forward. It seemed a path to reduced anxiety, and I could surely use that. Letting go of the abstract idea that at some point my life would be more complete than it was that very moment felt like letting go of some sort of underlying, constant fear I wasn't aware I had. Standing in the center of the Serengeti, it was apparent: I would benefit from balancing my abstract human thoughts with the visceral, phenomena-centered viewpoint of the animals that lived there.

Phenomenal is defined as that which is amazing. It also means that which is directly observable to the senses. And what began as a tour of extraordinary sights had evolved into the story of how—in an abstract, digital world of overspecialization—I was becoming the expert witness of my own life. When I returned home—as I did for months at a time, in between one- and two-week phenomena chases—I brought an expanded, global sense of wonder to bear on my own backyard, alongside my family.

"They are going to cross," David said, nodding toward wildebeest that had lined the dirt road. Their pulse would quicken as they ventured out, but once they were back in the grass, it would slow. They'd move on, in every sense of the phrase. David picked up speed, determined to reach camp before dark. I turned to watch the animals brave their crossing, but all I could see was a cloud of volcanic dust rising in our wake.

CHAPTER 1

METAMORPHOSIS

I AM FRANTICALLY SEARCHING FOR MY NEWBORN SON, ARCHER.
I'm on my knees. My hands are slipping across cold hardwood floors. I
grope my mattress's metal frame, the legs of his crib. I've already thrown
all the covers off my own bed, convinced he was suffocating in down.

When my panic reaches an apex, I wake up.

Sleepwalking. Night terrors. I have no idea what to call these episodes, but they have become a regular part of my life. More than once, at
sunset, I have wept knowing I was assured another sleepless night to
come. Sometimes, I cry into the night, watching my son nurse in his
sleep as my husband, Matt—a bookish woodworker with a collection of
self-designed tattoos—snores nearby.

Matt does not parent at night. That was established early on. Though
I'm already back at my day job—teaching writing classes between nursing sessions—he is working with power tools. Sleeplessness and power
tools are not a good mix, and anyway, Archer wants milk. I am the sup-

ply. He is the demand. We are sharing my body. I am his ecosystem. He is mine. And it feels like we're clinging to each other for dear life. Matt is in our orbit, but he has become a distant planet.

When I am fully awake, I see Archer safely sleeping in his crib. I glance at the notebook where I record each of his nursing sessions so that I'll remember to rotate sides, lest my raw breasts began to bleed, again. He is nursing nine times every twenty-four hours, a system that means he is attached to my person, suckling, almost constantly.

I hear his every movement, each breath. I read too much about Sudden Infant Death Syndrome. I cannot relax. I have not slept more than three straight hours since he was born, but I am especially shaken by the night's episode, which has actually brought me to my knees.

My mouth is dry. My hands press against hickory floors.

I rise to get a glass of water that my body will, in time, turn to milk like holy wine.

Dawn won't offer assurances. Days feel like hour-upon-hour of living underwater: the outside world muffled, every movement slowed to a languid speed. My friends tell me I seem to be handling things well. Things being the fact that my colicky son does none of the quiet, cooing lap sitting that seems so common in other people's babies.

I wonder if it's because I am afraid to tell the whole truth—what happens beyond the hours I spend staring at my son in wonderment, amazed at the miracle of his life. I love and marvel over him as if he were my own heart pushed into the world and, still beating, set on top of my chest. Yet I cannot help but mourn the loss of something I can't quite place. I have an inner emptiness—literal and figurative—that I've never felt before. It's as though nourishing his life has built a new chamber in my body that is now cavernous and empty, waiting to be filled.

I make my way into the living room without turning on any lights and walk toward a window, half expecting to catch sight of a bobcat. I

see only the river below, a distant forest, and the hill leading to our garden plot. I feel like I am the only being awake in the world and—despite
the fact that I have just doubled the number of people I share a house
with—I have never felt more alone.

To his credit, Matt perpetually tries to bring friends back into our lives
with more regularity, but his attempts—often grand, as in "Oh, did I
mention I invited ten people over for dinner tomorrow"—don't always
go over well. In fact, they often lead to arguments and, to my chagrin,
me throwing fits and—in my worst moments—food. Are these out-of-
control reactions the result of hormones, exhaustion, or are they proof I
am becoming someone unrecognizable?

I hold Archer, literally, all day long. He will not lie in a crib without
crying and I—struggling with feelings of confusion, spousal resentment, and guilt over things I can't quite pinpoint—cannot leave my baby
when his face is wrenched. So, he sleeps on me. He plays on me. Constantly. Sometimes, especially around dinner, even this does not quell his
crying episodes. I sing. I dance. I cry.

I have no hope of ever sleeping again. I have no hope.

I develop tendonitis in my arm. It hurts when I twist it to put him
down, punishment I accept for thinking I might be able to go to the bathroom without a companion. I forget to brush my teeth. I don't shower. I
can't figure out how to balance these simple things against my need to
feel I'm doing a good job—the right things, what I'm *supposed* to do.

When a friend tells me that her baby takes three-hour afternoon
naps, about how she's concerned her child might be sleeping too much, I
have a lurching physical reaction. I do Internet searches that lead me to
terms like "wakeful baby" to explain why my experience is so very opposite. I find articles about wakeful babies being of higher intelligence,

having a keen sense of curiosity. I want to believe them, but I suspect these articles were penned by parents like me as a form of solace in an excruciating time.

Finally, one day at around the six-month mark, I admit to myself that I am going to have a nervous breakdown if I don't take a shower each morning. I turn on a white-noise machine and put Archer in his crib. His tiny features crinkle like tissue paper being balled. His complexion turns crimson. I turn the water on and try to relax, impossible in my near-psychotic state. I hurriedly rinse my hair—which has begun to fall out in clumps as my body attempts to readjust hormonally—and I run back to him.

My friends, mothers, tell me that I will slowly get my life back. I don't believe them. My biggest fear—my secret fear—is the same one that plagued me years ago when I took a soul-killing receptionist job to quell my parents' concerns about health care coverage: This is what my life is going to be from now on. Only, I no longer have the solace of a reception area full of New Yorker archives. It is impossible to read while nursing, because the rustling of pages wakes Archer from his tenuous bouts of postmilk slumber. So, I sit. I stare at walls.

The woman I once identified as myself seems to have ridden off into the sunset. I am having a complete breakdown of faith. Faith in what, exactly, I do not know.

Have you ever heard the saying about how a mother is someone who, upon seeing there are only four pieces of pie for five people, declares she never did like pie? Before I was a mother I thought this quote was sweet. My own mother, a retired elementary school teacher with a sweater for every holiday, is selfless in this way. But when a friend posted it on her Facebook page halfway through my son's first year, it made me unreasonably upset. The mother probably baked the pie. Why not just cut the freaking thing into smaller pieces so everyone can have a taste?

When Archer turns eleven months old I begin ordering books about no-cry sleep solutions, but I am beginning to think it might not be such an awful thing to let him cry it out at night. I have cried myself to sleep for months. Something isn't right.

One night, when Matt finds me wailing in unison with our son, he tells me I should take a break because my emotions aren't good for Archer. Only then do I understand I've entered a phase of my life when people seldom consider what might be good for me. Even *I* somehow don't feel it's acceptable for me to think about my own needs—physical or otherwise.

Not long after Matt chastises me for crying, I tell him it's time for Archer to go to his own room. I want him to feel safe and secure, but I have given so much of myself I feel hollow. An actual shell of my former being. And if I have no enthusiasm, no wonder, no want for life inside of me, how am I going to nourish my child?

Matt and I survey the home we designed and built together, putting in hard labor at night and on weekends. I suggest that we move Archer into the guest room, but Matt is convinced that he should go in a smaller space that once served as his office.

"It's cozy, womb-like," he says.

After a little hemming and hawing, I finally agree, and he builds a changing station using scrap wood from one of his job sites—strips of walnut, oak, and wormy maple. On the night Archer moves into that tree-lined, womb-like nursery, farther afield from his former residence—i.e., me—he starts sleeping. Not all night, but for several hours at a time. Finally, I understand what he's been trying to tell me all along. He needs me, but he also needs some space.

I can totally relate.

. . .

Months pass. Each week, I get a little more sleep. Thirty minutes. An hour. Two hours. I am still breast-feeding, and I am still night walking—stumbling into Archer's room, cradling my swollen breasts, convinced I am holding him after a feeding session only to find I'd already put him down—but my floor-level panic sessions have become sparse. I am upright. I am coming back into the world of the living. Sort of.

I'm an odd bird, you see—a mix of my mother, who rarely leaves the house, and my father, who cannot stay seated for more than ten minutes. Even before Archer's birth, I hardly ever went out to socialize, but I often took trips farther afield. It's unlikely I'll meet you downtown for taco Tuesday, but I might very well join you for a trip to Tahiti.

Archer makes this tendency tricky.

I spend most of my evenings watching computer-streamed television shows that don't require me to think. But as the months go by, my ability to stay awake increases. I start reading the news again. I begin to allow myself to dream improbable dreams. I pull up Web images of far-flung phenomena. Because my memory has been racing along the ridges of the Appalachian Mountains I call home, tracing the migration corridor of the monarch butterfly, seeking the promise of my own rebirth.

Nearly the entire monarch population of eastern Canada and the United States migrates to Mexico's Transverse Neovolcanic Belt to wait out winter, traveling up to 3,000 miles from their respective homes. Their needs are so specific, almost all of the approximately 250 million monarchs that make the pilgrimage each year can be found in a small, mountainous swath of land in Michoacán and, to a lesser extent, the state of Mexico, where oyamel firs grow at high altitudes.

A monarch's life span is only two to six weeks in the summer months, but those born in late fall live for an unbelievable seven to eight months. This generation is responsible for carrying on their species' migratory legacy. The butterflies traveling to Mexico are four to five generations removed from the butterflies that left the mountains the previous spring. But they always return to the same vicinity, and often to the very same tree their ancestors left the year before.

Scientists believe the monarchs mark the trees in some way, but they do not know how.

In 2007, three years before Archer was born, I visited the El Capulín Monarch Sanctuary on a magazine assignment. The site was deep in the Sierra Madre Mountains, beyond the orbit of Mexico City field-trip buses and day-trippers. I was joined by a driver, Paco, and travelers including the Matthews family—Judy, Donald, and their son, Dan, a second-grade teacher with a penchant for Hawaiian shirts.

Judy and Donald, hobby naturalists from New York, had spent the last fifteen years of their lives working as volunteers for Monarch Watch, an educational outreach program of the University of Kansas. The Matthewses told me they had a garden they cultivated with plants other people might try to eradicate from their manicured lawns. They were especially careful to nurture milkweed, which the monarchs depend on for reproduction. This is where the butterflies lay their eggs, and the Matthewses were thrilled to think that the monarchs at El Capulín might have started their journey on the underside of a leaf in the family garden.

The Matthewses almost hadn't made it to Michoacán that year. Dan explained that his father was coping with an early stage of Alzheimer's disease and his mother's walking cane was required because she had Parkinson's disease. "It was looking like we couldn't come on this tour . . . but it was important that we come now," Dan said. "This might be their last chance."

In preparation for the trip, Dan's students had raised two butterflies to watch them go through their metamorphosis. One of the butterflies, Holey, formed its chrysalis on a book in a forgotten corner of the classroom. When he emerged, he had a hole in his wing. This deformity made the butterfly the kids' favorite. Dan recalled, "I have a video of the kids on the day we released the monarchs. The butterflies were just out of reach, and they were chasing them and calling out, 'Holey! Holey!' It looked like a church service."

The kids asked Dan to keep an eye out for Holey on his trip, but the odds of it made him roll his eyes. He said, "I mean, I didn't even think Holey would be able to fly."

The path to the monarchs' roosting site at El Capulín was hidden between a white house and a wooden hut surrounded by banana trees and grazing sheep. It was not a place you would easily find on your own unless you were a butterfly, and maybe not even then. There, just outside the village of Macheros, monarchs lived at the top of Cerro Pelón, or Bald Mountain, a dormant volcano.

At the foot of the mountain, *vaqueros*, or cowboys, stood by their horses waiting for us to choose a companion. We'd been warned that the sanctuary's roosting site was not accessible without one. I approached a tan horse with a black-and-gray-speckled mane. The animal, Flor, was short in stature, which helped calm my near-crippling fear of heights. But I was still nervous.

At dinner the previous evening, I'd explained my hesitation about riding horses and another woman on the tour said, "Sounds like you are having control issues." She was right. I didn't like being dependent, out of control of my own motion.

As Flor and I started our journey, I thought about how far monarchs travel. They move all the way to Mexico on air currents. They do not flap and flail; they soar. They would never make it across the continent before freezes if they used their own energy. It is because the butterfly leaves so much up to chance that it is able to reach its ancestral home in Mexico.

The relatively flat section of the lower trail leading to the monarchs' hibernation site was flanked by trees with very little underbrush, likely due to grazing livestock. The evergreens' trunks were impossibly straight. As Flor and I climbed, the brush got dense, and the path got steeper.

I began to wonder just how far up we were going, so I asked a nearby *vaquero* accompanying us on horseback, "How much longer do we have to ride?"

"Two," he said, making a peace sign.

"Two minutes?" I asked, hopefully.

"Two hours," he replied, amused.

I resolved not to ask any more questions I didn't really want to know the answer to.

Somehow, Flor and I began to take the lead, but it wasn't long before we reached a point in the path where Flor refused to climb. I looked up and saw a stretch of unearthed stone so precipitous that the trail took on a switchback pattern, as if we were being asked to crawl up a downhill ski slope.

Paco was riding behind me. "*Ándale!*" I heard him shout.

"*Ándale,*" I said to Flor, and she began to move.

I leaned forward until my body was pressed against the hard horn of my saddle. The trail was so coarse, so difficult to negotiate, that Flor was starting to sweat. I could see the hair on her neck beginning to clump. To our right was an endless green chasm. My life and Flor's were intertwined. If I had been nervous before, I was absolutely fearful now.

"Everything is okay," I told Flor softly, "*Todo está bien.*"

I repeated this over and over to placate her, to placate myself.

Flor pushed on and it was all I could do to hold tight. The path was narrowing. My shoes scraped against stone and tree trunks. I was holding the back of my saddle so tightly it was digging into my skin. I could hear horses clambering behind me, but I could not turn.

"*Todo está bien. Todo está bien.*" I said it until everything really was.

Finally, we reached the top of Cerro Pelón. The sun was coming out as I dismounted Flor. When I first saw the butterflies, I saw more than a dozen at once, and my enthusiasm grew with their numbers. It took a few minutes to realize the extent of what I was witnessing. To see one hundred butterflies against a blue sky was fantastic. Seeing one million swerving and soaring above me, realizing there were more in the trees waiting for the right moment to open their wings, felt like nothing short of a miracle.

Paco called out and instructed me to cup my hands behind my ears. He said, "*Escuché.*" Listen. And, as we stood there, I could hear the butterflies. Their wings against the air sounded like a light rainstorm falling on verdant forest. All of those paper-thin wings had traveled as many or more miles as we had, but I was still surprised to see that some of them were a bit worse for wear. They looked like faded flags, tattered and torn after a battle. Monarchs are valued for their physical beauty, but what is most beautiful about them is that they are survivors.

Only three colonized trees were visible from where we dismounted, though there were more butterflies resting in the understory. I was standing under a tree filled with monarchs when a cloud passed to reveal more sunlight. Bunches of butterflies above me began to let go of the branches they'd been desperately clinging to and poured into the sky; they brushed against my face and fell into my hair. The streams of cascading monarchs made the trees' branches look like ever-expanding arms reaching down to embrace me.

I was filled with an inexplicable surge of energy that made me want to laugh and cry at the same time. The butterflies were live orange confetti setting the sky ablaze. They were the beauty that cultures try to capture in stained glass windows, the elation people seek in religion.

They were an embodiment of hope.

The ancient Greek word for butterfly is *psychē*, the same word for soul. The Greeks believed butterflies were souls seeking reincarnation. All over the world butterflies have held an inexplicable amount of significance for diverse cultures. In Mexico, the widely observed Day of the Dead holiday has its roots in indigenous mythology. The P'urhépecha, also known as the Tarascan, believe that the first two days of November are a special time of year when their deceased loved ones are able to visit them, possibly in the form of monarch butterflies.

Historically, Celts believed women became pregnant by swallowing the souls of butterflies. Chinese culture indicates that butterflies are the joining of two souls, their wings halves of a sacred whole. And every contemporary American college student with a butterfly tattooed on her belly, ankle, or shoulder must have a different explanation for why she was drawn to the image.

In this information age, the monarchs' mystique is part of their appeal.

Despite recent advances that have led scientists to believe the sun plays a role in assisting the butterflies' navigation, it is unknown how the fragile-winged insects make the many decisions necessary to keep them alive as they battle storms and choose their moments of passage in high-stakes situations, such as crossing the Great Lakes. It is also a mystery as to how they find their way back to the very specific spots where they gather in Mexico's mountains in concentrations of millions per acre.

No single butterfly ever makes the round-trip from Mexico to the northernmost reaches of North America. Most of the males die near their ancestral breeding grounds, but female monarchs move north in the spring. There, they lay their eggs. Each subsequent, short-lived generation moves a little farther up the continent along corridors of wildflowers.

In early fall, the chosen generation reliably starts the migration cycle anew.

Wandering Cerro Pelón, I found Dan lying on a patch of open ground, playfully calling out for the monarchs to cover him. Judy was watching her grown son with a satisfied smile on her face. "God gives us more than we even know to ask for," she said.

Though I was raised a Sunday-school-going Lutheran, I usually shirked away when people started talking about God. I always imagined there were political, social, or moral motives at play rather than spiritual ones. Also, coming from North Carolina—the Bible Belt state where I was born, raised, and still lived—I was hesitant to use the word "God" because people from my part of the country often used it interchangeably with Jesus. And—while I thought the cultural manifestations of his handsome, bearded face brought a lot of people peace—I didn't think it was necessary to go through Jesus, or for that matter, anyone, to get to divinity.

I'd called myself spiritual but not religious since I was twelve years old. Yet, as I stood on that mountaintop at twenty-nine, I still didn't have a good grip on what that meant. But in the presence of open-hearted Judy, in that extraordinary place, I was actually starting to suspect that I had been limiting my way of thinking about the word "god."

Mythology mastermind Joseph Campbell wrote: "God is not supposed to refer to a personality . . . God is simply our own notion of something that is symbolic of transcendence and mystery . . . We are particles of that mystery, that timeless, endless, everlasting mystery which pours forth from the abyss into the forms of the world."

That, I could get behind.

It wasn't social or political. It was not a religious affiliation. But it was something.

I did not turn from Judy, and she had nothing more to say. Together, we stared into the day's abundance, appreciating the tangible rewards of our resilient, monarch-focused faith.

Dan, whose students were never far from mind, finally stood up and said, "I saw a butterfly with a hole in its wing just like Holey's, but, I mean, I don't really think it was Holey."

"You never know," I said. "It's pretty amazing that any butterfly with a hole in its wing could make it down here."

"I guess you're right. I took a picture. I'm going to show my kids. They'll believe it's him," Dan said, shaking his head, amazed. "Think of how many days we take for granted in our lives, but this is one day we will never forget. We will never be able to take this for granted."

The hours we spent with the butterflies passed quickly. Just before we left, I looked down and noticed the monarchs were casting shadows on the earth. They were turning the mountaintop into an inverted carousel night-light, their shadows moving slowly across the land.

Overlooking the surreal scene, I began to wonder how something this marvelous could take place year after year without millions of people clustering in these mountains along with the butterflies. I made a mental note to research nature's most spectacular shows, questioning: *If I'd never heard of this phenomenon, grand as it was, what else was I missing?*

When we departed, there were still millions of butterflies overhead. I opened my hand as if to touch the gliding creatures, even though I could have reached them no more than a star. There were so many monarchs at the top of Cerro Pelón that, when we began our descent down the mountain's trails, the butterflies seemed to chase us as we left, horse by horse. They followed along in the air to our right, gliding over the abyss I feared.

One of the guides, knowing my trepidation about horseback riding, looked at me, glanced at Flor, and then said, "It's amazing what we can do when we have to, isn't it?"

But when we hit our first acutely steep stretch of trail, I started to clench up. I called out to my fellow travelers, "I can't do this. I couldn't have made it up without my horse, but I think I'm going to have to walk down."

From behind me a voice called out, "You can do it. Just take a few deep breaths and get comfortable. Your horse knows what to do."

I took a deep breath. I considered how much farther I'd get if I had faith in my horse, just as monarchs have faith in the invisible breezes that carry them across the continent.

Flor struggled to find her footing on the rocky path. I wanted to scream out when she raised her head to express her own uncertainty, but I didn't. Instead, I released my grip on the saddle and placed a hand on her wiry mane. I leaned in to whisper, *"Gracias."* And together, we stumbled forward, into the unknown—which, for me, turned out to be motherhood.

I'm now nearly thirty-two years old. I've traveled, explored, adventured. I've built a house, married a husband, had a baby. I've done it all, happily, in that order. None of it felt forced; all of it was welcomed and celebrated. But there is an untraditional glitch in my very blessed, traditional trajectory. I can't get the travel, explore, adventure part off my mind.

Those things weren't just part of my youth; they are part of me.

But all the years of my life I've been told that motherhood means I'm finished with hard-core, challenge-myself-to-the-hilt adventuring. I'm married with a child. That's the adventure. Those roles will do all the challenging I need. Sure, there will be worthwhile things ahead of me, but, really, I'm in for the winter, and by winter I mean the season of discontent that will last the rest of my life. It's only natural to allow myself to become a little embittered now that my familial roles don't allow for the all-encompassment of my personal pipe dreams.

For a split second, I bought into this. But then I remembered how a friend once shared with me the fallout from her mother telling her, over and over again, about the sacrifices she'd made to have children. She'd reiterated them like tiny mantras, stories of personal loss offered as proof of love for her daughter. But the comments always made my friend think to herself: *Wow, she probably shouldn't have had children.*

Parenting is about sacrifice, that is for certain, but does being a good mother mean devoting every drop of my being to my child, or does it mean being true to my spirit in a way that illustrates that there is more than one way to live a good life? Motherhood affects everything, but does it have to change everything about who I am and what I choose to pursue?

Archer and I are forming a relationship word by word, day by day. And it seems like embarking on a pilgrimage might just be a way for me to do my part in our partnership. I give to my son of myself, as I hope he will someday choose to give to me, but he is his own being. I am my own being. And I fight the idea that my life is no longer my own. I have to think like this because, as Archer grows, it will be increasingly true. I have given birth to a person with free will and my success as a mother, my personal gauge of success, will be how far, how brazenly, he ventures into the world—coming back to me as I will always return to him.

But since his birth, my world has collapsed into a series of rooms with central heat and a supplemental woodstove. I've been living in a black hole, feeling guilty that my curiosity—my need to venture afield—isn't going to go away. The list of must-see natural phenomena I compiled after witnessing the monarch migration seems to read like a map that might lead me back to myself, a way of fortifying the natural-world connection I made in the presence of butterflies.

I need to take a leap of faith. For my sanity. For my marriage. For my son. I want to look back in ten years and think *I can't believe this is my life* in a good way, a wondrously astounded way, rather than a *woe-is-me* way. I don't want to wait and wait and subconsciously resent my life or, worst of all, my son—my beautiful, blessed boy. That, perhaps more than any of the *tsk-tsk* looks and comments I am opening myself to from the outside world, is the greatest danger of not embarking on the quest I've dreamed up. I am going to pilgrimage to some of the world's most dazzling phenomena. I don't know how I'll make it happen, but I am going to do it.

When Archer suckles one breast and refuses the other during our ritual one morning, I feel a bit rejected and relieved. The next day, when I offer him my milk, he laughs at me as I lie on the bed, offering up my body. He makes the American Sign Language symbol for milk, a grasping motion reminiscent of milking a cow. Archer wants a bottle. He is weaned. I am inexplicably saddened. I will miss his nuzzles, the way he patted my breast when he was hungry.

He has inspired me to marvel at our joined bodies the way I yearn to once again wonder at all the world. But, now that he is eating solid food, it is time for me to start at the top of my phenomena list. I am going to reimagine my life by doing the unimaginable, and I am taking my husband with me. We need more than a vacation. We need rejuvenation, electrification.

So, with Archer happily settled into a room at my parents' house,

Matt and I head for the airport. We're thankfully financed by a travel magazine assignment, my first since Archer's birth. My father holds my son in the crook of his arm, and Archer waves good-bye, repeating his favorite new word: "Go! Go! Go!"

The syllables rain down like a blessing.

CHAPTER 2

BIOLUMINESCENCE, PUERTO RICO

February/March 2011

TWO DAYS LATER, MATT AND I ARE STANDING IN A NARROW AL-
leyway in Isabel Segunda—on the island of Vieques, Puerto Rico—when
a stranger approaches to tell us that he's channeling the power of the
ocean. Crazy? Maybe. But we're here on a similarly far-fetched quest—
to swim in a celestial sea. I tell the man, who introduces himself as Charlie the Wavemaster, that the Milky Way will soon crackle and shimmer
as it slips through my fingers. Bits of stardust will cling to my hair.

I hope Vieques's Mosquito Bay, or Bio Bay, will be as grand as I'm
imagining. Plankton-induced bioluminescence—which appears to mirror stars in the night sky—occurs spontaneously across the globe, but
no site on earth hosts the phenomenon with more regularity than the
southern coast of Vieques. In 2008, Guinness World Records named Bio
Bay the brightest in the world.

Charlie, a gray-bearded man who is wearing a baseball cap and handkerchief headband, seems delighted by our plans. He says, "The Bio Bay, it's all about vibrations. You slap the water and it lights up! It's inspiring! The water holds so much awe!"

I smile. That's exactly what I'm hoping to find here.

Charlie is holding a long metal pole. I gesture toward the rod. He says, as if he's surprised that I have to ask, "Oh, this is my magic wand!"

A ferry from mainland Puerto Rico approaches in the distance. Charlie taps his wand on the ground near my feet. "I'm putting out vibrations right now. Feel it?" There is a dull resonation under my sand-encrusted flip-flops. Charlie says, "Vibrations affect everything and everybody all the time. All the way up to the divine!"

A yellow butterfly hovers above us. Charlie uses his free hand to point out its fluttering wings. He stops his vibration making and pulls the rod close to his chest, saying, "Hey, what do you get when you multiply two negatives?"

"A positive?"

"Yes!" Charlie says, pleased that I'm playing along. "Everything," he says, "comes out a positive if you look at it the right way!"

Vieques, which is located roughly seven miles from the main island of Puerto Rico, is a place where it hasn't always been easy for residents to see the bright side of things. In the early 1940s, thousands of residents were forced from their homes when the United States Navy expropriated roughly two-thirds of the twenty-two-mile-long, five-mile-wide island for artillery storage and military training. In the following decades, Vieques was the site of perpetual military training involving munitions that delivered doses of napalm, lead, depleted uranium, and a cocktail of other contaminants. In 2003, when the navy ceased bombing, nearly 18,000 acres of the island were designated as a national wildlife refuge. This move has kept residential activity concentrated in a narrow swath of land in the center of the island, preserving its status as one of the least developed in the Caribbean.

In 2005, the Environmental Protection Agency added Vieques to its Superfund National Priorities List, officially making parts of the island hazardous-waste sites. This designation made Vieques a supremely unlikely tourist destination. But the navy's toxic legacy has proven no match for the island's more than fifty undeveloped beaches where—on a busy day—visitors might share a crescent of sand with one or two other intrepid souls. Tourism is on the rise, but the cadence of local life still dominates the streets here.

Matt and I begin the climb back into town. Charlie follows. Together, we walk through Isabel Segunda—the larger of the island's two towns, with a population of roughly 2,000—in full view of its bustle. Cars blast the thump-de-thump of reggaeton. Neighbors chat through barred windows with people on the street. Young men in athletic clothing ride bareback on horses guided by rough, twisted rope. Roosters run wild through the scene, dodging hooves and tires.

Everyone passing, almost without exception, gives Charlie a hearty hello or thorny glance that reveals respect, bemusement, or disapproval of his one-man, wave-channeling work. Charlie, as it turns out, is somewhat of a local fixture. He's a full-time Wavemaster. I can't comment on the practicality of his work. All I know is that he's putting out a good (there's just no other way to say it) vibe.

We stroll a few blocks into town before Charlie bids us farewell. Just before he slips into the driver's seat of a borrowed pickup truck he says, "There are so many mysterious ways and miracles in the world. There's so much involved you could never understand it all."

As he drives away, I can hear his metal rod echoing in the truck bed like a tuning fork.

. . .

It doesn't take long to realize that exploring Vieques requires a car. The island, which doesn't have a single traffic light, is also devoid of taxis. We catch a *público*—part of Vieques's limited public transit system—and head for Maritza's Car Rental.

The island is stitched together by a series of unmarked, one-lane roads. Our minibus races by turquoise and hot-pink houses, past a church hosting a tent revival, along fences of slender branches and barb-wire intertwined with hibiscus vines. Each time a car appears up ahead, we enter a contest of wills. Who'll guide their tires off the blacktop first? Which driver is going to yield? Locals tend to favor small compact cars and work trucks. Visitors are immediately identifiable in the late-model Jeeps that have begun to proliferate.

After I fill out the paperwork necessary to secure a Jeep Cherokee—which turns out to be several years newer than the vehicle I drive back home, not exactly a positive on an island where driving is considered an adventure sport—I inquire about Vieques's speed limit. I haven't noticed any signs posted. The attendant looks shocked by my inquiry, as if she's never been asked about these regulations. In fact, she looks like she's never even considered them. She shrugs. "I don't really know. Maybe 45?" I must look concerned about the looseness of this estimation because she adds, "Don't worry. The horses will let you know how fast to go."

Here, horses trump Hondas. The animals often appear wild, but the clip-clop of metal shoes and the brands burned into their coats reveal that they are at least semitame, domesticated. They sometimes chase cars alongside roads and, along with prehistoric-looking iguanas, can often be found leisurely sunning in the middle of streets.

The rental attendant says, "When people want to ride the horses they just go out and catch them." She makes a lassoing motion and explains that, sometimes, if people cannot locate their own horse, they'll wrangle whatever animal they can. In this situation, proper etiquette requires the borrower to set the animal loose in the middle of town. This way, the owners are sure to find out that their free-range friend has been released.

As I turn to go, she says, "I know it seems strange, but the horses here get sick if they're penned in. We don't know why, so we let them be free. It's the only way they will be healthy. It's what makes them happy."

Matt and I stop in Isabel Segunda to gather supplies—grilled cheese sandwiches and guava pastries that fill our pristine Jeep with powdered sugar. As we drive out of town, signs of development completely disappear. Increasingly, there are more and more horses grazing on the grassy knolls. They are pleasingly plump, and it's hard to imagine that anyone comes this far out of town to lasso.

We're on our way to see a collection of bunkers that appear on our cartoonish tourist map as hobbit hovels. The abandoned military bunkers are covered in peeling paint. Despite their novelty, they're not that exciting, so we take off in search of plantation ruins, which are marked only by a hand-painted sign. After spending thirty minutes or so exploring crumbling brick buildings on foot, we get back in the Jeep. I'm ready to go back to the hotel for a nap, and Matt knows not to get in the way of my slumber. Still, when he notices a small path near the ruins, he can't resist. "I bet there's more to see down here!" he says.

Branches brush against the sides of the vehicle. I thrust the tourist map out the window and lay it against the side of the car in an attempt to protect its paint job. There's a prolonged screech from the driver's side. Matt, ever cool, says, "I didn't notice that thing."

"You mean that *tree?*"

We both laugh. Maybe my hormones are finding balance. Perhaps there's something else at play. All I know is that I feel more warmth toward him than I have in a long time. It's now clear that the road isn't a road, but we've gone too far to prevent damage and can't turn around. The path is too narrow. "Let's keep going; this has got to lead somewhere," Matt says.

I don't say anything. The situation is ripe for bickering, and we've avoided that thus far. This actually feels like some sort of breakthrough. I've been so focused on my son and myself, I haven't given enough thought to the sort of stress our marriage has been under. I'd wanted to shout "no" when he turned down this road, but I'd refrained, trying hard to fight his observation that I'm now a naysayer to everything he wants to do. (Currently on the list: Get a puppy, a basketball goal for our gravel drive, a microbrewery.)

We could have just gone to the beach today. But we didn't. Matt is a fellow wanderer. Curious without my incessant, sometimes debilitating sense of hesitation. I'm more than a little nervous about our upcoming rental charges, but this experience is reminding me that Matt's willingness to take risks is one of the reasons I married him in the first place.

"Maybe I should turn the radio up?" he says.

"Okay."

I clutch the car seat. Matt notices and tells me, "All we can really do is relax and hope for the best."

There is absolutely nothing that can be done at this point sans machete. My stress isn't doing us any good, and my paint-job-protecting map got caught on a briar. I don't loosen my white-knuckled grip on my seat, but when Matt turns the radio up, I slowly bob my head to Caribbean tunes, and we push on.

. . .

Just before sunset, we meet up with Garry Lowe in the parking lot of a convenience store. Not long ago, Garry was a fly-fishing guide in Colorado. On a whim, he decided to return to Puerto Rico—his mother's homeland and the site of good boyhood memories—to start his own enterprise, Vieques Adventure Company.

Garry, a lanky guy with a level of animation that rivals that of a caffeinated stand-up comedian, says, "I really shook up my life when I came down here. It was like Boggle!" He hops around, pretending like he's got a hand full of dice, and then points to the ground, to indicate he's just rolled a series of letters in his imaginary board game. He shouts, "L-I-F-E! This is my life! I won! I'm on the water 200 days a year, and work isn't like work at all!"

Garry runs biking and fly-fishing tours on the island, but his real claim to Vieques fame lies in his innovative use of clear canoes. His polycarbonate boats give people who are unwilling to swim in the Bio Bay at night an idea of what it might be like to be immersed in its unique aquatic wonders. Tonight's group gathers in a puddle of yellow created by the headlights of Garry's passenger van. He suggests a last-minute run into a nearby market to use the facilities, saying, "The circus will begin soon! Curtain in seven minutes! Hurry!"

When the crowd—a mix of all ages—emerges from the store, Garry hangs his head as if in mourning. He's spotted a teenage boy in too-tight swim trunks toting a new bottle of bug spray. "I asked you not to use any of that stuff!" Garry laments. He points to the store and says, "Go in and wash your arms. Scrub them!"

"Really?" the boy asks, bewildered by Garry's sudden shift from fun-loving adventurer to schoolmarm.

"Yes!" Garry says. "I know you don't want to kill anything on purpose!" He shakes his head. This is the sort of thing he fears most. "I'm not a tree-hugging kind of guy, but I do think that humans have a habit of wanting to save something after it's already gone. Everything we put on our bodies has the potential to kill the dinoflagellates. Shampoo, deodorant, sunscreen. All of it."

A substantial loss of the photosynthesizing plankton would disrupt the Bio Bay's food chain and result in decreased oxygen levels. It would also snuff out conservationists' hope that—through careful regulation and vigilant guiding—tourists can safely commune with earth's remaining bioluminescent bays. There are about six left in the world, and Puerto Rico is home to three.

Garry's watch beeps. Usually, island time means something like "hang loose, no worries," and in daylight hours this is true on Vieques. But at night, the demand for tours, especially Garry's, is too great to wait for stragglers. "We're still missing one," he says, dismayed, as the pink-armed, bug-spray-free teenager hops into the van. "I feel bad she's going to miss this," he says of the no-show before putting the vehicle in gear. "We'll be there in four minutes and forty-eight seconds!"

When we reach the put-in site, Garry puts on a headlamp to show us around. His boats are all outfitted with red lights so that he can keep track of his crew, the color chosen for its benign nature. Any amount of white light has the potential to disrupt the plankton's circadian rhythm, the biological clock that lets them know when it's time to glow.

Once Garry has safely positioned everyone in canoes, he hops into his own opaque kayak. Almost immediately, the wake alongside our boats is illuminated. I feel as if I'm paddling through neon blue champagne bubbles. I put my hand in the water. When it's immersed I can see my fingers, outlined in tiny, round orbs of light. When I raise my hand to the sky it is camouflaged by its own spontaneous twinkling.

Garry has located a buoy and invited the group to gather around him. He explains that the dinoflagellates are neither plant nor animal, but rather, as the Latin origins of the word "bioluminescence" indicate, they are living light. Garry says, "They use the same chemical as lightning bugs. They're both trying to talk with light, just in different ways."

A rope connecting our boats hits the water in a metered motion, setting off liquid sparks. The group is abuzz with questions. Someone asks, "Would the water still glow if I took some in a jar and put it on a shelf in my house?"

"It wouldn't last," Garry says. "It would just be water in a glass if you took it away from this place. They call this a microbial stew . . . It's special because of what's at play. It's just like with people: You're going to thrive if you're where you're supposed to be."

He straddles his boat and recounts a childhood trip to La Parguera, a bioluminescent bay on mainland Puerto Rico that has nearly lost its luminosity due to degradation. "La Parguera has been dead for a long time. Even when I was a kid, the closest you could get to the water there was when they poured it bucket-to-bucket to show you the glow," Garry says. "At some point, it might not be possible to touch the water here anymore." The group is quiet as we turn our boats toward land.

We paddle close to shore and wait in a swaying cluster as Garry calls us in, one by one. A woman who has revealed she's staying at the only gated resort on the island says, "I'm a hopeless paddler. My nails were getting in the way and I didn't want to break one." Behind us, a fish jumps and lands in a pool of light. Coquí frogs whistle from the surrounding wetlands. When Garry indicates that it's the hopeless paddler's turn to say good-bye to the bay, her voice softens. She says, "He's right, you know. It's amazing that we're allowed in here at all."

. . .

The next morning, at Garry's suggestion, I walk along the picturesque
main boardwalk of Esperanza—the smaller of the island's two towns—
until I reach the Vieques Conservation and Historic Trust, an unassum-
ing building set back from the road. I make my way through a museum
of indigenous Taino artifacts before entering an educational center
maintained by the trust's director of community affairs, Mark Martin
Bras. He emerges from a side door holding a giant stuffed squid, which
he cradles under an arm when he reaches out to shake my hand.

Mark's duties at the trust include educational programming and acting as liaison for the organization's research partnerships with universi-
ties, but he moonlights as a guide for Island Adventures, one of the
most popular guide companies on Vieques. "I've seen people get religious about the bay. I've seen people cry. Adults start to talk like children," he says. "They're not losing intelligence, they're just disarmed.
Nature has the power to completely disarm people. Most of the time we
live outside of that power, but the bay returns it to us."

Mark, who grew up on the main island of Puerto Rico, still remembers his first visit to the bay. He was eight years old. He says, "I'd been
to beaches, but I'd never seen anything like that. It challenged what I
knew of the world. I remember a disappointment in the future that not
all water glowed."

I follow him into a tiny dark room with a giant wooden submarine
in the middle of the floor. The room was created to teach local school-
children, some of whom have never had the opportunity to float in the
bay, about the natural history of bioluminescence. He says, "It's difficult
to get people to care about something they don't understand." During
his educational presentations, Mark often shares a slideshow featuring

some of the earliest written observations of bioluminescence—including quotes by Aristotle and Pliny the Elder, an early naturalist who observed, in AD 77, "There are sudden fires in the waters."

Pliny is often credited with the first human use of bioluminescence, though natives of the West Indies—who stuck bioluminescent beetles to their toes as ground-level flashlights—may have beaten him to the punch. Still, it's impressive to think that, while Pliny's countrymen were walking around Rome with open-flamed torches, he was free-spirited enough to illuminate walking paths with a stick rubbed in glowing jellyfish slime. Fellow Romans were not always kind at the sight of this eccentricity. "He wasn't hanged or anything," Mark says. "But they thought he was strange. Really, he just saw nature differently than other people at that time."

Mark turns on a black light and the room becomes a psychedelic fantasyland. He points out a black-and-white photograph of a dinoflagellate that has been enlarged under a microscope. The image has a purplish-pink tint under the black light. I study the plankton for a minute before exclaiming, "It looks like a human heart!"

He walks over to examine the familiar shape. Finally, Mark says, "You know, it does. It really does!"

Near dusk, Matt and I join Mark on one of Island Adventures' repurposed school buses. We're on our way to the bay's main entrance, which is located inside the public beach compound of Sun Bay. The sides of the bus screech out as branches claw at paint. When the vehicle finally reaches its destination, a clearing roughly twenty feet across, a woman in front of me says, "Those would have been great sound effects for a horror film! Actually, this whole trip would be a great plot for a movie."

She changes her tone to that of a mock announcer: "They went to see the dinoflagellates, and they never came back!"

We leave the bus and stumble to find our footing as we're guided, in single file, onto narrow metal boards leading us onto an electric pontoon boat. Once on board, people seem desperate to photograph the bay, though the bioluminescence is not yet visible. Mark asks guests to turn off their flashes and warns, "There is a gap in technology and the bay."

There are very few photographers who have been able to document these waters in a meaningful way, and rarely do they achieve good results without digital alterations. In a world of Google maps—when it's possible to virtually fly over the Eiffel Tower and the Grand Canyon on your lunch hour—the bay remains a you-had-to-be-there experience.

Mark raises his arm to gesture toward a hilltop neighborhood visible from the water, saying, "Light pollution is one of our greatest enemies here." Street lamps obscure the bay's brilliance, just as they do stars in the night sky.

One tourist—who is still struggling to photograph the bay despite Mark's comments on its elusiveness—calls him over to ask if he wouldn't mind turning up the boat's lights a little. She doesn't yet understand what she's looking for, but she doesn't want to miss capturing it when it appears.

Mark says, "That's not coming from the boat. That's the bioluminescence you're seeing out there."

The woman, still struggling with the concept, says, "There's no light?"

"No *artificial* light," Mark says.

From the boat's perspective, high above the water, the bioluminescence reveals the back-and-forth patterns of fish swimming, squiggly lines drawn in their wake.

Mark points toward the surrounding mangrove forests, which shed nutrient-rich leaves, help maintain the bay's heightened salinity, and build islands as they strain sedimentation. He says, "Mangrove trees actually create land." He directs our attention to the silhouette of a hillside and says, "See that? It used to be water all the way up to the mountain." A level mangrove forest, creeping into the bay's placid waters, is just visible in the evening's fading light.

Someone asks, of the bay's narrow, ocean-gulping mouth, "Will the mangrove ever close the opening?"

"Well, it could, but humans would never let that happen," Mark says.

He continues: "There is a story. I don't want anybody to think I agree or believe in the story, but it goes like this: When they came here, the Spanish thought this was the devil's water, so they put rocks around the mouth to keep the devil in."

Two chemicals that produce the plankton's light—luciferin and luciferase—were named after Lucifer, the fallen angel. Mark says, "Historically, most people who were writing things down were thrown toward evil more than good. They had the idea that bioluminescence was too surreal to be natural."

He gives a small sigh and continues: "I know people have a desire for mythology—and it has its own beauty—but I think that story takes away from the mangrove and nature. It gives humans the credit for creating this."

Our slow-moving pontoon comes to a stop. It's time to swim. We quietly stargaze as we wait our turn to use the boat's ladder. When a cloud threatens to cover a section of sky to our left, Mark pulls a laser pointer and shoots it into the heavens: "Before it goes away, there's the king of the gods—Jupiter! And there's Orion's torso!" He traces its body—celestial belt, outstretched sword—and then, without pause, he abandons his set course to trail a shooting star with his red laser.

"Do that again!" someone calls out, as if Mark might be able to manipulate the sky above.

I approach the edge of the deck to see swimmers kick their legs and flail their arms. They appear as iridescent butterflies shimmering in an inky sky. I clip a slender piece of foam around my waist and enter the darkness. The water is warmer than the air. It feels near body temperature, and when I am fully submerged, I am surrounded by a cloud of liquid electricity. I am speaking to the water through movement, sign language, and it is responding with visual cues.

Not far from where I'm treading in a tornado of light, a man—clean-cut and seemingly not prone to saying words like "dude" and "awesome"—is carrying on as if he's on hallucinogens, shouting, "Look at the hairs on my arm! Look! The hairs on my arm!" He dips his arm in the bay and lifts it for everyone to see. His hair has become a catchment of flickering pulsars. "It's so weird! Like I'm covered in stars!"

When Mark announces that it's time to get out of the water, a collective groan rises. I'm saddened and slightly relieved, given that, despite the overwhelming magic of the experience, I've squandered a little too much of my swim envisioning how we might all look from the depths below. I streak my way across the bay, climb the boat's ladder, and grope around for a towel.

Back on shore, when people begin to make their way down the gangplanks, Mark shouts after them: "Don't forget to tell people about the lights!" He isn't talking about the soul-stirring bioluminescence. He's reminding us to take inventory of our far-off corners of the world. "More light," Mark says, "isn't always better."

During our last day on Vieques, Matt and I decide to take a daylight tour of a mangrove forest. We're part of a large crew, but we're attentive as Carlito Cruz Morales, a twenty-something with wavy black hair, gives a brief kayak paddling lesson. When he's done, a fellow guide, Michelle McNerney, who's sporting a slender hoop in her nose, disseminates life jackets.

Under the afternoon sun, deep areas of the bay look like tea that has just begun to steep. The group falls into loose formation as we travel to the far shore, a mass of mangrove. It's unclear how we're going to pass through the forest's tight aerial root system. I am within a foot of the mangrove and still I do not see a clearing large enough for a human body, much less a boat, to pass through.

Carlito hops out of his kayak. The water barely reaches his chest. "Abracadabra, Rastaman! Open sesame!" he shouts dramatically as he moves a few dangling prop roots to reveal a tight passage.

He pushes the first craft through. The tunnel seems to close itself behind the kayak. The mangrove might not be home to a plethora of spiders, as one fellow boater had feared, but it hosts a healthy population of tarantula-size arbor crabs. They scamper along the roots as I pull my paddle into my boat.

This mangrove forest is relatively young, with most trees standing at roughly twenty-five to thirty feet. During hurricane Hugo, it lost many of its mature trees, some of which were more than sixty feet tall. "After Hugo, the bay didn't glow for six months," Michelle says. "The conditions just weren't quite right."

We've traveled roughly half a mile into the mangrove when we reach another open section, a watery roundabout. Clumps of spongy silt float up around us. Carlito jumps out and thrusts his hands into the water to produce a huge clump of earth, which he plops on top of his head as the group looks on, aghast.

He begins to work it into his long hair. "What's good for the dinoflagellates is good for your skin and nails!" He continues his mud bath, clearly delighted by the group's collective recoil. Each time he pulls a handful of muck from the water, a sulfuric stench wafts over our flotilla.

He looks slightly alarmed when a military-looking cargo plane flies by overhead. "I haven't seen an airplane like that in a long time," he says. Carlito grew up with the military presence. He says, "I used to sleep every night to the sound of bombs. Boom! Boom! It thundered every day without rain."

When the plane is gone, Carlito dips back into the swampland. Still reminiscing, he explains that one of his favorite childhood haunts was a beach where purple and orange coral formed rainbow cliffs. To his chagrin, it was located in a former military zone. "Sometimes, when they were bombing, I wouldn't go there," he says. "Other times, they still said I couldn't go there. I did anyway. But then the protests began."

People opposing navy activities on the island—including well-known activists such as Al Sharpton and Robert F. Kennedy Jr.—were regularly arrested for acts of civil disobedience between 1999 and 2003. The movement was spurred when a local man was killed by an off-course bomb, an incident that incited international rage. Carlito said, "When things got bad, I couldn't go to my beach at all. I would have gone to jail if they'd found me there."

Carlito hops back into his boat to lead us though the mangrove. As he paddles, he mentions that some of his friends are advocating a local movement to build a bridge to mainland Puerto Rico. "People always say, 'I hope Vieques gets a Kmart' or something like that, but I say take two dollars and go to the mainland on the ferry. It's all there."

He negotiates the mangrove passageway gingerly, moving root-to-root slowly, so that his boat doesn't hit the oysters below. He says, "I know Vieques will change, but I want it to stay like this—quiet. A bridge would make the island different. If we have more people, we need bigger roads. Bigger roads mean bigger neighborhoods and more cars. Nature will disappear."

A year ago, Carlito had a different outlook. He says, "I was sleeping. I was like 'Nature, who cares about that?'" But when he heard Abe's Snorkeling was hiring, he was quick to apply. He knew how to kayak because he'd grown up around boats, he knew how to snorkel because he was a fisherman, and he was familiar with most parts of the island because it was his home. Even so, when Carlito was hired, he still didn't really see any fringe benefits to working outdoors.

Over time, his feelings began to change. The perspective that many young people get from experiencing unfamiliar terrain was delivered to Carlito through the travelers he encountered. He says, "I started to wonder: Why, when people come here, do they say it's so beautiful? Why don't people want to leave? I changed my view to see a tourist view. People come wanting to know a local like me, but I want to know them. How do they see this place?"

We're nearing the end of the mangrove tunnel. Carlito sweeps his hair into a loose bun on his head and continues, "Before, I didn't understand that you don't need money for the most beautiful things. A smile? Free! The beach? Free! Surf? Free! Free things for me are enough. That's what people come here for, what they really need—the free things. My island isn't developed, and that is a good thing."

When we exit the forest, Carlito says, "When I started working here I didn't know how these wonderful trees worked. Everything here is important . . . All my life changed when I starting sharing my island. I'm no *santo*—how do you say, saint? But I'm a better person since I got to understand this place."

We're in full sunlight now, back in the open waters of the bay. Carlito turns his boat to make sure that the rest of the group has made it out of the mangrove. After he's counted the brightly colored crafts to make sure everyone is accounted for, he resumes his course, falling silent as we paddle a snaking passageway crafted by trees.

The water becomes choppy as we round cliffs of white coral on our way to a small beach accessible only by boat. When I drag my kayak onshore, I plant my paddle as a flagpole. A middle-aged man, who's in Vieques as part of a trip around the world with his wife, pulls up beside me and does the same. We sit in the sand as Carlito and Michelle sort out snorkeling equipment. Around us, bits of sun-bleached coral lie scattered about like bones thrown from a fortune-teller's hands.

The man, well-traveled and obviously well-heeled, says, "It's unbelievable this place is still here." But it's really what *isn't* on Vieques that's amazing. Even now, eight years after the navy stopped bombing the island, there are no chain restaurants or stores. No fast-food restaurants. No golf courses. He says, "It's like the whole island is fifty years behind." He pauses, glances around the otherwise deserted beach, and reconsiders, "Or maybe it's fifty years ahead."

Visitors to Vieques are warned against collecting shells—mortar shells, that is. A major portion of the eastern end of the island is closed due to unexploded ordnance and cleanup efforts. Disconcerting, to be sure, but at the moment my major concern is finding a safe place to step, not out of fear for my own safety, but for that of the coral below. One false move could snuff out hundreds of years of growth. Preventing this sort of catastrophe is harder than it might seem to a seasoned snorkeler. Though I've grown up around water, I've never taken to flippers.

As I flail, I watch Carlito's movements under the water, learning. He turns his head slightly to look at me, and he moves his hands to indicate that I'm trying too hard. I'm moving too fast. In order to last in these waves, this far out, I've got to relax. The world is muffled as I plunge my head into the water. I stop my desperate kicking. I don't have the energy to keep fighting. Slowly, I catch on. My hands fall to my side, and I gently propel myself forward. I'm not exactly graceful, but I'm in transit.

A good portion of the coral at the mouth of the Bio Bay is dead. Unfortunately, it's not a surprising discovery. Unusually warm waters have led to the death of roughly 40 percent of Caribbean coral over the last decade. But there are signs of life on the sea floor here. Brain corals, named for their uncanny resemblance to one of the most complex and least understood parts of human anatomy, appear every few feet. They are small specimens of a species that can grow to be six feet tall. I wonder if the reef also suffered during Hugo, if these marigold-colored corals are a hopeful sign of its regeneration, but Carlito is too far away to ask.

To me, the bottom of the sea floor looks nearly barren—small bits of sea grass and kale-like plants growing from a chalky bottomland. To Carlito, it is still a place of bounty. He reliably finds less-than-charismatic living creatures to share. When he pulls a small sea urchin from a piece of coral, he asks me if I'd like to hold it. I study its spiny surface and extend my arm. Its weight reveals a surprising density beneath its spiny appearance. When the creature presses into my palm, I feel anchored, grounded, despite the fact that I am not tethered to terra firma. Carefully, I hand the urchin back to Carlito. He passes it around until everyone willing to hold it has had a turn. Then, he slips beneath the waves to return it to its home.

As we begin to propel ourselves toward land, it becomes apparent that the tides have taken us much farther than I realized. We're far from shore and my flippers have, once again, begun to seem like a burden. I feel hopelessly restrained, and I've lost sight of Matt in the crowd, identities hidden by masks and the bulge of mouth spouts that look like dorky headgear. My legs are cramping, and my throat is burning. Michelle is following the group in a kayak to provide emergency assistance, but I don't want to call her over.

The water is shallow, but if I put my flippers on the coral below, it will die. I'm seconds from admitting failure, calling for help, when I feel a hand on my back. Matt has seen me struggling, and he has reached out without being asked.

I have the oddest feeling, a realization, really, that I've been wanting him to do this for over a year. He'd long been telling me that I should take a night, go out to dinner with friends, hand Archer over without guilt, but I couldn't. The confusion over what my life had become—the sleep deprivation, the hormones, the resentment—had been too much for me to navigate on my own. I'd wanted him to step up, to not make me feel like a failure for asking. I had blamed him for not noticing that I was drowning, but I should not have been afraid to ask for parenting help any more than I should have been embarrassed by my need for a little tow from Michelle's kayak. Matt and I make eye contact through our plastic goggles, and we nod in unspoken understanding. He keeps his hand on my back until we reach shore.

On the beach, we dine on sandwiches that have been stowed in soft-sided coolers. Michelle pours guava juice into small plastic cups, and I mention that I'm disappointed that I haven't yet tried fresh coconut milk on the island. Carlito, overhearing, says, "Coconut? We can have that here! This is freedom island!" He turns on his heels. "Come with me!"

A few other interested parties trail behind, including Michelle. "Nobody can climb a tree like Carlito!" she announces. We walk down the beach, over patches of dried sea grass that crunch under our bare feet. When I point out a tree with large coconuts, Carlito says, "That's a good one!" Then his eyes scan the bottom of the tree. He says, "Looks like it's been protected by some scary stuff."

The understory around the tree is the most prickly and daunting I've seen on the island. Bits of hardened, dead reeds appear as chest-height nails. Still, Carlito is deterred for only a moment. By the time the rest of the group reaches our spot on the beach, he's already out of sight. I point to the brush.

"He's in *there*?" Michelle asks, concerned.

Suddenly, Carlito's head rises above the reeds. He puts his arms around the tree—as if he's asking it to dance—and he lifts himself, so that the pads of his feet are against its trunk. Then he begins to climb. He's a blur of hands-feet-hands-feet. His movement is so fast, so graceful, I almost don't have time to admire his form until he's in the upper area of the tree. He tosses coconuts over the brush so that they roll down the embankment, all the way to the beach. They each come to a halt at our feet, unharmed. Michelle looks up at Carlito in admiration: "That kid likes a good challenge." She gathers the coconuts under her arms, and we head back to where we've left the boats.

Carlito emerges from the foliage without a scratch. He takes the smallest coconut and pounds it against a piece of driftwood that has been doubling as our dining table. Finally the green outer layer breaks, and he peels it back to reveal coarse, cream-colored fibers. Carlito cracks the interior shell with his thumb, pressing in as if he's opening a tabbed soda can. He hands the coconut to me. "Anything in there?"

I take it with both hands and hold it over my head. Nothing. I lean back farther and hold the coconut higher. It's dry. Carlito looks disappointed. "We will try another," he says.

Michelle hands him a larger coconut. "It's heavy," he says as he hits it against the silvered branch. When its leathery green skin hits the wood for the second time, the coconut begins to spray, liquid shooting in every direction. Carlito jumps up and brings the exploding orb over my head. Coconut water shoots into my hair and onto my face. "Drink!" he says.

I open my mouth to catch the mild, earthy streams. "Somebody hand me a cup," Michelle says. I gulp the water for a moment before stepping back so that she can gather some of it. This isn't exactly the sort of relaxed, colorful-umbrella-garnished, sipping-out-of-a-straw sort of coconut experience I'd expected. It's better.

Launching kayaks into a churning ocean at dusk doesn't seem a terribly safe idea, but it's the move we're making. I can barely see the silhouettes of my fellow boaters. They're moving forward in sync, paddles like clock hands ticktocking us into the future.

As we paddle toward the Bio Bay, fighting currents to stay on course, I can make out Mark's pontoon boat. I also see a series of red lights slipping across a distant portion of the bay, an indication that Garry has already arrived for his evening paddle. But our group is still out of reach of the bioluminescence. These waters, at the bay's gulping mouth, are still more ocean than mangrove.

I put my hand in the water and let it act as a rudder for a moment. No light. The breeze of the beach disappears as we move into the bay. The waves also cease. When we're in range of the mangrove forest's spindly root system, our rocking world becomes serene. Just as I am lulled into appreciating the bay for its simple, everyday beauty, just when I get a little too comfortable, the dinoflagellates appear. Despite all my previous encounters with the water, I'm startled by its presence, so mysteriously lovely that it's hard to accept as an earthly scene.

"See the glow?" Carlito says. "It's starting!"

When the entire group is in earshot, Carlito asks, "What would you do if you were holding a coconut and it suddenly became one hundred times bigger than you?"

"Drop it?" someone offers.

Carlito laughs. "Well, you'd probably get scared and run away. That's what happens here. The dinoflagellates use the light as defense, making themselves look bigger than they are so things will leave them alone." He puts his hands together to form the rough shape of a dinoflagellate and starts to chant: "Defense! Defense!"

This is one of the explanations scientists have derived for the phenomenon. Other hypotheses include the idea that the shock-and-awe reaction is actually intended to attract large predators so that whatever is threatening the dinoflagellates will be eaten before it has a chance to chow down on them. There's also a small contingent of scientists that believes dinoflagellates' bioluminescence is an evolutionary holdover made unnecessary by environmental changes. I find this scientific footnote particularly enthralling. It's not often that you find a single-cell organism creating beauty for no reason at all.

The group goes wild, mocking fans at a sporting event. They echo Carlito's cry: "Defense! Defense!"

Our boats knock with dull thuds as we attempt to break loose of each other. I lower my hand and let water pool in my palm before lifting it at an angle so that it flows down my arm, which is temporarily transformed into the tail of a shooting star. Then I lean against the kayak's neoprene seat to study the sky. I'm pleased to see the Milky Way with unmistakable clarity. It feels like a crack in my consciousness.

My moment of quiet reflection is broken when Matt, who's behind me, hits his paddle against the water's surface— roughly, as if to splash an invisible foe—spinning plankton rain down on the bay's glassy surface like an explosion of fireworks in a moonless sky. The eruption is bright and surprisingly far-reaching.

"Do it again!" someone shouts in the distance. He obliges.

A chorus of wonder follows: "Look at that! Oh, my! Incredible!"

At first, I'm a little contentious. But when I hit my own paddle against the water at the request of another boater, I am rewarded with a parade of sparklers, and I forgive the disruption. In fact, I am suddenly and unexpectedly grateful for it.

Others join in with their paddles—their own magic wands—and we become a flotilla of Roman candles set ablaze. Our rumpus splashing drowns out the voices of other groups on the bay, and the aura of pollution over Esperanza seems to dim in comparison. We watch as nebulous rings of living light ripple out, beyond our line of sight, adrift in an expanding universe.

CHAPTER 3

CATATUMBO LIGHTNING, VENEZUELA

September 2011

I AM GETTING READY TO WIRE HUNDREDS OF DOLLARS INTO THE Miami-based bank account of a guy who knows a guy in Venezuela. This sounds beyond sketchy, I know. And the worst part is, it very well may be. My resolve to follow through isn't exactly fortified when my bank teller leans in and says, "Are you sure you want to do this?"

"No," I say. "But I don't know what else to do."

There are no hotels in the shallows of Lake Maracaibo, where the Catatumbo lightning—a near-continuous nocturnal lightning storm— rages more than 300 nights a year. But there are stilt villages, or *palafinos*, near the mouth of the Catatumbo River, which feeds the lake. They house populations that see more lightning than any other humans on earth. This is where I need to be to really experience Catatumbo lightning, the next phenomenon on my list. But navigating in-country airlines and booking passage with Venezuelan fishermen, who live hours away from landlines, presents a problem.

Naturalist Alan Highton is one of the only tour operators in the country that travels to the Catatumbo region. The American expatriate, who settled in Venezuela after marrying a national, has earned the nickname Alanconda due to his prophetic abilities to find snakes in murky water. He's offered to buy my domestic plane tickets and boat passage if I send him fees in full. He's also suggested that I wire some extra spending money. After all, Caracas has one of the highest per capita murder rates in the world. Do I really want to show up in one of the most dangerous cities in Latin America with wads of cash in my pocket?

In his e-mail requesting half a month of my teaching salary, he wrote: "Of course, that takes trust . . . It's an option." Sure, good faith is always an option, but not necessarily an attractive one.

Miraculously, I'm able to send the funds because—just after beginning my quest in earnest—a publisher accepted a book proposal outlining my pilgrimage to wonder. A few months ago it seemed I'd never write again. Now, I have the opportunity to write nearly full-time.

The protective bank teller rat-a-tats on her keyboard, glancing up every so often, as if to make sure I haven't come to my senses. I imagine how her concerns for my sanity would soar if I told her about the typhoid pills I'm taking with my dinner this week or the sore spot on my right arm from a yellow fever vaccine that came with a legally required warning from a nurse, who towered over me yesterday, saying, "This could be a lethal injection."

This banker thinks I'm reckless, and she doesn't know half of what I'm up to. But I've been feeling increasingly brazen lately. And my newfound courage is changing me in ways I'd never expect—at home.

I've been letting Archer explore more intrepidly, and it hasn't gone unnoticed. At a recent dinner party, Matt told our dinner companions about finding Archer standing on top of the kitchen table, shouting with the unfettered enthusiasm of an explorer who'd just reached the top of a previously unscaled mountain. "I opened the door and Leigh Ann lunged toward him so I wouldn't see what she was letting him do," he said. "It was so out of character!"

I'd been embarrassed for Matt to see me let Archer run wild, afraid of being judged a bad mother. Unfortunately, I'm afraid the story made our friends, parents of two, think just that. "I once had someone's five-year-old climb on our kitchen table," the mother said, shaking her head. "You just can't let that sort of thing go on for too long."

But what if I let it go on forever? Archer is going to learn social norms and the limits of risk—I tell him about them every day—but I'd like him to know what it means to challenge himself as much as what it means to challenge me.

Before I left for Puerto Rico, Archer had weaned himself. He'd started talking. He'd begun sleeping through the night. But I was still in mourning for a life I'd thought I'd lost, the sacrifices I was making. It wasn't until I went to Puerto Rico that I began to imagine that my life might actually have the potential to become larger than it had been pre-pregnancy, and I don't just mean because of the joys of parenthood.

When I came home from that trip, something was different. I cried when I saw my son with his fine, golden-halo hair. The tears were, at first, of the how-could-I-have-left-him, look-at-what-I-missed variety. They soon turned to something else. Relief. He had allowed me to go. He would let me leave again.

When my father handed Archer to me on that first day back, I kissed his cherub-soft cheeks. And, for the first time since we locked eyes seconds after he emerged from my womb, I felt like he saw me. Something had shifted. I was no longer an appendage. I wasn't his right hand, he seemed to realize; I was his right-hand woman. That day, I accepted that occasional absences, journeys that allow me to be true to myself, my spirit, have the potential to make me a more present mother.

And motherhood, in turn, might just be making me a braver woman.

Watching Archer discover the world is my greatest joy, but I've still got some discoveries to make outside of the ones he has to show me, in places that are not child friendly. The fact that I'm not planning to take him to Venezuela is perhaps the only part of my upcoming travel plan that seems sensible. He'll be taking nature walks and making county fair visits with my parents while I'm out of the country—accompanied by even-keeled Matt, who agrees I might actually have some valid concerns about this particular trip.

The State Department's warning for Venezuela is one of the diciest I've read. The cautions start at the airport and don't let up: "The embassy has . . . received multiple, credible reports of victims of 'express kidnappings' occurring in the airport. . . . The road between Maiquetía Airport and Caracas is known to be particularly dangerous. Visitors traveling this route at night have been kidnapped and held captive for ransom in roadside huts that line the highway."

Huts. For kidnapping. *Are you kidding me?*

The Catatumbo leg of my journey is just beginning, but it's already reminded me of something important that I tend to forget: Foolish acts and bold adventures almost always appear, especially in the beginning, to be the absolute same thing.

Matt and I have been with Alan Highton for two days—slowly working from the peaks of the Venezuelan Andes to the shores of Lake Maracaibo—when he nearly poisons us. We're dining in a restaurant that is completely open to the diesel-powered street, at a large wooden table with leather-upholstered chairs. Alan ordered, going to the counter alone, and we were presented with chucks of chicken on silver platters, small tamales wrapped in green leaves, and mounds of boiled yucca, a starchy root vegetable.

Alan—who has shaggy salt-and-pepper hair and lips that are almost always lined with the brown residue of *chimo*, a pre-Columbian tobacco paste—gestures toward the communal plate of yucca as I stuff another bite of it in my mouth.

"That's toxic, you know."

The dense, mealy root suddenly turns bitter. I'm poised to spit it out. "The skin, it's full of cyanide," he continues, as I gag. "You have to peel it and wash it well to make it eatable."

Luckily, Alan assures me, it seems the restaurant has done a fine job preparing our feast. I attempt to regain composure. I'm still getting used to his guiding style. He has a way of making me feel simultaneously well taken care of and completely on the edge of catastrophe. He puts everything out there, all the time.

This supremely forthright nature, I now realize, might be one of the reasons I chose to go with him in the first place. His promotional materials include lines like: "It is not a tour for those who look for luxury or rest. The climate is hard and the activities, of long hours, cover day and night." We signed up anyway. So did several nationals, including Romo, a seventy-something theater professor from the highland city of Mérida.

After lunch, we pile back into a passenger van to roll past plantations of palm trees and pastures where water buffalo flick flies with their beef-stick tails. When we come across a flag representing the state of Zulia, which bears a lightning strike, a member of the group explains that it was the lightning he witnessed in Miami, Florida, that inspired him to seek out the Catatumbo. It is known to nearly all Venezuelans as a point of national pride and is credited for its heroic role in several battles, including the nation's war for independence, when the lightning revealed invading ships to allow patriots to defeat Spain.

"Ah," Alan says, "Florida is one of the world's lightning hot spots."

An estimated 1.4 billion lightning flashes occur on earth each year. Roughly 30 million of them flash over the United States. Florida has the highest number of strikes, Alaska has hardly any. The Democratic Republic of Congo in Central Africa has more than any other nation in the world, but recent National Aeronautics and Space Administration (NASA) studies have revealed that no inch of earth gets more lightning than the Catatumbo Delta.

Benjamin Franklin is credited with being the first modern scientist to systematically go about proving the electrical nature of lightning. But despite his extensive studies, he conceded that he didn't understand how clouds became electrified. Franklin thought bioluminescent waters—like those of Vieques—might actually be electric, an earthly source of energy that fueled lightning in the sky. But subsequent research led him to believe that living organisms were producing the waterborne light. He reasoned, in 1747, that "it is indeed possible, that an extremely small animalcule, too small to be visible even by the best glasses, may yet give a visible light." This hypothesis, furthered by the generations of scientists that came after him, provided a basis for modern bioluminescent science.

Amazing, isn't it, the things we find when we're looking for something else?

Generations after Franklin hung up his kite and key, scientists still don't know for sure what causes electrification in clouds. The running theory has long been that it's due to charges created by ice particles colliding in clouds. The Catatumbo isn't thought to be different from the lightning that splashes over Oklahoma City—or my very own home—

in terms of physics or chemistry. But its reliability and geographic fixa-
tion set it apart. It is so consistent that locals depend on the atmospheric
phenomenon—known colloquially as the Lighthouse of Maracaibo—as
a navigational aid.

A few people have been watching this hot spot, the term for
lightning-active places, from a distance. Steve Goodman, of NASA, is
one of them. He is interested in lightning—be it in the Catatumbo Delta
or elsewhere—because of its potential to save lives. Someday soon, scientists like Goodman believe, lightning might give early nocturnal tornado
warnings. They might not know for sure what creates the sparks, but
they've figured out that lightning-free zones in thunderstorms usually
occur just before supercells start swirling, creating black holes in otherwise lit areas visible from space.

In 2015, NASA, in collaboration with the National Oceanic and Atmospheric Administration (NOAA), has plans to launch a Geostation-
ary Operational Environmental Satellite, which will have a real-time
lightning mapper onboard. Goodman thinks severe storm warnings in
the United States will be improved by 50 percent when it launches. This
means that, in the 2011 storm season alone, lightning—which took 25
U.S. lives—had the potential to save 275 people from tornadoes with its
Morse Code–like flashes. It is an ancient language we're only beginning
to understand.

Boys in plastic sandals chase our van, hawking coconut cookies. Behind
them, shirtless men laze at roadside kiosks, gnawing on mangoes as
juice drips onto bare skin. It's several hours from Mérida to the shores of
Lake Maracaibo and there are few corporate establishments along the
way. Coffee is served via skinny teenage girls who stand in the center of
the road with push-top metal containers. As we pass a dump truck full

of artfully packed green plantains, Romo launches into a bit of local folklore that was passed down to him from his grandmother. "She was a peasant," he says, "and she lived close to nature."

His grandmother knew the old ways. Romo tells me she sipped water from dried, hollowed out gourds and sought the wisdom of shamans. She once explained to him that this region was full of lakes because of a forest sprite who came down from the highest mountain in the Andes with a clay pot, which he gifted to an elderly couple. "Take this," the sprite told them, "and pour a little water as you walk between the mountains. If you do this, you will have eternal life."

So, the couple spent the night pouring water. Their puddles, tiny offerings, grew to be lakes in the darkness. Villagers from all around awoke to find that the region was rich with water, sources of life. They wanted to thank the couple for what they had done, but in the morning, when the sun crested the surrounding mountains—so tall they were sometimes mistaken for storm clouds on hazy days—the elders were gone. Romo looks at me and says, "They'd dissolved into the lakes, understand?"

Plenty of things have dissolved in Lake Maracaibo. In 2011, the Organization of Petroleum Exporting Countries (OPEC) named Venezuela the most oil-rich nation on earth. It has more oil than Saudi Arabia. Almost all of it lies at the bottom of Maracaibo, a virtual stew of prehistoric animal bones, zooplankton, algae, and long-lost dinoflagellates, the organisms that Franklin once thought might have the capacity to electrify. In death, maybe they do.

When Romo's grandmother first told him about the Catatumbo, he searched distant horizons like a child looking for Santa Claus on Christmas Eve, and with no less a sense of magic. Soon after he began to pay attention, he saw bits of light in the distance, explosions that appeared as if from another world. He hadn't known to look for them, but they'd been there all along. It was a realization that forever shaped how he saw the world.

The last time he witnessed the lightning he was an adult, staying in a hotel a four-hour trip from here. Romo says, "I am not a timid person, but I felt a fear, a supernatural fear, like something coming from the collective unconscious that night."

This lightning-born fear and awe runs throughout history and cultures. Thoreau wrote: "The ancients called it Jove's bolt, with which he punished the guilty, and we moderns understand it no better . . . Science assumes to show *why* the lightning strikes a tree—but it does not show us the moral *why* any better than our instincts did . . . Men are probably nearer to the essential truth in their superstitions than in their science."

Romo seems to agree. He hasn't come to Lake Maracaibo for scientific answers. His push for discovery is of a spiritual sort. "I was that storm," he says of his last encounter. "I lived in it, through it. My grandmother was with me that night. I thought to myself, the nest of that phenomenon must be close to here."

His terminology brings to mind the mythic thunderbird and its lightning-shooting eyes. Giambattista Vico, a philosopher in the 1700s, suggested that humankind's earliest notions of God arose out of lightning and subsequent thunder. It was thunder, he thought, that first introduced early humans to a greater power. Joseph Campbell believed that lightning was one of the first divinations of nature and the all-encompassing cosmos, an early symbol of divinity.

Romo plays with his necklace, a brass medallion just visible in the mass of white hair that's bursting forth from his half-unbuttoned dress shirt. The circular necklace is divided with four lines, the cardinal directions. He flips it in his stubby fingers and says, "Being in the lightning that night was like being in an earthquake. It seemed to come from the ground." He shakes his head, remembering. "There were moments that night when it felt like the lightning was coming from everywhere."

In the village of Puerto Concha we find men sitting in dusty jungle clearings, playing cards. We'll travel by boat from here, tracing a dark river into the lake. Our group clusters on a cement pier that has a large hole in the middle. I can see water sloshing below us, shining through exposed rebar. Ferns grow around rough cement.

In the flurry of e-mails exchanged when planning this trip, Alan told me that he was going to hire three boats, though we needed only two. He thought it would be safer. Bandits roam these waters, and they've been known to rob fishermen in the middle of the lake.

One of the small boats Alan has secured features a motor covered with a large red T-shirt. It might be intended to block out the fading sun, Alan explains, or it might be to make the new motor look less desirable, you know, to *pirates*. "Don't worry," he says, "nobody's ever stolen a motor from a tourist boat." In classic form, he adds, "Not a lot of tourists go out here, though. They get nervous because of guerrillas and drug trafficking, but that's on the Colombian side of the river." This offers little comfort since there's nothing but lawless jungle and open water between us and the border.

Loaded in our vessels of peeling paint and webbed fiberglass, we move away from the fish-scale-littered streets of Puerto Concha onto a narrow river swathed by jungle. The sun, the air itself, is so hot it hurts. I adjust my weight on the boat's seat, which has been padded with broken down cardboard boxes reading "Country Club Brand Whisky." We begin to move at a steady clip.

Romo looks at me and puts his fingers to his mouth and kisses their tips. "*¡Delicioso!*" he says of the breeze. And it is tasty. My skin begins to cool. I lean back and scan the trees for monkey tails that hang from low branches like strange, coiled fruits.

In the distance, a boat approaches with a driver wearing a long-sleeved shirt tied around his head to obscure his face, like a mask. All three of our boats' motors start kicking exhaust as we slow to move through an area of the waterway that's nearly overgrown with hyacinth. The motor fumes are thick. I begin to cough.

"That's a black-tailed hawk," Alan shouts, pointing to a bird soaring through the haze.

I don't follow his gaze. I'm a little more interested in the motivations of the *bandito* who's barreling toward us. I gesture toward him and Alan says, "The sun is brutal to the guys out here. They wear shirts over their faces to protect themselves." The masked man speeds past us, and all around, the river screams with life, thousands of insects appearing as shadows on the undersides of leaves.

"Near the horizon line," Alan says, "you can see a few storms beginning to form. It's rare to see a storm in the Catatumbo Delta during the day." This is a place that saves its secrets for after dusk.

We follow the Puerto Concha River to its mouth, where we bound over waves into an ocean-size lake. There is no pleasant zipping. We're wave hopping and my less-than-swashbuckling attitude is experiencing even more of a setback. The boat moves *zoom-boom-boom-boom* across the water. I grip the side of the boat and Matt's leg, crouching down as if to make myself more aerodynamic. It doesn't work.

I have two hours to go, and I'm losing my mind. I know this for certain when I hear strange music tingeing the whipping static of wind. Classical opera. It's coming from behind me. I have feared kidnapping bandits. Instead, I got Romo.

He's pulled his chest-length white hair back with a bit of leather twine, and he's wearing a wide-brim straw sun hat tied under his chin in a neat little bow. His voice is strong and dramatic. I laugh through clouds of my tangling hair. This rough, butt-bumping, pirate-braving voyage has turned into one of the finest, oddest, most refined moments of my life.

When Romo stops singing, Matt leans in and says, "I can't hear very well. My ears still haven't popped!" We've descended thousands of feet in elevation over two days, and the barometric pressure outside of his ears is greater than that inside. It's a sensation that serves as a reminder that our bodies are constantly neutralizing our relationship to the atmosphere. But, sometimes, it's hard to keep up.

Alan's mentor, scientist Julio Lescaburo, believed that unique barometric pressure systems, or atmospheric pressure, in the Catatumbo Delta are the origin of its namesake phenomenon, and Alan does, too. Nearly every morning, according to Alan and Julio's observations, winds reliably blow off Lake Maracaibo onto the Andes. While aloft, they cool on mountaintops cold enough to host tropical glaciers. Then, just as reliably, in the evening, the changing pressure systems of the lake call the winds back, where the cool pressure system of the Andes meets with the warm, moist pressure system that has been simmering in sunshine. When they converge over the lake: *Kaboom!* Lightning.

One popular counter-theory is the idea that high concentrations of methane gas over the lake somehow increase conductivity in the air. This idea, formulated by Ángel Muñoz of the University of Zulia, has been adopted by one of the Catatumbo's most vocal promoters, Erik Quiroga, a Caracas-based environmentalist.

Quiroga has introduced legislation that would make the Catatumbo lightning the first UNESCO World Heritage Weather Phenomenon. It's a request that received quite a bit of international press when the lightning temporarily disappeared in 2010. The incident made the lightning itself seem suddenly endangered, though no one could reliably identify the threat. Alan maintains that the lightning's disappearance was because of an El Niño that created drought conditions that extended the dry season, when the phenomenon reliably takes a brief annual hiatus. Quiroga, for his part, thinks deforestation and subsequent erosion along the Catatumbo River—which alters ecosystems—might have had something to do with the historic disappearance.

During the phenomenon's hiatus, *The Guardian* reported that UNESCO had no plans to declare the Catatumbo region a World Heritage site because "electric storms did not have a site." But in the case of the Catatumbo, this isn't true. It may transcend the terrestrial and our understanding, but if there's one thing—and there may be only one thing—that's known for certain about the Catatumbo lightning, it's that it has a home. We're almost there.

"Welcome to water world!" Alan shouts as we enter the village of Ologa, home to 300 perpetual seafarers. We're in a shallow, where houses are perched above the lake on wooden stilts. They look like water-walking spiders. Most of the unexpected structures are built with plank lumber, floors nearly falling into the lake-sea. Others are constructed of rusty tin and branches covered in bark that looks like elephant skin. The pre-Columbian homes encountered by early Spanish and Italian explorers weren't all that far removed from what we're seeing here today. They reminded the Europeans of the canals of Venice, Italy. This is how Venezuela, or Little Venice, is popularly known to have gotten its name.

In the distance, beyond the stilt houses of Ologa, there's a swampy island full of coconut trees. It's roughly as long as a football field and as wide as a suburban street. Beyond that, there is only the flat line of the horizon, punctured by the outline of a distant oil platform. All around the village's stilted homes, in what amounts to watery front yards, there are men standing in waist-deep water. They're shaving in broken shards of mirrors, and some of them have chests covered in soap suds. Children splash each other below platforms full of frothy fishing nets. A woman stands in an open doorway, raising her hand in greeting.

Alan lives, part time, in a house that sits a little apart from the others. It has a cement floor, which makes it a luxury accommodation among the mostly recycled-wood huts. When we dock, the boatmen busy themselves, unlocking the recycled-metal shipping-container doors of the house and separate kitchen, which is the size of a small closet. It has a rare patch of walkable swamp behind it, connected to the stilt house via a small cement bridge.

Coolers—filled with solid blocks of ice picked up at a factory alongside the road to Puerto Concha—are our only refrigeration, and water comes from a blue rainwater tank that's located on the backside of the house. One of the teenage boys in the group suggests that we could bathe in the lake like the locals do, but I can't get past the fact that the house's sewage system—like that of all the houses within sight—isn't actually a system at all. It's a hole in the floor. This is something Alan aims to change. He'd also like to add solar panels to limit the need for the generators that provide huts with electricity.

"You feel that the wind is different now," Alan says, taking off his mesh sun hat. "It's beginning." He points toward the lagoon side of the house, which has a wraparound cement porch. The wind is coming from the mountains now. When Alan is in Mérida, he can tell what time of day it is by watching the town's flags. He knows it's late evening when they start to blow toward the lake.

Alan instructs everyone to gather around him in the plastic chairs that the boatmen have brought onto the porch. We oblige and he pulls out a laminated topographical map of the lake. A small strait connects it to Tablazo Bay, which leads directly into the Gulf of Venezuela.

"These are NASA readings of lightning," Alan says, holding up a tie-dyed-looking chart. "This is the first show." He points to a red splotch over the mouth of the Catatumbo River. Then he directs our attention to the second show, which is centered on the lake. "See that dot in the center?" he says. "That's where the lightning is concentrated." It looks like a bull's-eye. "January, February, March, you don't see much lightning, but the rest of the year this storm is here."

Quiroga and others have touted the Catatumbo as one of the greatest ozone producers on earth. But this only serves to sully the phenomenon's reputation in many scientific circles, since the type of ozone produced by lightning is a greenhouse gas. This tropospheric ozone—like methane and fossil fuels—is a player in global warming. Though there's no clear connection, the fact that all three of these are present at the center of Lake Maracaibo—in amounts that might be greater than anywhere else on the planet—is something no one has seriously looked into as far as Alan and NOAA and NASA representatives know. Now, I'm no scientist. In fact, I'm about as laid out as a layperson can get. But I find this downright flabbergasting.

I initially felt crazy for putting the Catatumbo on my must-see list, but I now think it's sort of insane that more people aren't out here with me—especially people that might have the background to figure out what the Catatumbo has to teach. Even I feel confident in declaring that there's something magnificently interesting happening here. And I have yet to see my first lightning bolt.

Alan would like to host researchers at his stilt house, but he has thus far not received many inquiries from scientists or even storm chasers. He's contacted some well-known American meteorologists in the States to garner interest, but they often dismiss him. I suspect that they might actually think he's a little crazy.

He shuffles charts against the rough cement floor of the porch and begins to ramble in Spanish that challenges my basic language skills. I become distracted by a wooden boat full of children. They're inching across the channel between Alan's house and the rest of the village, navigating open water. A boy, who looks no older than seven, is pushing the craft over to us with a long stick. When they reach the house, the boatmen circulate bread stuffed with dry cheese and guyabano jelly, and the children accept their servings hungrily.

They cluster together on the cement floor and lean into Alan's words. Alan has observed the Catatumbo phenomenon to have two episodes and epicenters. NASA satellites have, too. It's actually the second storm, which is located near the center of the lake, rather than the one over the river, that's the strongest.

A little boy—face smeared with jelly—starts to whisper to his companions, but one of the girls shushes him. When Alan finishes his talk, the children turn their attention to the charts scattered on the ground like debris. They are not unfamiliar with the world beyond Lake Maracaibo. Few houses other than Alan's have lightning rods, but many of them have circular satellites for television. Still, the telenovelas from Mexico and sitcoms of Hollywood give a skewed perspective of what the world beyond the lake is really like. The children, all siblings and cousins, are in agreement: The idea of year-round, uninterrupted darkness— a deadened night sky—is amazing. And, maybe, just a little bit scary.

The rest of the group has gone to bed, but I'm keeping watch with Alan. He thinks it might be time for the lightning's late-night episode—which will actually be the first we've witnessed—to begin. It's just before midnight.

"The center of Lago de Maracaibo is where everything converges," Alan says.

He's talking about the winds—those coming from the mountains, which give the air a lofty boost, and the sea breezes that slip through the lake's narrow strait—but the way he says it makes it seem like he's talking about something greater, something spiritual. Maybe he is.

"I believe what the pre-Columbians believed," he says of lightning bolts. "I think they're spirits communicating with us." He shakes his head. "You know, I've had so many coincidences happen out here that it actually sort of freaks me out."

The most affecting happened without him even knowing. He was preparing to photograph the phenomenon, as he always does, when he saw a cloud in the shape of a giant white-feathered wing. The way the cloud reflected on the water made it appear to be half of a flight-worthy pair.

When he showed the resulting photograph to his daughter, telling her he thought the image looked like angel wings, of the sort he'd seen in Bible stories as a child, she was amazed. She asked when the photo was taken. Alan told her, and they both gasped at the significance. Exactly one year from the night he took the photo, his youngest granddaughter had lost her life to leukemia. "I hadn't realized that until I looked," Alan says. He puts a splayed hand on his temple and leans against his plastic chair, face hidden in shadows.

"I've told my family to come out here after I die," he says. "I've told them that they're going to see the most spectacular lightning show of their life when I'm gone."

He grows quiet, saying that he hopes he hasn't shared too much. It sounds weird, he knows. But, tonight, he's feeling a little more reflective and open than usual because it's his birthday. He's forty-eight years old.

We stare into darkness, waiting. Nothing happens.

Then, thunder!

No. It was Romo.

The other group members have retired to hammocks, but Romo, wearing only bikini underwear, is lying belly-down on the cement bridge between the house and the tiny island. He's fallen asleep with a blue flip-flop hanging from his left foot, as if he fell there. Another abrupt, opera-size growl of a snore makes me jump.

Alan laughs and says, "It does sound a little like thunder."

Romo may be the most dramatic person I've ever met, even in his sleep.

Above, a double moon ring forms before our eyes. It's a fairly rare, reflective ice-crystal phenomenon that's traditionally thought to be an indicator of bad weather. As the bands expand, it appears that the moon is blowing rainbow-tinted smoke rings. Alan is appreciative of the sighting, but he's not surprised. Stuff like this is always happening out here.

It was in this exact spot that he witnessed the 1998 solar eclipse. He says, "A phenomenon like that makes you feel strange. It makes animals go nuts. I met these eclipse hunters once and they told me that an eclipse is the oldest recorded event on earth." As the story goes, there were two armies on their way to war when, suddenly, the sun disappeared. "They thought it was a sign from the gods," Alan says. They were awed into peace.

"It was 400 BC; they can tell when it happened down to the second because of the cosmos. That's the reason life exists, because the cosmos are so perfect. If the sun changed its temperature even a little, we'd be toast." Alan leans forward in his chair. "It's that sort of thing that can make you believe in God."

Alan turns to look at me, breaking his sky gaze for the first time in a long while, and he says, "I feel really privileged to exist. I don't understand how or why I'm here. It's not like when I'm talking about my body; I'm talking about my soul. I believe we are something more than expression of self."

This transcendence of self—ego—is what many religious traditions are about. It's a major tenet of Buddhism, the religion Einstein thought was perhaps best suited of all organized religions to serve science, which tends to value the body of work created over time more than the insights of an individual. There's really little room for ego in the long arch of discovery. No matter how far one ventures in a lifetime, how much knowledge or insight is gained, there's always more to be known.

Einstein felt there were three sorts of religiosity. The first two were the religions of morals and fear; the third he called "cosmic religious feeling." He understood this state to be one that had no dogma and no God conceived in man's image, a way of thinking that allowed for failure and encouraged the sort of curious doggedness required of scientists and creative people. It was spirituality that transcended understanding, an embracement of mystery and the impulse to explore it. "In my view," he wrote, "it is the most important function of art and science to awaken this feeling and keep it alive in those who are capable of it."

Some people, it seems to me, attempt to fall away from their egos, to transcend into cosmic religiosity, via yoga or meditation. Others, like Alan—and, I'm increasingly realizing, myself—are seeking the same sort of experience in nature at its most spectacular, in moments that inspire a sort of temporary yielding of fear and expectation to awe and acceptance.

A sense of wonder is, I think, what Einstein meant by a cosmic religious feeling. And that is really what I'm seeking on this journey. It's an admission of human frailty and the perfect magnificence of earth, the universe, time, in a way that removes the masks of humankind's many religions to reveal their connectivity, the fact that we are—in the end—one.

Romo is the first to awaken when the lightning begins a few hours later. He greets everyone on the porch with a lightbulb-shaped lantern balanced over his head, symbolizing a moment of enlightenment. "*¡Tengo una idea!*" Romo says. "I have an idea!" The jokester, still wearing his bikini underwear and nothing else, starts to giggle.

He's the opening act. We're in for quite a show.

The clouds are lighting up the sky like giant rice-paper lanterns, strikes hidden in the clouds. These obscured flashes are known as sheet lightning. The absence of thunder makes these appear as what many people—including me—have long called heat lightning. But it's just the distance—the viewers' perspective—that makes it seem silent. Somewhere, the sky is screaming as air molecules are ripped apart by extreme heat.

A bolt—vivid and unshrouded—suddenly appears directly before us and shoots nearly straight to the ground, where it seems to hold for a very long time, a solid column of plasma. Lightning bolts are typically less than a half inch in diameter, but these appear as wide as the Mississippi River.

"*¡Qué bueno! ¡Qué bueno!*" Romo shouts, suddenly serious.

A rooster crows from somewhere in the village, and the lightning does make the night appear a faux sort of dawn, orange and yellow light illuminating the sky with forceful regularity. They expose the atmosphere—red toward the bottom where pollutants allow only red spectrum light to pass, and a phosphorescent blue toward the top, where the air is cleaner. The crown of the strike looks like pure fire, a butane flame.

A rush of wind blows across the island and Alan says, "That's good. It's growing. Come on!"

There are two storms in front of us. Three now. They're getting stronger.

The wind picks up and the cloud-to-ground strikes become cloud-to-cloud. When a bolt of lightning flashes across the sky, filling the entire palette of night, we all cry out. The phenomenon shoots across the sky, forking in four different directions like a mapped nervous system.

"Bravo!" Romo screams. "Bravo!"

I'm so exhausted, I feel nearly nauseous with fatigue. What's more, each time I turn to go into the house to get a long-sleeved shirt to prevent malarial mosquito bites, the lightning flashes even bolder than before. I turn, it shouts. It's almost as if it's tapping me on the shoulder, saying: The show isn't over.

Matt offers to go in my stead—out of kindness more than concern about tropical diseases—but I urge him to stay. There's too much to see here. And—unlike everything in our regular schedule at home, which allows only brief contact when passing the domestic baton—we're going to see it together.

"All that concentrated energy!" Alan shouts.

"¡Mira! Look!" Romo shrieks.

The sky is a labyrinth of light that's shooting north, south, east, west, but its structure is so complex it's impossible to see where it begins or ends.

I close my eyes as I stand on the stilt-house porch. The air smells of swampy earth. I can hear the water lapping at the island's ragged shores and the stilt-house's cement pilings like the hull of a boat. My senses feel attuned. I'm living three-dimensionally. This, I realize, is what I'd been missing in those early days of Archer's life. It had been so cold outside and I'd had a fragile infant. I'd been suddenly thrown into the visceral cycle of life and death in labor, but as a nervous new mother, I was rarely going outdoors.

I was more connected to the cycle of life than ever before, but I'd never been more isolated from its larger stage. The hunger I've had—the deep-seated one that I've been denying because of my who-am-I-to-ask-for-more outlook and my fear of being judged a kook for talking about spirituality—extends even beyond that, I think. In my childhood, I spent countless hours exploring nature—collecting wild mushrooms, sifting slick pebbles from streams. I spend much more time mining the Internet now. I have allowed myself to fall too far from grand shows of beauty.

But I am here now. Right here. Right now.

I open my eyes again. I watch the light of a hidden strike rise in the sky, cloud-to-cloud, spirits rising. The earth feels oddly charged with meaning, and truth and mythology seem to blur as in magical realism. The voices of ancestors crowd around us, crackling and cackling in what locals sometimes refer to as "rivers of fire."

Flames fork overhead, in what scientists call spider lightning. They web the stars, like a game of connect-the-dots. Then, I see a strike zig-zag across the air, pausing at each star step. Zig. Zag. Lightning bolts are usually too fast for the human eye to catch, but when intracloud lightning goes on for long enough, it reveals itself. This strike is going the distance. I'm able to watch it transpire. Lightning has been known to travel more than a hundred miles, but as far as Alan knows, there've been no studies on distance here. It seems to go on forever. What I'm watching is not a flash. It is an electric progression, a slow knitting of bone, a white-hot shard of marrow slicing through the darkness to give the flesh of night something to cling to as it takes shape.

"Tumbo, tumbo! Rumbo, rumbo!" Romo shouts to my right. He sounds like a sorcerer tending a cauldron of roiling energy. Above, bands of pink gold jump across the lower atmosphere, arching like the backs of Lake Maracaibo's freshwater dolphins. They swim toward the heavens and back down again. Romo paces the uneven ground, half naked, his long white hair flying wild. He whistles through his teeth melodically, and his songs are carried by the wind. The bolts don't stop until sunrise.

The following evening, dinner is local fare—there's really no other kind out here: bottom-feeding fish baited with chicken heads. It's served tuna-salad style, mixed with boiled eggs, and it's better than it sounds, salty and filling. We sing "Happy Birthday" to Alan as winds whip at the hammocks, turning mosquito nets into festive, gauzy streamers.

"Anywhere else in the world," Alan says, "and these winds would push the storms into a different position." He shakes his head at enduring mysteries. Then he pushes away from the table. "Now," he says, "for the celebratory fireworks!"

There are a few flashes in the distance, lightning hidden behind clouds. The epicenter appears to be just over the Catatumbo River, where drugs are trafficked in its light.

Romo is seated in a plastic chair. He lifts his arms and begins to wave them like an orchestra conductor. The flashes begin. "Ping. Ping. Ping. Rum. Rum. Rum. ¡Pada! ¡Pata!"

His hands explode into the air, trying to mimic the lightning in the distance. It has become a silent symphony. There is no thunder—the storms are too far for that—but the light has become nearly constant now.

"There are five storms out there!" someone shouts.

"Maybe six," Alan says.

The storms appear as a line across the sky, following the curvature of the Catatumbo River. The lightning has turned the sky into an instrument of light. I move my fingers as if I'm playing the piano while Romo continues his own embodiment of the phenomenon.

"Oopa!" he shouts, hooking his right arm like a boxer. "¡*Muy bien!*"

"Try to count how many you see in a minute," Alan tells the group and we go silent. I lose count somewhere around forty. There is too much light, too much happening at once. Flashes from the different storms are bleeding into each other. Sometimes, spontaneous strikes occur in unison, their origin shrouded by the clouds. The fact that we can't see their genesis only serves to make them more beautiful. It's as if the clouds themselves are on fire.

"*Cien*, one hundred!" someone shouts.

Romo doesn't try to count. He doesn't seem to have the need to quantify. "¡*Tada*! ¡*Tada*!" he shouts, pinging his hands in the air, ringing invisible bells.

"Try to turn your head to follow the flashes and you'll find you're shaking it," Alan says. "It's cool!" To the left. To the right. Left. Right. It's like trying to count flames flickering in a campfire. We can't keep up. To even attempt is dizzying.

Just after midnight, as Alan has predicted, the storm fires up in the middle of the lake, on the other side of the house. I'm half asleep when I encounter Alan, who shouts: "This baby's on top of us! It looks like it's going to be massive! There are often minihurricanes here, and the night is young!" He begins to sing the Doors' *Riders on the Storm*.

For the first time since we've arrived, it begins to rain over the village. The storm is no longer something to watch from a safe distance. Here, there is no shelter that is so far removed from the elements that one can feel totally safe, completely cocooned. No matter how many hatches you batten down out here, there's no way to escape the storm.

"Thank God," Alan says. At first, I think he's just excited about the force of the winds, the ever-increasing power in the sky. But then he adds, "It'll fill up the rainwater tank. We were about empty, dude." Lightning: danger and savior.

The sky flashes. "Whoa, here it comes!" Alan shouts. The water laps. Alan jumps a little in place. The lightning is everywhere now. Romo is laughing like a madman. Hearty laughs, laughs that you might expect from a man whose snores could be mistaken for thunder.

"That's only about eight kilometers out," Alan says, pointing at the sky.

I feel a mosquito on my back. Pulling it from my flesh is like removing a needle. In the swamp, trees turn to shadows, their palms skeletal, backlit and sinister. Even the boatmen, used to the storms, have gotten out of their hammocks for this. They hop in their crafts and move them toward the bulkhead of the island so that they won't smash against the house.

Horizontal bolts rip through the sky. We're all on our feet now. When a particularly loud bolt crashes, I let out a little scream. The rest of the group laughs, but, on the next strike, a few of them follow my lead. "This too shall pass," Alan says.

He appears the happiest I've seen him since we met. He shouts, "There are spirits in these clouds! Spirits!" I actually have a sense of otherworldliness myself, though I'm coming to understand this world— a blue dot on the cosmic map—as magical as magic can be. Maybe, I think, the lightning doesn't bring so much a message as an opportunity to listen to our own fears, questions, doubts, needs. In the end, no source of light is as important as what it illuminates. No thunder is as loud as its resounding interpretation.

A bolt lights the porch. The group giggles nervously. Alan says,

"Sometimes the bolts are so constant that, if it's not raining, you can go onto the island and read a book by their light." It is, of course, something he's actually tried.

Sans Alan, our whole group is in a cluster now, which goes against NOAA instructions to separate so that if someone is hit by lightning there will be survivors to go for help. But, on Lake Maracaibo, this rule doesn't really apply. There's nowhere to go, no help to be had.

I'm relieved when Alan decides to join us under the awning, until I realize he's just ducking under to get his tripod. When he steps into open air with the three metal rods, a bolt illuminates the jungle beyond, bright as day. I can see bark on the trees just beyond the cement bridge, previously unnoticed.

"It's interesting how the thunder here sounds so different than the thunder in Mérida," Alan shouts. "There, it just bounces off of the mountains, but here . . ." A high-tone boom cuts him off, barreling across open water as lightning strikes the center of Lake Maracaibo once, twice, oh, I don't know, *a thousand times*.

Romo is already in performance mode, doing a graceful mash-up of tai chi and yoga in the swamp, when I wake up the next morning. He seems to be tracing the circle of the full sun, his palms pressed toward the sky like sun-soaking butterfly wings. Matt is sitting on the porch with a cup of coffee in his hand.

"Pretty wild night," I say, helping myself to fresh-cut papaya. I fix him a plate, too. This is something I don't always do at home, where Archer's needs are my first concern. The trip has been full of many small, soft moments between us. These days, we're both reaching out.

When I hand him his plate, he says, "I think what makes us most nervous about lightning is the fact that we can't conquer it. We'll never be able to hold it in our hands no matter how hard we try."

He pauses to savor a bite of overripe fruit before continuing. "The lightning," he says, "it's what you'll never get back. Watching these storms is like spending the night in life and death. A strike of lightning is a moment in time. We get thousands of moments, but the lightning reminds us that they're all temporary."

Now, this is not the sort of table talk we have over breakfast at home. In fact, when we're in the daily grind, we hardly have time for talks about who's going to pick up milk and bread. But this is one of our lightning-strike moments in time. The Catatumbo phenomenon has jolted us out of our routine, our ritual, our comfort zone so completely that it's impossible to imagine ever settling back into it quite as deeply as we'd been before.

Alan stirs in his hammock. He emerges to join the group for *arepas*— fried corn pancakes—and eggs scrambled with tomatoes and onions, which is curiously called *perico*, or parrot, possibly an ode to the dish's brilliant colors. The connection comes close to home as a scarlet macaw lands on the roof not far from where we sit, the sky momentarily splashed with a vivid, living rainbow.

"This is another cool part of the storm sequence," Alan says. "You get that gnarly storm at night and then this!" He waves toward the morning's unblemished sky, and then he sets about whittling a brick of hardened *panela*, a regional confection created by boiling fresh sugarcane until all that remains is its essence.

The *panela* is covered with wasps, their dark bodies pierced by brilliant yellow streaks. Alan brushes them off as if they're harmless houseflies before pushing caramel shavings into his coffee. Then, he offers the wasp-covered block to me.

The insects look like living lightning. I hesitate. Alan notices.

"These guys can really hurt you," he says. "But they rarely do sting."

I laugh and extend an open hand. The *panela* is earthy and rich. I fill my cup and return to the block, daringly, again and again. Why wouldn't I? All of life is a trust fall, and I'm awakening to the thrill, rather than the fear, of being suspended midair.

CHAPTER 4

VOLCANIC ERUPTION, HAWAI'I

November 2011

MY UNDERSTANDING OF HAWAIIAN HULA HAS, UNTIL RECENT-ly, been limited to Hollywood portrayals and tourist luaus. But when I discovered that the dance is considered a direct conduit to the goddess of fire, Pele, who lives in Kīlauea volcano, I decided that the next phenomenon on my list might be better explored via gyrating hips than geological surveys. That's why I'm headed to the Big Island of Hawai'i to see the volcano in action and attend the Moku O Keawe Hula Festival, where I'll learn about hula as an expression of nature-based Hawaiian spirituality. Then, I'm slated to join up with a hula *hālau*, or hula school, performing an actual crater-side offering to Pele. But my departure is still two weeks away.

Today, I'm hanging with Archer.

Some people think a seven-course meal is the pinnacle of culinary pageantry. I suspect these people have never dined with a two-year-old. Archer can make a one-course meal last for nearly an hour. He sings to it. He caresses it. He squeezes it just to feel the sensation of it between his fingers. He paints the table with it. He paints himself. He explores the texture, savors the flavors, plays with the colors. Dinner isn't composed of food groups. It is the creaminess of mashed potatoes and the oozing satisfaction of soft-enough-to-smash green beans.

Food often ends up on the floor and, during the messiest of meals, the wall. This is exasperating. It's also strangely beautiful. Unless we're in a hurry.

I'm not necessarily in a rush on this fine fall day, but I am hoping to check the mail. This seems like a simple task, one that shouldn't take much effort or cause frustration, I know, but checking my mailbox is easy like lunch with a toddler is quick. The box is located roughly a quarter mile from my house, down a gravel road that makes getting to and from my place in winter—and for nervous drivers, in summer—a challenging prospect.

I used to be able to strap Archer into a big-wheeled stroller, but he's gotten too curious for rides. He bucks like a baby bronco if I try to get him in the thing. I'm longing for a beeline; he's more interested in actual bees.

Our road is a curve cut into a mountainside, and it's the fringes of the path that Archer is drawn to. It isn't long before he is ahead of me. He throws out his arms and screams: "Outside!" It's the sort of enthusiasm some kids reserve for ice cream.

We stop by a drainage ditch that Archer has taken to calling his "garden." He studies weeds as if they're flower-show roses. I try to convince him that there might be something interesting in the mailbox when we get there—a letter from his grandmother, a magazine with pretty pictures—but he's insistent on continuing in the opposite direction.

I've been holding the arm of his coat. But, tired of trying to control a situation where there isn't any immediate danger, I let go. He takes off. I follow.

When we get to a small wooded area, he yells, "Pine forest! Path!" and shoots off into sheltering trees. There are three stumps on the trail, memorials to trees sacrificed to show us the way. They are covered in bristly moss. Archer touches it and quickly recoils as if it might bite him. Then he starts to chuckle. There's really no other word for it. He smiles smugly until his eyes are slits, and he throws back his head.

"What are you laughing at?" I ask.

"Laughing at the trees waving," he tells me. I look up, at the spindly arms of the pines. They look like big-haired cheerleaders enthusiastically waving green pom-poms. I start laughing, too.

He climbs on a stump. I throw my hands up and shout, in supreme Archer fashion, "Be the tree!" He smiles and stretches his arms to the sky, elbows turned knots on a limb; fingers, splayed pine needles. This spontaneous game, I soon learn, might be fine pretraining if he ever expresses interest in learning the Hawaiian art of embodiment otherwise known as hula dancing.

Ancient Hawaiians identified so closely with nature that there was a term for every observed phenomenon, no matter how small. Winds were named based on their subtlety. Raindrops, their size. Lava flows, their shape. These site-specific observations have been passed down for millennia through myth-heavy *oli*, or chants, and dance.

Hula is, at its core, a collective sort of muscle memory.

During my first morning on the Big Island, I dine with a woman who has the ability to morph into twisting flows of lava. At least, she does when she's dancing. Keikilani Curnan—a soft-featured woman with long brown hair and lips coated in coral-colored lipstick—is a *kumu* hula, or hula teacher. She can, with the flick of a wrist, turn herself into phenomena of all sorts. And, as a keeper of Pele's stories, she is—according to Hawaiian tradition—the closest one can get to meeting the fire goddess made flesh.

It's actually a fluke that I'm having breakfast with Keikilani today. When I was checking into the Waikoloa Beach Marriott, the receptionist realized that Keikilani—teacher of the *hālau* I've ultimately come to see, days from now, miles from here—worked in the sales office of the very hotel I was standing in.

Maybe geography really is destiny.

Hawai'i—declared a state in 1959 after an overthrow of Hawaiian monarchy—sits in the center of the Ring of Fire, a horseshoe-shaped area of volcanic activity anchored by the Pacific Basin. The Big Island was constructed by five major volcanoes: Kīlauea, Mauna Loa, Hualalai Loa, and Kohala. Kīlauea is a shield volcano, categorized by its gentle lava flows. Through them, Pele's presence can be found everywhere.

Keikilani, native of Hawai'i, sees Moku O Keawe as an opportunity for hula dancers from outside of the islands to get to know the place they're dancing about. She explains that the festival is a celebration of the islands as not only the center of volcanic activity on earth, but also the center of the hula world. "We reference this place as the *piko*, or belly button," she says. This is more important than one might think.

"To Hawaiians," Keikilani says, "your gut or intuition, your navel, is almost more important than the brain. You know when something is right or when you feel something is good." She puts a hand on her belly and moves it up her chest until it rests on the top of her head. "When it needs to," she says, "that knowledge flows up."

She is—without hesitation—telling me that she comes from a culture of navel gazers.

To call someone a navel gazer on the mainland is to say that they're narcissistic, self-absorbed in their introspective pursuits. This perspective, I realize, might be the very reason I've come to think of a spiritual life as some sort of luxury. I'm suddenly struck by the irony of a culture that seems to point to personal spiritual quests as somehow selfish when, in the end, those journeys, like the discredited belly button, are ultimately a search for connectivity.

Hawaiians don't use the word chat. They say, "talk story." So, I ask Keikilani to talk story about her upcoming performance at the Halemaʻumaʻu crater. "Everyone wants to dance there," she explains. "That's where Pele resides." Keikilani rubs her hand along her arm as if she's trying to warm herself. "I've got chicken skin just thinking about it!" she says, using the Hawaiian term for goose bumps.

Keikilani was born into a dancing dynasty. In 1938, her mother was crowned the first Queen of Hula. At eighteen, she briefly went to Hollywood, where she got a small part in an MGM movie. She ultimately returned to Hawaiʻi and married a man of Irish descent. Keikilani may have inherited her mother's moves, but she got her father's blue eyes and chestnut hair. They're part of the reason she originally became interested in hula. "I was teased as a child because of the way I look," she says, "but I *am* Hawaiian."

Though dancing has always been a way for Keikilani to assert her cultural identity, it wasn't until the late seventies that she began to understand it as a moving sort of prayer. "Some people just want to learn to dance," she says, "but others want to experience the *mana*, spiritual power."

Mana is something her mother, despite her crown, never quite understood. One day, when she was in her nineties, she called out to her grown daughter, who was rushing out the door to dance class: "Where you going?"

"I go to hula," Keikilani reminded her.

"You're *still* taking hula?" her mother said. "Don't you know it all by now?"

Keikilani smiles at the memory, and she gives me a sideways glance: "But you see, there is no end to the hula, no ultimate mastery," she says. "Hula is an ongoing thing."

She nods toward my cell phone, where a digital photo of Archer stares at us from the screen. "It's like parenting, yeah? It doesn't end and it's always changing. You're learning, but you're also creating. There's new hula music being created and there are new chants all the time. This is all part of the birthing."

My radio-equipped headset can't mask the *thwamp, thwamp* of the heli-copter's whirling blades. They've turned the sun into a strobe light. The nose of the craft is glass, and when taking off, I feel like I'm floating rather than flying. There goes the blue car, the white bits of bleached coral placed on the dark ground as geological graffiti. There goes the strip of asphalt that's been overtaken by stone. There goes the earth itself.

I'm touring via helicopter to witness the volcano's lava production. I'm also interested in seeing Hawaii's *kīpuka*, isolated areas of foliage surrounded by lava. From above, these sparred patches of land look like green arks sailing in dark, hardened seas. Once the molten lava flows around them have cooled, birds and winds will carry their seeds to re-populate desolate landscapes. My pilot's name on this *kīpuka*, or seed ark, tour is—I kid you not—Noah.

Only 5 percent of Hawai'i is populated. From the air, it's a lunar landscape. This made the Jersey-based honeymooners I met at the heli-port feel like they'd been duped by brochures. It makes me feel like I've been granted access to space, though I do agree with the disgruntled groom: The whole island looks like a construction zone. Probably because it is one.

On the North Carolina coast, where I went to high school, people worry about eroding waterfront lots. Here, there are landowners concerned that their seaside property might suddenly be located inland. Kīlauea has added more than 500 miles to the landmass of Hawai'i since 1983. The coastline is ever expanding.

We're moving toward the eastern side of the island, home to the rift zone. This is where earth's internal hot spot becomes a visible-to-the-naked-eye phenomenon. Our destination, Kīlauea, has been active—as far as volcanologists know—since its formation roughly 300,000–600,000 years ago. The volcano has two main areas of action, Halema'uma'u, Pele's home, and Pu'u'O'o, an east rift vent.

When we pass Mauna Kea, Noah says of the volcano, "It's almost like it's satisfied with how big it is and it's taking a break." Currently, it holds the title of largest volcano on earth, though some volcanologists believe that Kīlauea will ultimately rival its height.

Hawai'i becomes geologically younger before our eyes; old lava flows stream into new. Noah points out a highway where plastic-smooth lava, called *pāhoehoe*, laps at asphalt like a frozen black tide. It's a flow from the 1800s with a smooth surface, rock solid all the way through. Rockier lava is called *'a'a*. The island is a mix of the two types, which are chemically alike despite their differing appearance.

Noah takes the craft over monkey pod and albizia tree canopies that look like lily pads from the air, over rusty rooftops, macadamia nut plantations, and Hilo, the largest town on the island, named for the way its flows appear braided. Finally, we reach the edge of a tree line. Here, there is only lava. Miles of it.

Noah nods toward the hard-baked moonscape and says, "Try to picture this before the eruptions. It was forest all the way down to the

ocean. Then flows began consuming this area and forming that cone."
He points to PuʻuʻOʻo in the distance; its rim is sort of off center, like a
semicrushed dunce hat.

In the 1980s, the area below us was covered in houses. Then, one day,
a crack opened and started spewing lava. The ground seemed solid one
minute, a curtain of fire the next. Without giving many signs of its plans,
the earth dilated and new land was born, consuming a neighborhood of
200 homes.

This cone was formed over decades, magma cooling and building
itself. From above, it looks like an open mouth with the cherry of a cigarette balanced on its lower lip. The flat land around the crater is full of
salt-flat-style cracks, and smoke is rising from nearly all of them. An
overnight rain has soaked into the ground and the moisture is coming
out as steam. The place looks like a black sea full of whitecapped waves.
To make things even more surreal, it's hard to tell the vog—volcanic
emissions that look like fog—from the morning's low-hanging clouds.
Smoke emanates from everywhere.

"Everything here is linked together," Noah says. "What we see on the
surface is connected to what's going on under the surface."

He twists around to get another look at the surrounding landscape.
There's no safe way to get to it from the ground. "This is an old lava
system. It's actually amazing to see it smoking like this," Noah says.
"You can see that it's still hot, and it goes all the way down to the ocean."

As Kīlauea grows, it forms complex plumbing systems underground.
Sometimes, when pressure is right, lava is pushed out of the main crater
in dramatic shows, but most of the time, the volcano works its island-
building magic behind the scenes, moving through underground tunnels. When these tunnels become dormant, they will be known as lava
tubes, capillaries-turned-caves, created by fire.

Noah shakes his head: "There's a lot going on under there that we just don't even know about." He points to the east where he's observed a lava tube forming. "Let's go see what it's doing today," he says.

We find a spot where magma is exiting the tube system. Its flows are pure orange on a black canvas. Odd iridescent silver-streams surround them, too hot to form crust. I can see where the surface layers have hardened and been pulled forth by new flows.

After he's made a few rounds to make sure I get a good look, Noah moves on to the most famous *kīpuka* on the island, an oval of tropical forest that was once the center of the Royal Gardens subdivision. By 1990, pretty much every house in Royal Gardens had been destroyed by lava. Today, there's only one left standing. It belongs to Jack Thompson. He still lives there.

Thompson's house sits in the center of a *kīpuka*. It's miles from another patch of green. He used to ride a motor scooter across lava and remaining roads. But, in time, all the roads were covered. Then the nearest town was destroyed. Now, according to Noah—who picks Thompson up from time to time for dentist appointments and rare, can't-grow-it-in-the-garden grocery runs—Hawaii's most famous hermit still makes infrequent hikes across landscapes that could devour him at any minute.

I look down at the totally intact wood-sided house, its roof a dot of red in a small island of green, and imagine the ghosts of hundreds of other houses lying under a hardened mat of lava. I flick a handset switch that allows me to communicate with Noah: "It's a little wild that the only house the volcano didn't take belongs to the only person who would stay, isn't it?"

"You're right," he says, somewhat taken aback. Later, when we're back on the ground, he'll tell me: "I've made this flight multiple times a day for years and no one's ever said anything like that. They're usually more focused on how crazy Jack must be for living there." It's only then that I realize I've been talking about the volcano like it's in control of the situation. But isn't it?

In a 1955 eruption of Kīlauea's rift zone, barriers were erected on the island to divert flows from destroying two separate plantations. But, ultimately, they found different routes and took both properties anyway. Diversions are little-researched and expensive to erect. So Pele continues to choose her course without much human resistance. Here, going with the flow is a metaphoric *and* physically observable thing—often simultaneously.

We have no way of knowing that, just months from now, Pele will decide that it's time for Jack Thompson to move on. He'll catch a ride on a helicopter as she takes the last standing structure in Royal Gardens, along with its *kīpuka*, which had already spread its seeds.

Noah flies the helicopter over the coastline where Royal Gardens' lava tubes deposit their magma to create land that will, over time, be eroded to create habitat for coral. But, for now, the ring around this island is a drop-off into 15,000 feet of water. It's too young for life to cling. These are the black cliffs of Hawai'i, land created in my lifetime. The entire island is still a child in the geological scheme of things, a monument of newness, every plume of its smoke screaming, like a toddler in search of an audience: *Look at me!*

At some point the eruptions here will stop, giving rain a chance to weather this down. This area will be forested again, and a different crater will start erupting. Noah says, "When that change is going to take place we don't really know. It could go for twenty-eight years or it could stop next week. Hard to say."

To many, this would be a nail-biting sort of ambiguity, but to Noah, it seems to be more than okay. Change brings joy, gains, happiness, blessings. It brings loss, hardship, and tragedy, too. But the underlying sentiment of conversations I've had thus far on Hawai'i seems to be this:

Accepting change isn't fatalism; it's a jump-or-be-dragged-into-it part of the holy process.

"Everything here is part of a big cycle," Noah says, "a cycle we can see."

He points out tiny dots of green below, ferns just beyond the orange-black of fresh flows, the first growth to emerge. 'Ōhi'a lehua trees, which are native to Hawai'i, often follow. There are thirteen climate zones on earth. This 4,000-square-mile island hosts eleven of them. It's proven a perfect canvas for evolutionary creativity. Ninety percent of plants on the island are endemic species, those that grow on Hawai'i and nowhere else. Endemic species derive from seeds that grow here, unaccompanied by the species that threatened them in their homelands. In Hawai'i, they relax. Berry bushes lose their thorns. Nettles shed their stinging parts. The island's isolation breeds a chill sort of diversity.

The nose of the helicopter is pointed so that if we flew in a straight line we would fly over all seven of Hawaii's inhabited islands. Conversely, if we took a right, we wouldn't hit land until we reached Alaska, more than 3,000 miles away. "Big picture, we're just a tiny little rock and we're in the middle of the largest ocean on the planet," Noah says.

Hawai'i is, geographically, the most remote place on earth, but Pacific explorers found it as early as AD 200. In ancient Polynesian culture, everyday people—not just biologists—understood the natural world so well that they recognized patterns inherent in it, and this may have been what enabled the discovery. "They developed this idea that there was land here by watching the migration of birds," Noah says. "That's what gave them hope."

We fly over landscapes shaped by earthquakes, erosion, landslides, collapsed lava tubes, photo-worthy waterfalls. These scenes are the progeny of ancient flows that have had time to break down, where the elements have made the soil loose enough to accept seeds. The Hawaiian islands are at their most luscious in their latter phases of life, just as fruit is sweetest on the verge of rotting. Every mile we travel brings more green.

Noah says, "The forest below us used to look like the barren landscape we've just seen. But this is the change that's possible." He nudges the helicopter toward younger flows. It's time to head back. "We'll be full circle pretty soon," he says.

By the time Captain Cook got to Hawai'i in 1778, making the first known European contact, it seemed unbelievable that Polynesians navigated based on their observations of birds, stars, winds, and waves. But, still, Cook and his crew were likely nagged by curiosity: Could it be true? Would I have had the fortitude to set out with no compass? If I tried, could I learn to use my senses to read the sea?

It's something lots of people ask. Danny Akaka can assuredly answer: Yes.

In 1999, Danny—a Hawaiian *kahu*, or spiritual leader—was part of an eight-month traditional canoe voyage to Chile's volcanic Easter Island. His crew used traditional Polynesian star-compass navigation to travel the globe. At Keikilani's urging, I've joined up with him for a group tour of the Mauna Lani resort, where he serves as director of cultural affairs.

He's wearing a tucked-in Hawaiian shirt and glasses that turn amber when he's standing in direct sun. In his revered role as a *kahu*, he has performed blessing ceremonies at high-end resorts, biodiesel stations, and highway openings. When the Dalai Lama visited the state, Danny was chosen to represent Hawaii's spiritual heritage. He's known for earnestly saying things like: "We're all strings on God's ukulele."

There are roughly 400,000 deities in Hawai'i. Danny says of the deities, "When you call on all those parts to come together, that's the whole.

Holy, to become whole." *Holi* is an Old English word, derived from *halig*. Whole. Complete. In traditional Hawaiian culture, it is understood that everything in the universe is part of this completion.

But many of the deities and ancestor names of Hawai'i have been forgotten over time. Though they have been experiencing a renaissance along with hula, some residents of the Big Island recognize only one of the ancient deities: Pele. "Pele is talked about very carefully still because she can see and hear everything," Danny says. "She's been quite active, so she's survived."

Danny begins to walk fast and it strikes me that I don't know where we're ultimately headed. This bothers me. I'm calibrated for destination. It's partly why I've been imagining divinity as some sort of beam-me-up-Scotty experience. But maybe transcendence isn't about leaving. It's about being present. Life is a performance piece. Like dance and song, the art is in the process. Like hula and *oli*, the process is the prayer.

"Christianity," Danny tells me as our strides begin to match, "tends to go straight to the source. But to get to God there is a process. There's the acknowledgment of the ancestors, the addressing of the land. You've got to go through all of that to get to the purpose of why you're here."

Ma ka hana ka 'ike. In the journey of the task is the knowledge.

Danny's wife, Anna, a slight woman in a floral sundress, is walking nearby. She points to the sky, as if the air might be visible if I look long enough. "'*Ōlauniu*," she says; "frond-piercing wind." It is a wind that lives only on this coastline, only on this island.

When we near a hut surrounded by primary-colored kayaks, Danny and Anna spot a visiting elder they have been looking for all day. They ask the group to wait while they greet him. Anna approaches him and lifts her arms upward to unravel a yellow lei that's been wrapped around the brim of her sun hat. She places it around his neck.

Danny gently leans forward, piercing what I perceive as the man's personal space, until the two are standing forehead-pressed-against-forehead. He inhales. Dramatically. Audibly.

This is a traditional Hawaiian greeting. It represents an exchange of spiritual power between two people. In Hawaiian, *alo* means being present together. *Hā* is breath, the sound every human makes when exhaling. It is a greeting meant to acknowledge that we all share the same breath of life.

Aloha.

I've been breathing on people, and people have been breathing on me. Not in an intentional, *aloha* way, but in a you're-spitting-on-me-in-coach-class sort of way. Maybe this is why I am losing my voice. Or maybe I'm suffering from the effects of vog. I've seen herbal supplements advertising relief from its harshness in local magazines. Or maybe my vocal cords are just irritated from all the mold and dust that flew from the shell of my *ipu*—one of the sacred gourd drums used in hula—when I crafted it in a Moku O Keawe workshop. In any case, all chatter has fallen to the back of my throat. And, as anyone who knows me can attest, that means there's a whole lotta story-talk rattling around in there.

Earlier this morning, I drove to the village of Volcano from the Kona side of the island, starting out before 7 a.m., taking Saddle Road, a route that was only recently opened for rental cars like the Jeep I'm using. It was like driving on a trackless roller coaster. There were more cinder cones than cars, more signs for sacred places than speed postings.

Volcano is famed as an artist colony. It's home to poets, painters, weavers, and potters. The Roman god Vulcan, after whom volcanoes are named, was the god of welders, who represented the constructive, creative side of fire. The welders in Volcano—and there do seem to be more here than in an average township—are mostly sculptors. It seems more than coincidental that Pele, goddess of fire, is also the goddess of creativity, mother of flow.

Keikilani's *hālau* will be performing on a stage of earth and stone, directly across from the Halemaʻumaʻu crater. I've been told we're only yards from a steep drop down, though nothing is visible beyond the performance area because of fog and vog. The girls are changing in the traditional *hale*, a hut of waxy leaves tied onto posts via coconut fiber. It's part of the performance ground at Volcanoes National Park. The grassy area in front of the stage is full of onlookers, mostly locals with umbrellas and grass mats, teenage girls with bare feet covered in leafy debris.

It looks like the performance area has been filled by an offstage smoke machine by the time Keikilani appears. She is wearing a long white robe, and her head is encircled by muted flowers and silvery sagelike leaves. Outside of Hawaiʻi, hula schools are likely to be commercial endeavors, but on Hawaiʻi, many *kumu* are part of a genealogy that stretches into antiquity. Each genealogy might be considered a genre with characteristic nuance. Keikilani's genealogy, her family tree, is known on the islands for its exceptionally fluid movement. "What we're showing today has been passed on from our hula family," she tells the audience.

When her students appear, they're wearing *pāʻū*, hula skirts that are smocked at the top to leave copious gathers around the thigh. They have the same shape as traditional skirts made of ti leaves. If a camera adds ten pounds, a *pāʻū* skirt would add twenty, which is perhaps why Hollywood turned the traditional *pāʻū* into grass skirts, which—like coconut bras—can offend in Hawaiʻi. Dancers following the spiritual protocols of traditional hula never bare their *piko*, their belly buttons. Doing so, Keikilani has told me, would reveal too much of their power.

The dancers—each wearing a fuzzy crown of native lehua flowers—perform a series of songs that can be followed, with imagination, through cycles of the moon, hands thrown around their heads. There are also stories of wayfarers paddling, invisible oars appearing in the dancers' fists. Their *kumu*, sitting on the side of the platform with their *ipu*, chant. Every so often, the group chants back. But their main job is to communicate with Pele through their dance.

Cultural ecologist David Abram has studied oral-based societies in depth. "While persons brought up within literate culture often speak about the natural world," he writes, "indigenous, oral peoples sometimes speak directly to that world, acknowledging certain animals, plants and even landforms as expressive subjects whom they might find themselves in conversation . . . Obviously these other beings do not speak with a human tongue, they do not speak in words. They may speak in song, like many birds, or in rhythm, like the crickets and the ocean waves. They may speak in a language of movements and gestures, or articulate themselves in shifting shadows . . . Language, for traditionally oral peoples, is not specifically human possession, but is a property of the animate earth, in which we humans participate . . . They feel the ground where they stand as it speaks through them. They feel themselves inside and a part of a vast and steadily unfolding story."

I'm beginning to feel it, too.

I watch as the *hālau* becomes a mass of churning lava, a single wave in an infinite sea. There is a song about sunrise in Volcano. Hands hit the ground. Heads shake. Gourd rattles are a flash of red and yellow feathers. The dancers fall to their knees, as if they're submitting to the sky. The older girls trade their gourds for water-smoothed lava stones, earth-turned instruments. They tap pieces of Pele in the palms of their hands.

The chant tells of Pele's move toward the island's Puna district, where she reaches the sea, her boundary. The dancers' red skirts spin around them as if they are a flow of lava. Red, the color of Pele. Red, the color of life blood. The dancers' clothes are covered in circular splotches of

yellow and black. Their swishing hems give the appearance of a creeping flow of lava. Their skirts are bunched like fresh flows pushing forward, breaking through older, cooled layers. They are past, present, and
future in one. *Wā*, the Hawaiian concept of now.

The dancers' hands are smoke, hips are hot, feet are twisting, churning points of contact with the earth. And then, fluid as lava, they pour
off the stage, flowing back into the *hale* from which they came. When
the last girl has disappeared, I go over to greet Keikilani, hot-pink-laced
high-top sneakers flashing from under her traditional *muʻumuʻu*.

"Leigh Ann! My new friend!" she shouts, waving so excitedly that
kukui-nut necklaces rattle against her chest. Before I can explain the
disappearance of my voice, an onlooker approaches Keikilani. She has
recently moved to Volcano from the mainland, and she'd like Keikilani's
permission to paint from some photos she took of the *hālau* today.

Painting, she explains, has been helping her integrate into the island.
"Whenever I paint it helps bring things into the physical," she says. "It
helps me explore the feeling of a place. I paint things I don't necessarily
see. They're the things I feel. I think art helps you feel a place and it
makes you part of it." Keikilani nods, understanding. This is what hula
does for her.

She gives the woman her blessing and invites me to join the *hālau*
for lunch, guiding me over to the thatched-roof *hale* to wait while she
checks on some of her younger pupils. I hover by the structure's gaping
door with a purse-and-*ipu*-holding boyfriend. When a wayward dancer
walks by us, feet turning on the grit of loose lava pebbles, he points
to the ground and says, "I always get God bumps when I'm barefoot.
I think that's why the dancers don't wear shoes."

I furrow my brow and throw out my right hand like a question mark.
I've had no fewer than five people get chicken skin with me since I've
been here. Still, the God part throws me a little. He laughs: "I call it that

because it's a reaction I have when I feel the spirit. It's how we communicate for real."

Jaak Panksepp, a neurobiologist studying how music triggers emotion, proposes that goose bumps—chicken skin, God bumps, whatever you want to call them—are a physiological response handed down by ancestors who had a cold-evocative reaction to being separated from loved ones. In other words, he thinks it might be a physical reaction to the craving for connection. And it isn't limited to physical connection with people. Sometimes, goose bumps are brought on due to an overwhelming sense of awe, the sort of wonder one might experience when in the presence of a wondrous natural phenomenon like, say, a volcano. God bumps might just be a physiological response to the oft-satirized, navel-gazing, and wholly real human yearning to be at one with the universe.

When Keikilani reappears, she tells me that she needs to stop by the Volcano Arts Center to say good-bye to a friend. Keikilani tells the woman that she's going to take the girls to see Pele before they leave the area. Her friend immediately begins rubbing her arms. I can see what's coming. Hawai'i is a seriously pimpled-out place.

"Oh, ho!" she says. "I get chicken skin every time I go! I could almost cry at the thought of it, and I see it all the time!"

Recently, she says, the sound of the churning lava was so loud she and her husband were convinced there was an eighteen-wheeler barreling across the island. I muster all the vocal-cord vibration I can to whisper: "You can hear it, actually hear the volcano like you'd hear the ocean?"

"Oh, yeah," she says. "It sounds like breathing. Tūtū Pele was breathing really hard that night. She was so loud, my husband and I jumped in the car to see if I could catch sight of her."

"Tūtū?" I whisper-croak.

"Grandmother," she says.

· · ·

The *hālau* is staying at Kīlauea Military Camp, a government-run compound of small stone buildings that's been in operation since 1916. It's
intended as a place of rest and relaxation for military families, and it has
the feel of a summer camp with creaky screen doors. The living room of
Keikilani's cottage secured by a student from a military family—has
been designated a gathering place. Lunch is potluck, a mix of the cultures that have contributed to modern Hawai'i—part Polynesian, part
Japanese, part Hamburger Helper.

Over a paper plate full of potato salad mixed with rice noodles, Kika
Kahiluonapuaapiilani Nixon, a small, forty-something woman who has
shark-tooth tribal symbols tattooed on her calf, gives me the scoop on
the gathered *kumu*. "A lot of *kumu* are like Hollywood in teaching
dance," she says, "but not these *kumu*. They go deep. They teach the
spirituality of hula."

Kika's *kumu*, Alva Kamalani, often takes her students to experience the phenomena they're dancing about. They slip into little-known
lava tubes and chant so that their voices resonate. They swim in storied
ponds to splash each other, laughing as they master the art of embodying
sacred waters.

Kika takes a bite of a sushi roll and says, "By knowing these places and
their phenomena, we can better become them. And then, through our
dance, we get to take people there who might never get to go otherwise."

Alva, a large woman with a spiraling gray bun perched on top of her
head, has taken the chair beside Kika. The *kumu* says, "In hula, understand, we're not dancing about lava. We *are* the lava!"

Kika smiles. "We get to see it all, be it all . . ."

"And eat it all!" Alva says, playfully, pointing toward a box of cookies
on the kitchen counter. She gestures to a woman seated near the buffet

that she'd like an extra serving. Then she turns her attention to me. Her expression makes it appear that she's going to break out in laughter at any moment, but her words are sincere: "We know we're blessed to be here," she says. "It's a blessing that extends to everything!"

I lean in to whisper that it seems people are saying things just as I need to hear them, that I can't stop seeing connections everywhere I look now. Alva nods, "You know this stuff. But you're putting it all together now. What you *thought* was, what you *see* is."

Ike, in Hawaiian, means "to see." It also means "to know." To experience the physical is to understand it in some way. Traditional Hawaiian spiritual practices—of which hula is a part—still begin with the phenomenal: direct observation. It's the essence of the philosophical discipline of phenomenology, the study of consciousness from the first-person field of view, which can be traced back to Aristotle, a scientist philosopher who depended on his own senses to make use of the world and believed that theory mattered only when it could be applied to day-to-day life. The school of thought was popularized by philosopher Edmund Husserl in the early twentieth century. He believed that direct experience, or the phenomenal, is the origin of all human knowledge and meaning.

This is, of course, at odds with much of modern science, a pursuit that has convinced us that human senses are subjective and, therefore—in a world that values the peer-reviewed abstract more than the first-person visceral—unreliable. But Hawaiian culture doesn't seem to subscribe to this. Not even in this technological age. *Maka'ala, Makawalu, Mākaukau*, the local saying goes. *Be alert to the physical. Be alert to the spiritual. Then you will be ready.*

Quietly, I tell the women about my drum-making experience at Moku O Keawe. My instructor, Kalim Smith, explained—in between cutting and grinding instructions—that the *ipu* is a cosmology to have and to hold. The seeds of the gourd, scattered through the sky, become stars. Its pulpy innards, clouds. The smooth exterior of the emerging drum—polished during high tide with handfuls of sand—can be viewed as the solid dome of heaven. Through the process of creating the instrument, I acknowledged that I was connected to them all.

In hula, implements are considered an extension of the body. It is the same sort of thinking that allows dancers to become the phenomena they're dancing about. It's the ability to morph, change, evolve. It is spirit given to physical, observable form.

When I jokingly point out the curious reality that I created a drum voice and lost the use of my vocal cords the very next day, the women don't laugh and they don't look bewildered by the wild connection. It's almost as if they've been waiting for me to make it. "The *ipu is* your voice," Kika says. "You speak through it now."

Alva nods and adds, "It's an extension of you. Everything is, understand. You're having trouble with your voice right now because you've extended it so greatly through your *ipu.*" I imagine my voice unfurling like the outer edges of this island. In my imagination, it looks not unlike the films I've watched of lava hitting the ocean, where magma cools into giant orbs and then cracks under the weight of itself, continually, like dinosaur eggs hatching fire in the depths of the sea.

After plates have been cleared and the kitchen counter made bare, I shyly bring my *ipu* from my Jeep to comply with Keikilani's request to see what came of my time at Moku O Keawe. When she sees my drum, she proclaims it beautiful and gently taps it like one might test the ripeness of a melon.

"I want them to show you how to use it," she says, gesturing toward her students, who are lounging on the floor texting and playing card games. She waves to get their attention and asks: "Who will help Leigh Ann learn to play her *ipu?*"

I'm surprised when a handful of them abandon what they're doing to help me hone my voice. A young girl, maybe fifteen, slaps the *ipu* with her palm and taps it with fingertips as she moves it around her head, her torso, making it appear as the rotation of the sun. The rest of the group—six or so—chant as they swim across the living room, arms turned to glinting waves. We're underwater, swimming in a sea of surreal magic.

They twirl the drum. They pound it. When they hand it back to me, after half an hour of dance, Keikilani guides my hands with her words, instructing me on how to make my gourd vibrate with the same resonance. "Not on the bottom," she says, "on the side."

I reluctantly drum-sing: Palm, *tap*. Palm, *tap*, *tap*.

I gain confidence, pound a little harder, a little louder.

Palm, *tap*. The girls smile. Palm, *tap*, *tap*.

"Good sound!" Keikilani exclaims.

When Alva works her way around the living room, saying her goodbyes, she draws me into a hug and holds me for a long time, inhaling. It feels like I've been taken into a cloud. "Don't worry," she says when she finally releases me. "You'll get used to the new shape of your voice. The awkwardness you're experiencing is just a consequence of growth."

Her floral *mu'umu'u* swishes around her bare feet as she moves toward the front door of the cabin. I raise my hands to my throat and touch my heart with an open palm to indicate that there's more I'd like to say, that it pains me not to express myself as fully as I would like. She nods, as if to confirm she's heard what I have not spoken.

Volcanoes emanate sound at frequencies below the threshold of human hearing. These elusive vibrations are known as infrasound. Through infrasound, Kīlauea's Halema'uma'u crater sings.

Well, actually, it chants.

Milton Garcés, a geophysicist with the University of Hawai'i, says, "Kīlauea has a beautiful voice, a sound that's very unique." His job is to make infrasound audible—and visible—via microphones and computer screens. The scientist, who refers to himself as a Sound Hunter, says, "What we think of as silence doesn't exist . . . Our bodies are absorbing vibration all the time . . . There's sound you can't hear but you can feel, and that's infrasound."

It's fascinating stuff, and it's given me a new party trick. The next time I hear someone couch an I'm-getting-a-vibe comment with *I know this sounds crazy*, I get to say, "Actually, it sounds like geophysics."

All volcanic processes—like the churning of lava and emission of hot gas—create sound, some audible, some infrasonic. Garcés begins his work by making eruption recordings in the field with specialized microphones. He then uses computers to process recordings of slow infrasonic vibrations until they're fast enough for human hearing. Keikilani's friend compared Pele's surface-level voice to labored breathing. But when Garcés listens to Pele's underground, ever-pumping heart, it sounds like a cathedral-quality pipe organ.

Pele's infrasonic chant wasn't known to exist until early 2000. Some scientists actually suspect that every place on earth has a distinctive, infrasonic song. The whole planet sings. The Halema'uma'u crater is just one of its more dramatic rock stars.

This brand of mysterious music isn't just the domain of volcanic phenomena and earthquakes. Hurricanes, tsunamis, tornadoes, and the aurora borealis—which just happens to be the next phenomenon on my list—are all academically acknowledged as having their own infrasonic pulses. It's really quite a bit to digest, this science-based idea that we really can pick up vibrations. Good vibrations. Bad vibrations. Sound we can *feel*. And it doesn't all come from geologic and atmospheric phenomena. Garcés says of infrasound, "The earth, like us, is constantly stimulated from without as well as within . . . The whole planet vibrates and we're actually pretty intimate with how it does that if we listen to our bodies. Our mother's greatest gift, the heartbeat, is infrasonic. We have this coming out of the womb. We realize that we are not alone."

We are never alone.

Katy Payne, an acoustic biologist, was working with elephants at a zoo in Oregon when she felt something that she describes in her book *Silent Thunder* as a "throb and flutter" in the air. In addition to rumbles she could hear, she sensed other rumbles. Her intuition led to the discovery that elephants communicate through infrasound, that 12,000-pound animals have been screaming all around us for millennia and we never knew—just as we didn't know the volcano being chanted about was actually chanting back.

In *Silent Thunder*, Payne notes that Indian mythology was full of references to strange phenomena of the sky that could be traced to elephants. She wrote: "No one who knew elephants was entirely surprised by our discovery. 'Of course!' they all said." It's something they knew—figuratively or, maybe, via vibration, physically—all along in their gut. And there are other creatures that have infrasonic conversations. Spiders, for instance, are known to pluck their webs like banjo strings and tap their bellies like drums.

In 2003, a group of British researchers realized that church organs also have the potential to emit infrasound. The BBC reports that when they did a controlled experiment, pumping infrasound into a concert hall, they were able to "instill strange feelings in the audience . . ." Some shivered and felt there was a ghostly presence in the room, others were suddenly reminded of emotional loss.

Richard Wiseman, a psychologist from the University of Hertfordshire, said: "It has been suggested that because some organ pipes in churches and cathedrals produce infrasound this could lead to people having weird experiences which they attribute to God . . . This was an experiment done under controlled conditions and it shows infrasound does have an impact, and that has implications . . . in a religious context and some of the unusual experiences people may be having in certain churches." Not to mention the chicken-skin experiences of nature— where there are island-size pipe organs playing all the time.

Approximately 10 percent of the world's population live within obvious reach of an active volcano. But, even if you're not near a volcano, its activity—infrasonic or otherwise—can affect you. In 1991, Mount Pinatubo in the Philippines erupted and sent twenty million tons of sulfur dioxide and ash into the atmosphere. They circled the globe for three weeks. And just as erupted particulates can travel the world, so can vibrations. There are corridors in the atmosphere that catch sound, too. Garcés says, "There is a wall of sound that originates on earth and goes all the way to the edge of space."

Charlie, the Wavemaster of Vieques, is seeming less insane and more prophetic all the time.

Vibrations affect everybody and everything all the way up to the divine!

Oh, Charlie, if your neighbors only knew!

When the 2011 Japanese tsunami took place, the earth shook. The. Entire. Earth. First came a seismic wave, a vibration from the ground. Then there was rip-roaring song that turned our planet into a rolling stone, our atmosphere into a concert hall.

It sounds impossible.

It sounds like a huge orchestra tuning its string instruments with increasing velocity.

I know this because Garcés has a recording of the seismic shift and wave that made the planet tilt right off its axis. And I don't mean that metaphorically. I mean that as in a shift of roughly eight centimeters.

This axis adjustment made our days move a little faster. And I don't mean that metaphorically, either. I mean that as in it shortened the 24-hour day by roughly 1.8 microseconds.

Garcés says of the event, "The world moved in ways we didn't even think was possible . . . We're still learning how the world works. We're definitely not masters of the universe . . . The world has always [changed] and is always changing. And we can see it, but we can also hear it."

Things change more rapidly and palpably on Hawai'i than they do most other places. After leaving Keikilani's gathering, I check into my room at Volcano Lodge, where I find a quilted welcome book waiting for me. It contains the logistical information one might expect, along with a list of attractions. Midway down the page, a listing has been covered in black ink like secret sections of a government document. I can't make out what's underneath. So, of course, I immediately want to.

I walk the short gravel path to the lodge's dining hall, a retrofitted YMCA bunkhouse circa 1938, to find the innkeeper, Lorna Jeyte, sitting in a corner booth near an oversized fireplace. Lorna, in her seventies, has the jazzy energy and style of someone who's twenty-five, and her bobbed hair reveals metallic purple earrings that flutter when she talks.

Somehow, despite the fact that I can't raise my voice above a whisper, Lorna and I hit it off. We order snacks from the inn's gourmet menu, and she gives me the scoop on the blacked-out documents in my room. The site in question hasn't been overrun by hooligans or closed by the county. No, the beach, one of her favorites on the island, simply just doesn't exist anymore.

When Lorna learned that the beach was going to be taken by lava flows, she didn't get upset; she packed a picnic basket and grabbed a bottle of wine. Her mother was still living then. It was a cold night, so Lorna wrapped her mother's wheelchair in blankets and they took off for the Pacific. She brought extra scarves to protect their lungs from volcanic gas.

When they reached the beach, they realized they weren't the only ones who'd felt the urge to come one last time. Dozens of people were there to say good-bye. It was a sacred area in Hawaiian culture—the flows ultimately destroyed a 700-year-old temple—but it was special in other ways. This was where couples had first revealed their love, where children had taken their first steps, where ashes of family members had been scattered to the wind. It was well known as the site of monthly full-moon parties. And Pele was coming for it.

But instead of mourning the imminent loss, the residents of Volcano celebrated the arrival of Pele. The goddess had built the beach, and she would take it away. They talked story about how they were blessed to be alive—at that very moment—to bear witness. They toasted to the dark sand of their beach, acknowledging that it was, itself, remnants of flows that had come before. They celebrated all that had been and all that would be again. They laughed and sang and hugged each other in the lava light that was illuminating the coastline like dripping candle wax. And when lava flows reached a nearby stand of trees, they left. "Coconut trees have a tendency to explode when the lava hits them," Lorna says.

She has just bought a small lot on the jungle-covered coastline of the nearby Puna district, where she plans to build a small cabin that will allow for more time spent swimming in the island's thermal pools and lava-warmed ocean lagoons.

Yes, Puna is paradise. It's also an open-air arsenal.

The Big Island is divided into Zones 1–9. The most likely to be hit by lava is Zone 1. Lorna's lot is in Zone 2. She probably won't be able to get insurance for the cottage she plans to build, and she admits that the whole venture is more than a little risky. But it's the realization of a life-long dream.

"If not now, when?" she says.

The following day, I think of Lorna when my hiking guide, Taj Flora, points to a knee-high, torso-size lump of coal and says: "These weird protrusions are all trees." We're standing in the middle of a charbroiled forest. "Every now and then," he says, "a tree will actually survive." We walk by a fruit-bearing tree that is, miraculously, still standing. Taj tells our group of roughly fifteen hikers: "I call that the god of the forest's last stand against Pele."

It is, in essence, a *kīpuka* of a single tree.

Taj, a slender thirty-something with straw-straight brown hair, leans down to the volcanic sand we're walking on and scoops up a handful. He pushes black grit around his palm until it catches on small bits of emerald-looking stone. "Olivine," he says.

"Did you know that was there?" someone asks.

Taj shrugs. "Once you know about olivine," he says, "you see it everywhere."

He tells us that a meteor made of the stuff once crashed into the island. He shakes his head: "It's the only place they've ever seen that much olivine and it was on a meteorite flying by this island, an island made of olivine. Seriously, it makes you wonder." He points to the cooked earth, the surface of an island that is anchored to an ocean vent. "All the amino acids that make up life start down there." He oscillates his arm to point to the sky. "Well, actually, they start up there. We're all stardust, right?"

According to science writer Nigel Calder: "Nearly every atom in the human body . . . was fashioned in stars that formed, grew old and exploded most violently . . . And from the rocks, atoms escaped for eventual incorporation in living things . . . phosphorus and sulfur for all living tissue; calcium for bones and teeth . . . No other conclusion of modern research testifies more clearly to mankind's intimate connections with the universe at large and with the cosmic forces at work among the stars."

I've always considered this sort of science-speak to be over my head. Now I'm coming to understand it as part of my head. It's dizzying. It's thrilling. It's making me feel like I've been underestimating my starborn, flesh-and-bone body in some way.

The human body biocycles just like plants, animals, and volcanoes. A full 98 percent of the atoms that make up our bodies are replaced within a year. There is only a very small percentage that stays throughout one's entire life. Most of the atoms that do are woven into DNA like flowers tucked into a braided lei.

We continue walking, moving onto lava that has hardened, creating a field of lava stones that look like stair steps and arches. "Could this collapse?" a hiker asks Taj, who responds, "Well, there's always the possibility."

Taj has a habit of making dangerous treks. During a recent lava-blowing-eruption of Pu'u'O'o, he snuck into restricted areas with friends to get the action on video. What he remembers most about the experience was the smell. "It was like cooked earth," he says. "I don't know how else to describe it." Some geologically minded friends have told him that it might have been brimstone. He shares his favorite Mark Twain quote about the island: "The smell of sulfur was strong, but not unpleasant to a sinner." The group laughs.

Taj directs us into a nearby kīpuka, and as soon as we step into the trees, the lava's sun-baked surface turns to rich soil, the detritus of all sorts of things. Life pours forth around us. The leaves seem to envelop us like a traditional Hawaiian offering of sacred foods wrapped in cool ti leaves. In an instant, the hard, brimstone-born earth softens.

Taj stops to point out the curved purple fiddle of a uluhe. The creeping fern's color is a defense against ultraviolet rays. "This symbol," he says of its spiraling head, "is really important in the Polynesian culture. It represents new beginning."

"*La vida*, life!" says Nellie, a group member of Puerto Rican descent.

Another nearby fern is at a further stage of development. "See how it bisects," Taj says. One spiral becomes many.

"It's like a butterfly emerging from its cocoon!" someone exclaims.

A breeze stirs as we start walking again. "The sounds of the trees," Taj says as the forest acts as a towering wind-harp. "The sounds of nature."

Trees have the capacity to communicate via infrasound and audible voices. Biologist Diana Beresford writes: "All trees of the global forest produce a fingerprint of sound. This sound is as individual as the iris is to the eye or the thumb-print to the hand . . . The sounds—both audible and inaudible—of the pine are sharper when compared to the rounder sounds of the red oak."

I think of the sacred feeling I had in that Mexican forest, the sound of the butterflies' beating wings, the whistling of pine trees. Beresford articulates: "Infrasound . . . is registered as an intense emotional experience. This experience is quite often felt in the cathedral of the forest."

Maybe that God-bump guy was onto something.

I pant a little as we begin our ascent to a lookout that will offer one of the only on-the-ground views of Pu'u'O'o. And under a swaying canopy of leaves, I realize the wind through branches sounds like human breathing. Once I make the comparison, I can't stop hearing it. *Alo-haaa. Alo-haaa.*

And, just like that, I get it. *'Ōlauniu: the wind that pierces the palm frond.* I'd imagined that it was named because of its geography, but maybe it was named for its voice. Even the hardened basalt stone of the volcano reveals its shape in song when wind caresses its contours. I recall the sound of the *'Ōlauniu* brushing against the slender, piano-player-worthy fingers of the palm frond. It was a percussive rhythm, the song of shaking maracas.

If I spent enough time here in this landscape of volcanic ash formations, or on the island's eastern coastline, I would likely recognize the voice of a given terrain as I would the voice of Matt, Archer, anyone I've ever loved. We are, after all, just players in a grander orchestra.

"The human body," Beresford writes, "is built like a large cello." This design, she believes, amplifies low-frequency sound waves. In other words, we resonate with the earth. And modern science decrees that the vibrating air that we take in—even when we're driving down the freeway or sitting in a skyscraper—is full of oxygen that's been exhaled by distant, singing trees.

We reach the lookout that allows us to see Pu'u'O'o. The crater is a distant line of gray smoke, an umbilical cord that begins as fire in the core of the earth and ends as a ghostly gray plume infusing open sky. Taj takes the leaf of a lehua in his hand. The lehua is notable for its ability to close its stomata—or pores—during a volcanic eruption. It instinctively protects itself and waits for the gases to pass. Once the danger is gone, the flowering tree begins to breathe again. It's one of the only plants on earth that can do this.

Taj tells us that some botanists think the lehua is the oldest flowering tree on the planet. The plant is famed for its ability to grow with great physical variation, always remaining the same genetically. He says, "It takes many shapes. It has many forms." Just like lava. Just like Pele.

The goddess has been known to transform into a beautiful young woman, a craggy old lady, even a white dog. She constantly reinvents herself as she shapes the land, weaving herself, her story, into stone— malleable as it is. Magma is, after all, solid and liquid at the same time.

The group rambles around the small overlook and Taj launches into a story about Pele's attraction to a demigod she noticed one day when he was in the forest cutting firewood. "She thought this guy was hot stuff," Taj says. Pele transformed herself into human form of great beauty to offer herself to the demigod, but he already had a lover so he graciously declined. Distraught, Pele kept her eye on the demigod, and when his love appeared, Pele came ablaze with jealousy. In her wrath, she turned him into the ugliest tree she could imagine—the gnarled trunk of a lehua.

The demigod's lover was inconsolable. She begged for Pele to trans- form him back into human form so they could be together. Pele, slightly regretful of what she'd done in haste, replied: "What I have done I can- not undo." But, to ease the woman's pain, she graced the tree with the lehua flower. It was through this beauty, the story goes, that the woman and her lover were reunited again.

When Taj finishes the story, he tenderly cups a red bloom in his left hand. The plant's hardy leaves gently rattle in the wind. "Hey," he says, "I have a proposition for you guys." He points toward a smoking caldera. It's a sacred site, and he'd like to take us. It would be only his second time making the pilgrimage. He's just gone through the cultural train- ing required of guides who travel there. It's a place where Pele is said to still visit occasionally. Do we want to go?

I'm already down the trail by the time everyone has agreed to the ad- ditional two-hour hike. Nellie is ahead of me. We're not the fittest in the group, but we might be the most goddess-giddy. Taj catches up and warns, "We're going over some places that are going to be unstable. You need to follow me. I can tell what's unstable from walking on so much of this stuff."

As we wait for the rest of the group, Nellie points to a nearby basalt flow and asks Taj, "Is this rock blue? Am I seeing blue?"

Another early-arriving group member teases as if she's hallucinating: "Give that woman some water!"

But Taj confirms that she's right. "Yes," he says, "what you're seeing is crystallized basalt."

Ahead of us there is a huge indentation, the sort of collapsed tube I saw from the air with Noah. "Think about this channel feeding the lava lake that was once here," Taj says. We follow him into the pit, into the very breath of brimstone. A fern hangs on the side of a glassy, black-stone wall. Taj walks up and puts his hand out as if he's aiming to pet a puppy. "Look at this thing!" he exclaims, tugging at its lacy leaves. "Look at how tenacious life can be!"

We scramble up a trail of breakdown from a collapsed lava tube until the passageway ends. It's taken us nearly to the top of the mount. "I'm going to ask permission," Taj says. To enter this place it is proper to offer a chant. And chant he does. *E hō mai.* He asks, in Hawaiian, to be blessed with the knowledge of this place, the ancestors, the stories that have been handed down. He holds his hands out and shakes them a little, like he's patting the ground around a newly planted sprig of botanical life. He means what he's saying. He's asking permission to see and be seen.

Taj pauses for a moment, as if he's listening for permission to pass. Maybe he is.

David Abram thinks this might not be as unrealistic as it initially seems to the rationalized mind. It is premature, he believes, to assume that our presence isn't experienced by a variety of sentient creatures—termites, bees, all kinds of things. He writes: "The material reverberation of your speaking spreads out from you and is taken up within the sensitive tissue of the place . . . The activity that we call prayer springs from just such a gesture, from the practice of directly addressing the animate surroundings . . . Volcanoes, bays, and bayous . . . participate in the mystery of language. Our own chatter erupts in response to the abundant articulations of the world: human speech is simply our part of a much broader conversation."

Finally, Taj says, "I think we're good. Let's go."

The caldera, collapsed land, is steaming from rain that's fallen through the cracks to find stone that's still skillet hot. "Stay away from the edge," Taj says. "It's really unstable."

We cluster around the cracks near the crumbling edge of the pit, and I put my hand in the slit of earth. It feels like dragon breath. It smells like rain falling on hot asphalt.

"I could stay up here all day," Nellie says when Taj indicates it's time to leave.

"Me too," I say, surprised to find that I can say anything. Maybe the steam from the vent has relaxed my vocal cords? Maybe it's a gift from Pele? And—taking into account all I've learned—wouldn't they be one and the same?

"This is the sort of place where you could really meditate," Nellie says. "When I come to a place like this I feel more spiritual than I do in my everyday life in New York. It's a connection." And she doesn't mean connection with lava and plants; she means a connection to each other. "We're all beautiful inside. We all have something to offer. Places like this give us time to reflect on what those things are. When I was younger, I would express myself. But then I learned people might take it wrong, they might think I'm weird. But I've started to move away from worrying about that now. Expression is important. But people feel uncomfortable talking about the things that really matter."

"Why do you think that is?" I ask, more forcibly, realizing that my voice—totally silenced at the beginning of our walk—has, since inhaling Pele's steamy breath, made a remarkable recovery.

"I'm not sure," Nellie says, "but I think we're here to talk about our spirituality, to support each other on this journey that we have."

Despite the fact that Archer is increasingly verbal, he often still communicates in blurs of physical action. Nellie, a grandmother, thinks young children—like awe-inspiring outdoor phenomena—have the potential to help us shed inhibition through their giving-it-all-I've-got physical conversation with the world around them. They can help us bring our spirits further toward the light if we let them. She says, "We express ourselves to children. We hug and kiss them. We show our love. We don't care if we sound silly. We let them see us at our most exposed. When you're with a child, you're just you. You return to your essence."

My essence. If I were to boil myself down, I might be left with a description like this: I'm short. I'm blond. I'm bubbly. And, trust me, no matter how endearingly it's used, "bubbly" isn't a word you want to see on a professional year-end review. To be enthusiastic is to be a Pollyanna, not-to-be-taken-seriously naïve. *Isn't it?*

When I've been called bubbly in the past, I've always thought: bubblegum, unsubstantial, inconsequential. But, on Hawai'i, bubbles are powerful. Bubbles are the language of boiling water and smoking-hot, molten stone. They're the foundation of primordial creation. They're what comes from stoking the fire in one's belly. And the fire—the passion of living, replete with uncontained, flailing hand gestures—is what it's all about. In a world that mistakes anything fun for fluff, in a culture that frantically studies depression but tends to dismiss happiness, I've been somehow mistaking shadow for substance.

As we navigate basalt stone, Nellie continues her Pele-inspired musings. "You know, a lot of people never share their feelings, their thoughts and experiences, their spiritual side." And then she tells me how she came to know this. There was a night in her childhood when her father found her crying. He came to her and asked what was wrong and she said, "I'm crying because you don't love me." He never showed affection. Not even then.

"His body was a capsule," she says. "He was afraid of expressing himself. He died, and I never got to know him. It's strange, you know, to have a parent—someone who gave birth to you—never really know you. I never really knew who he was either. He was never willing to make himself vulnerable."

As we navigate the basalt path, trying to catch up to Taj, who's gone ahead, I begin to wonder how an encapsulated man could have raised a woman like Nellie. I think about how—if I want to welcome the inevitable transformations of my life—I'm going to have to fully open myself to spirit-speak, to a seemingly cheesy-Earth-Momma vulnerability. I'm going to have to cede control—not just mentally or physically but also spiritually. As Plato once wrote: "We can forgive a child who is afraid of the dark; the real tragedy of life is when men are afraid of the light."

I ask Nellie: "Was your mother an expressive person?"

She doesn't answer right away. Instead, she talks story. She tells me that her grown son—a professional toy designer—recently painted a mural in her Long Island backyard. It's a Hawaiian landscape, and it includes three hula dancers. The women represent her and her sisters. In the middle of the scene, there sits a volcano.

"The volcano represents my mother because that is how I see her," Nellie says. "She's the one who really taught me how to live. She never held back."

. . .

When I arrive at Keikilani's cabin, to join the *hālau* on their trip to Hawai'i Volcano Observatory, I find a group divided. Some girls are practicing chants in a back bedroom, others are lounging on the living room floor, immersed in video games. When Keikilani directs them all out of the cabin's warm interior into the damp night air, one semisulking teen of the gaming sect shouts, "Aw, I was killing a zombie!" She recovers fairly quickly because, really, who needs computer-generated characters when a fire-breathing goddess awaits?

Keikilani counts the kids off into the cars of various *kumu*. I ride with Keikilani and one of the younger dancers in a small SUV with a silk lei hanging from its rearview mirror. As she drives, Keikilani tells us about a lava fountain she saw as a youth, a spewing cone that seemed to take cues from the paint splatter of Jackson Pollock.

"Which crater erupted?" her student asks.

"Pele!" Keikilani exclaims. "It was Pele's crater! It shot 1,200 feet into the air! I hope you get to see something like that in your lifetime," Keikilani tells her. Such eruptions are known to throw fine crystallized jewels and stuff that looks like *ipu* innards. The debris is referred to— even among hardened scientists—as Pele's tears and hair.

The parking lot of the observatory, which overlooks Pele's crater, is enveloped in vog when we arrive. The air is cool at 4,200 feet, and a low-hanging cloud feels like menthol vapor hitting the warm membranes of my mouth, my throat, my lungs. As we walk toward the lookout point, a stone wall that's a full mile from Pele, we spy the crater's glow. It looks like the sun slipping into earth at sunset.

Twain, after witnessing Halema'uma'u, wrote: "Here was room for the imagination to work . . . You could not compass it—it was the idea of eternity made tangible—and the longest end of it made visible to the naked eye!"

"It's getting redder and redder!" one of the girls shouts.

"That's so cool!" another says.

They are clustered around me, a shivering mass of hooded sweatshirts and flashlights.

"Look at my light!"

"Zoom in!"

They point their flashlights into the foggy night and proceed to have a Luke Skywalker–style sword fight with the slender streams of light, white threads weaving through the night. Finally, the *kumu* clap their hands to bring the girls to attention. "If you're chanting to the crater, where should you face?" one of them asks. Their haphazard formation changes and they fall into line so that their vocal cords will be directed toward the volcano. The girls slowly move into a tiny clump, some of them standing on a stone viewing platform.

"We're seeing things we chant and sing and dance about," Keikilani says. "So, let's do the best we can." Their chatter has dimmed to a whisper now, as mild as my voice has temporarily become.

"Just be quiet for a minute, first," she says. "Just watch."

It's what I've been doing for days.

The *hālau* and I gaze into the earth's navel for a few minutes until, finally, it is time to sing Kīlauea back to itself. I am encircled by the tiny dancers when they begin, each voice building one on top of the other until they make a sound so large, so moving, that the two sightseers who'd been near argument about what f-stop they'd need to get a clear photo of the crater are rendered mute, as I have been.

There are no flashes of light from the crater, only the subtle reflection of molten lava in a cloud of sulfuric gas, a hint of all the complexity that lies beneath. Each line of the chant is a flow of smooth lava, new slipping over old, building, strengthening, taking them higher. It is a show of transformation, life longing for itself in molten stone and the soft tones of voices just beginning to come into their own.

Matter can't be created or destroyed; it can only be transformed. It is a law of science. It is a tenet at the root of many religions around the world. It is at the center, the *piko*, of Pele's mythology. The caterpillar becomes the butterfly. The infant becomes the young woman. The young woman, the mother. The forest becomes the barren lava field. The lava becomes the forest. The star stuff of our lost loved ones becomes the flower of the lehua, reborn every time the vog lifts.

For many years, scientists didn't appreciate Pele's chants as anything other than entertainment. But in 2006, the U.S. Geological Survey (USGS) suggested that the orally transmitted story of a climactic battle between Pele and her sister was inspired by geological events in AD 1500. That year, the north coast of Kīlauea was covered by lava. "Such a flow is likely recorded in the oral tradition as Pele's revenge for what she thought was a lingering romantic liaison between her lover, Lohi'au, and her sister, Hi'iaka. The subsequent collapse of Kīlauea's summit is told as Hi'iaka digging for Lohi'au."

"Taken at face value," the USGS reported, "the change tells us that the caldera formed immediately after a huge lava flow, exactly what we scientists have come to recognize only recently . . . Had we been willing to believe Hawaiian chants about Pele and Hi'iaka, and oral tradition, we would have known this 100 years ago."

For all of my life, I've subconsciously—despite my best efforts and strong belief in the power of narrative—accepted the euphemism of "telling a story" as a way of suggesting that something is a lie. There is danger in taking mythology literally, of course—as all sorts of fundamentalism can attest—but there's also danger in ignoring the knowledge that mythological traditions have to transmit.

Joseph Campbell has said that when a myth is interpreted as biography, history, or science, it dies. But I wonder if Pele's unexpected twist might not be an invitation to rethink and redefine myth in the modern age. I don't think any of the poetry in Keikilani's dance is lost by looking at the historical or scientific knowledge it might have to share. In fact, biocycling and infrasound and *oli* unexpectedly mashing together has awed me beyond measure. Biography, history, science, and myth are not always separate things.

When Keikilani's girls tell the stories of Pele's journey to her current home, they are revealing not only the spiritual knowledge of their home place in a storied, subjective way, but also the intimate physical realities that their ancestors faced. In chants—enlivened history—these realities are not at odds; they're the same thing. They're practical, experience-earned stories that relay information and issue warnings. They're artistic illustrations of tellers' innermost landscapes and knowledge. And this braiding of scientific and spiritual knowledge is not limited to Hawai'i or Pele.

When the Fukushima nuclear reactors in Japan were first built, practitioners of Shinto—Japan's indigenous spiritual tradition—mightily protested their location. It was not in keeping with the directives of the *kami*, spiritual forces that resided in the land. But they were built anyway. Because, really, what *rational* engineer is going to take advice from *spiritual* forces? But if the sites had been in accordance with Shinto understandings of *kami*, they would likely have eluded the 2011 tsunami's grasp.

Scholars often refer to this sort of knowledge as the result of "indigenous ways of knowing." It's a body of wisdom that values millennia of holistic experience and subjective observation, whereas modern science often values controlled, objective data gathered in a shorter period of time. Both approaches are valuable, but it's clear which has been more valued.

What future disasters could be averted if we were to honor Shinto, Pele, other ways of knowing that occur throughout the world, as well as our own visceral knowledge? How can we collectively take seriously traditional knowledge, or even each other, when we live in an age where we're encouraged to discount personal observations, our gut reactions, ourselves?

When I learn of the Shinto warnings, dismissed because they were born not of repeatable, supposedly objective experiments but of spiritually bound communication with natural phenomena, I have a weird series of personal flashbacks that leave me reeling.

There's the God-bump guy telling me about how he feels the spirit through bare feet and me thinking *woo-woo*. Then, me finding infrasound data that says basically the same thing and thinking *wow*.

There's me, a couple of months ago, nervously dialing NASA to inquire about the Catatumbo lightning. Internally, nervously questioning: "Who am I, someone who barely passed a math course created for humanities majors, to call *NASA*?"

But in that conversation, there was a fissure made in how I perceive the world, though I couldn't recognize it then, so unconsciously dismissive have I become of my own experience. It happened when one of the scientists, after revealing the high points of his groundbreaking studies, shyly inquired: "Can I ask you a question?"

"Of course," I said, thinking: *What would this expert, this satellite-savvy researcher, possibly want to ask* me? And then this world-renowned lightning expert asked, about the most active lightning zone on earth, "What was it like there?"

To my knowledge, not one of the scientists I contacted about the

Catatumbo phenomenon had ever felt the winds of Lake Maracaibo. They'd never watched the far-reaching behavior of lightning at the center of the lake. They'd never smelled the bubbles of methane rising from its murky waters or inhaled the sweet scent of concentrated ozone. What's more, as far as I could tell, they'd never even talked to anyone who had. At the time, I found this odd. Now, I'm beginning to see it as an example of a larger trend.

David Abram once said, "The real truth, we have heard, is somewhere else; it is not in this world that our senses experience. Our physicists say that the real truth of things is hidden in the subatomic world. The molecular biologists now say that it is in the ultra-microscopic dimension of DNA . . . These are all worlds to which we feel we're beholden, but to which we don't have direct access: one needs very fancy instrumentation . . . to get at them. And so we take our truth from the experts with the instruments, and we forfeit our own power, our own access to the real . . . We hide ourselves from the most outrageous and mysterious truth of all, which is our ongoing immersion in this wild web of relationships." This is not to say that research conducted via remote satellites and in the confines of laboratories isn't important. Of course it is. It is lifesaving, awe-inspiring, enlightening. It is—to use one of Milton Garcés's favorite words—awesome. But what if we also sought and valued scientific *experiences* and spiritual *experiments*? What if we could begin to, once again, trust our most intimate ways of knowing alongside quantitative inquiries conducted from a distance? What if the phenomenal, defined as *that which is derived from direct experience*, could be accepted as phenomenal defined as *magnificent beyond belief*?

I know. Easier said than done. But recent days have introduced me to the notion that geophysics might be a god language and goddess chants might be geology. What might we learn if we created intellectual environments that encouraged scientists to value three-dimensional experiences—not just as data-gathering expeditions, but as visceral experiences that take all their knowledge and inborn, subjective senses into account as much as they do the abstractions on their screens? What might that curious-about-what-the-earth's-hot-spot-was-really-like scientist have seen or heard or felt on Maracaibo's waters that I did not? What might he be able to tell the rest of us about the curious global phenomena of lightning if he met the Catatumbo in person?

And, bringing it back to my oh-so-narcissistic navel: What does this all mean for me?

I can see now that the idea of removed rationality as more trustworthy and important than the phenomenal—that is, experiential knowledge, natural design, and my *piko*—affects me in some highly personal, unexpected ways: I have come to believe that I am a lesser authority in my own life. I have learned to distrust less-than-rational, nontechnical experiences, my own phenomenal knowledge. Because, to trust the senses—the mortal body—is to risk sounding crazy, especially, it seems, if you're a woman.

She's *seeing* things.

She's *hearing* things.

She's so *sensitive*.

Read: She's *irrational*.

And this I have internalized. Who am I to trust my body, my senses, my instincts? Who am I to know how to raise my child without consulting parenting books and up-to-date rearing studies? Who am I to try to find God outside of an institutionally approved, fully vetted doctrine? Who am I to think I can pursue impractical dreams? Who am I to be taken seriously? Who am I to think I'm capable or worthy? Who am I to . . . *Who am I?*

The very language we use to talk about our most intimate desires makes it seem as if we've been having a collective identity crisis. We want to *believe* in ourselves. We want to have *faith* in ourselves. It's as if we've begun—in a networked world that connects us to each other in ideas but not in body, in a culture that pushes individualism yet shames us out of navel gazing—to question our very existence.

"Without hula," Keikilani told me on the day we met, "you're disconnected in the universe." I'm starting to understand what she meant.

The Hawaiian word for identity is *ho'omaopopo*. It is translated as "to understand." It is through ourselves, our own experience, that we gain knowledge of the world. At least, for generations it has been. But in a world where we increasingly value the abstract and mechanical more than the spontaneous and creative, we are discouraged from valuing ourselves, our *piko*, our senses. We've come to see our perfectly patterned molecules, our bodies, as somehow antiquated and lesser-than, as if rationalized human engineering is superior to nature's design. As if we've accepted that we're just prototypes for soon-to-be-in-production, technologically superior robots.

As if our intellect is our only source of knowledge, the center of our abilities.

The medicalization of birth—a rite of passage, seen in most cultures as more spiritual, physical reckoning than pathologized procedure—shows just how deeply our distrust of visceral knowledge goes. Ina May Gaskin, perhaps the most famous midwife in the United States, once said in an interview, "There is an assumption that we humans are inferior to the other five thousand or so species of mammals in our ability to give birth to our young. I have always found it hard to accept this notion."

In Gaskin's practice, the cesarean rate is 1.7 percent.

The national average hovers around 34 percent.

During a late-pregnancy checkup, when I showed up at my OB/

GYN's office with a birth plan requesting no interventions unless medically necessary, the doctor on call said: "Look, it would be great if everyone could give birth in the woods, but most births require intervention."

Not some. Most.

I cried on the way home. Even Matt, who tends to be exceptionally
forgiving of tone, was disturbed by how the doctor spoke to me. That
night, I wrote an e-mail reiterating that I wanted to give birth in a hospital, not in the woods, and that all I was asking was for my body—
which had miraculously and thankfully been able to create life without
medical intervention—to be allowed to bring that baby into the world
without interference unless my child or I was in danger. What I didn't
know to say yet—what I was really getting at—was that I valued his
knowledge, and I wished he valued mine, visceral as it was. It's an e-mail
I never sent. *Who was I to question him?*

When I went into labor—two weeks after doctors *thought* I should—
it progressed slowly and irregularly. My doctor, a younger associate, told
me that he would usually recommend Pitocin—a drug that offers un-
naturally large jolts of synthetic oxytocin—to hurry things along. I asked
him to let my body work on its own and he agreed that it would be safe
to wait and see what it was capable of doing. But why was Pitocin rec-
ommended if it was safe—and statistically less likely to result in a cesarean section—for my labor to proceed without it?

I feared pain. But I knew that—in labor, unlike in situations of injury or illness—pain most often means that things are going right. I
knew that studies have shown that getting an epidural was likely to lead
to a cascade of interventions that were more likely to require the scalpel-
slicing of my uterus. I had trained to give birth like a pregnant woman
in boot camp. I'd done visualization exercises, walked a mountainous
mile a day in an unprecedented period of exercise. Yet one of the nurses,
after I'd asked her to stop her repeated offers of pain medication, told

me: "I can't stop asking because I just hate watching someone in pain when there's something I can do about it." How disembodied are we, as a culture, when someone who hates seeing people in pain thinks nursing laboring women is a suitable profession?

After nearly twenty-one hours of labor, nurses told me that hospital protocol suggested that they begin preparing for a c-section, because of a "lack of progress." I held up my finger, indicating that I'd like the nurse to wait as I rode through a contraction, a surfer on one of my own body's pain waves. When I regained my composure, I asked if ten more minutes of labor would be medically safe. She consulted with my off-site doctor, who agreed that it would be. Why was a c-section—surgery that is scientifically documented to present a three-fold danger of maternal death—suggested if my medical practitioners deemed ten more minutes of natural labor safe for both me and my son?

I didn't know why or how, or who or what might happen in those ten minutes, but I knew that—despite the irregular, abstract patterns on the monitors I'd been hooked up to as a precautionary measure—Archer was coming. He came. He came so fast that my off-site obstetrician almost missed the birth. "Could you just not push," the nurses said at one point, hoping that the doctor would get there before my son did. As if I had any say in the matter. As if the convulsions of my body were the doing of my rational mind.

As if my intellect was my only way of knowing.

All the nurses from the maternity ward were gathered in my room by that point. These were women who had attended hundreds of births among them. They had been with me through all stages of labor while my doctor consulted by phone. I couldn't open my eyes. But I could tell, even through the otherworldly pain of my body turning itself inside out, that those women were thinking: *Who are we to deliver this baby ourselves?*

What good are medical or technological or any sort of modern advances if we don't have faith in experiential knowledge to guide us? Too often we confuse technology with science, utilizing tools where we would be better off focusing on observed wisdom. How many times have I distrusted *my* visceral knowledge, the wisdom of *my* experience? Intuition—a form of knowing that bypasses rationality—has long been thought to be a pseudoscience. But what if—as Pele stories might advance science faster than science can advance itself—intuition is phenomenal, sensory knowledge that works in a higher gear than intellect?

It seems we've fallen away from our phenomenal wisdom, that gained through our primal—and by primal I mean perfectly designed—senses and ways of knowing that have been building, layer upon layer, for millennia. Body wisdom isn't something that exists in the romanticized past; it is a perspective of presence. What I thought, *was*. What I see, *is*.

In hula, this sensory self, this awareness, is acknowledged and appreciated. And there are advanced millennia of ancestral knowledge at every dancer's back—science and spirituality mingling in dramatic ways. In hula, every individual is honored as being part of a sacred whole, every dancer experiencing a Jerry McGuire–style, you-complete-me embrace from the universe. But me? I'm out here, umbilical cord cut, flailing, looking for experts to validate my intuition, my knowledge, my spirit, myself. At least, that's where I've been.

Hula is not my tradition, but it is showing me that I am part of a divine completion, and knowing this somehow makes me feel whole, *holi*. It is in the spirit of *aloha*, oneness, that I intuit divinity. We do not live outside or inside of nature. We are nature. We are not separate from each other—something the Hawaiians recognize by calling even non-relatives auntie and uncle—and our fates are intertwined, always.

I *know* this, of course I do, but I am beginning to *experience* it. I'm beginning to live out what I mean when I say, as I so often do: I'm spiritual but not religious. Religion is limited, whereas spirituality encompasses the world. My understanding of divinity is fluid, not fixed. But I haven't been trusting myself to properly bear witness to the universal everything-ness that plays out around and in me every day. I haven't been paying attention to the many becoming one before my very eyes, through my eyes.

What I *thought*, was. What I *see*, is. And it is phenomenal.

When the *hālau* finishes its chant, one of the girls makes a quiet plea to repeat it. Her friends echo the sentiment. I peer out into the dark horizon, light emanating from a hole in the earth that leads straight to the churning, molten, vibrating core of the planet. It looks like the last glowing embers of a campfire set to explode with a simple nudging of Pele's stick.

Throughout their song, the volcano has amped up its light. One of the *kumu* standing to the left of the group admires the increased activity, visible as a crimson reflection in a cloud of gas, ash, and soot. She says, "I think Tūtū Pele really liked that!"

The girl standing behind me whispers to her friend, a tiny seven-year-old wearing a leopard-print beret, "Did you *see* that?"

"Yeah!" she says. "There was an outline of a woman in there!"

They're claiming their observational powers. But who am I to claim I have *powers*? All signs point to: The Crazy Gourd Lady with a Developing God Complex. I guess it's something I'm going to have to get used to. Because Alva was right. My voice has expanded. It's unfurled in directions I didn't know it could go. And, in some ways, it isn't even what I thought it was.

My voice doesn't just reside in my throat or on the written page; it is expressed every moment I am alive. I am absorbing the infrasound of

volcanoes and earthquakes when I'm changing diapers, when I'm cook-
ing dinner, when I'm sitting at the kitchen table fretting about bills. And
when I am expressive, when I let myself fall into flow, to be creative, when
I believe in myself and resist holding back, when I don't shy from the
spiritual stuff, when I follow my bliss—when I talk with my hands so
dramatically that the people in an adjacent restaurant booth come by to
ask me if I'm a professional mime—I may feel nervously alone. But I am
simply joining the chorus of universal elements that are transforming
around and within me.

Because the iron that turns my blood red is the same star-borne ele-
ment that tints Pele's crater. More than half of the human body is composed of water. We're roaring ocean and sound-ferrying sky. Our hearts
are percussive instruments, our ears drum skin. We breathe in the atmosphere exhaled by the green earth, and we emit it as song and
speech and story. We might very well feel infrasonic vibrations and let
them channel through us as abstractions, smears of color across the me-
diums. We are creations and creators, art and artists, songs and song-
writers. The embodiment of spirit. Instruments of knowledge. Just like
Tūtū Pele.

The girls are chanting Kīlauea again, lost in their flow. I can feel the
hair on my arms begin to rise, as if pulled by the crater. As if internally
electrified. The *hālau* is not chanting *about* Pele, they are chanting *to*
her, and she is responding.

They utter: *Ha'a ana ka wahine Pele.*

She moans.

Uhi'uha mai ana 'ea.

Her plume shifts.

The girls will surely draw from this moment when they're dancing in
the coming years, morphing into fiery phenomena of all sorts. They
might even channel Pele in their day-to-day lives when they're called

upon to do things that seem beyond their mortal ability, when they begin to doubt themselves. At least, I hope they will. I'd like to think I might be able to find some of her fearless, inner illumination when I need it most.

These girls have spent hours, days, years of their young lives learning to embody this place, to kindle the essence of this sacred phenomenon in their own souls. Now, they are witnessing *it* transform into *her*, an image of their own likeness. They are seeing. They are being seen. *She is Pele. They are Pele. She is them.* And, from where we're standing, I swear, it looks for all the world like this volcano is unabashedly hips-twisting-hands-twirling hula dancing.

CHAPTER 5

NORTHERN LIGHTS, SWEDEN

February/March 2012

I'M ON A FLIGHT HEADED INTO THE ARCTIC CIRCLE, AND I have been seated next to a Japanese philosophy professor. His specialty? Phenomenology: the study of phenomena, that which appears. This school of thought—as I learned in Hawai'i—suggests that reality is subject to first-person perceptions. Given this experiential bent, I suppose it's no surprise that, like me, he is on a quest to see the northern lights.

Hirobumi "Hiro" Takenouchi took a visiting professorship in southern Sweden because he wanted to be situated near the auroral oval, a halo that encircles the polar regions of earth and provides conditions that allow for viewing the northern lights, otherwise known as the aurora borealis. It's his second effort in the northern part of the country. The first time he visited, he spent a week holed up in a hotel room, waiting for an apparition that never appeared. He's here to give the phenomenon another chance to show itself.

If you lived within the auroral oval—which encircles Iceland, northern Canada, Scandinavia, and Alaska—you would likely be aware that Japanese culture fosters a special fascination with the lights, which are created when solar winds from the sun slip past the earth's protective shield. Whole resorts are often booked by citizens of the tiny island nation. The country's interest can be traced back to the work of Japanese photographer Michio Hoshino. At least, that's how Hiro tells the story.

He adores Hoshino's photography, with its wisps of green celestial light, but he also appreciates how those images came to be. In the 1970s, the photographer heard tales of the lights and decided that they were something he needed to see in person. But this was before Google and travel advisor websites. Where would he stay? How would he find his way?

Hoshino wrote letters and sent them to towns across Alaska—the closest auroral region—addressed only with town names. Many people thought it was a ridiculous pursuit, but he pushed on until one of those shot-in-the-dark inquiries received a reply. It was from the mayor of a small Alaskan town who invited Hoshino into his home. The photographer accepted the stranger's invitation and ended up spending much of his adult life under the aurora.

Hiro believes the resulting images are beloved because they symbolize a man living according to his great passion. Hiro also respects Hoshino for his lay philosophy, relayed in essays. "What impresses me is not his work about nature," Hiro says, "it's about how he questions this scenery. He says, 'This is so beautiful I want to tell my friend. But how can I convey this? How can I express what is happening in front of me?' Because, once presented, anyone's personal experience becomes, to the other person, theory. But what they can see, what they can directly observe, is the way the phenomenon has changed me. If I first acquire the knowledge of a phenomenon, my loved ones will see it through me. They will see my way of living change."

Since I've spent most of my year on a phenomena chase, this, of course, makes me question: Has *my* way of living changed?

I have to admit, even this far in, my overarching quest is offering as many challenges as opportunities. Working and traveling and having a family is a tightrope-style balancing act. Sometimes I perform pretty well. Sometimes I don't. But when I start to question myself too heatedly about my Quixotic seeking, I think back to last summer, when my mother-in-law was visiting from the Midwest. At her request, we attended the local Lutheran church, a former mission that sought to save wayward mountaineer souls. It is still beyond the reach of asphalt, surrounded by woods.

Archer, not yet two, was railing against sleep when we arrived. I rocked him as hymns were sung. He crumpled bulletins. He wanted to get down. He could not be contained. Matt suggested that I take him outside, so I did.

We picked up speed as we neared the exit. It felt like we were making a getaway, dramatic as any runaway-bride romantic comedy. Archer started to giggle when sunlight hit his face. I started giggling, too. Then I unexpectedly teared up as if I were actually at a wedding. But the moment wasn't about commitment. It was about freedom. And the two aren't necessarily at odds, something I'm only beginning to understand.

No one expected Archer to sit still through the whole service, not even his grandmother, who is supremely bent on following protocol. In hindsight—emboldened by my lightning chase, fortified by Pele—I realize that I, too, had been fighting against perceived restraints. Why should the acceptance of antsy-pants not extend into adulthood? Isn't there a holy sense of purpose to be found in the search itself, at any age?

Not long before I left for my northern lights chase, I traveled with Archer to stay at my parents' house for a couple of days. Matt and I— short on child care—had been trading work hours, and I thought he could use a break. My parents, eager to spend time with their grandson, readily agreed.

It took a full day to get there. The following workday was excellent. Then, just as I clicked out of my dad's computer, I realized I had saved my draft in a temporary file on the unfamiliar machine. There were a few halfhearted attempts to recover it, but I knew it was gone.

"Maybe I was on the wrong track," I told my dad when he offered words of solace.

"This project is changing you," he said, surprised by my calm response. "You seem more centered somehow."

I think he's right. But maybe he wasn't seeing just me. Maybe he was witnessing the pounding of butterfly wings, the twinkling of dinoflagellates. Maybe his direct experience with me was informed by my brush with those phenomena.

Still, I'll never be a totally cool cucumber. The day after I lost that file—unable to go back to my writing without risking a nervous breakdown—I tried to follow up on plans for my next trip, a jaunt to Alaska for the aurora. Things weren't working out. Calls weren't being returned. And the ones that were didn't quite feel right. Nothing did.

I decided to use my precious time to do some logistical research. But instead of focusing on Alaska, as I'd planned to, I kept cruising websites about northern Sweden and Sámi mythology—the stories of one of the largest indigenous cultures in Europe. On almost every Swedish site I visited to learn about the northern lights, I found a Sámi shaman's drum.

Now, I realize that seeing a shaman's drum as a sign from the universe doesn't exactly scream "supercentered." But once you lose your voice to an *ipu*, it's hard not to find kinship with instruments of all sorts. Because of those drums, I kept digging. I made some calls. Everything started to, well, flow.

I know this all sounds pretty hippie dippy. But just when I think I've gone too far off the deep end with this whole listening-to-the-universe bit, I'm seated next to a Japanese phenomenology professor and I throw up my hands. There's something bigger than me at play here.

I brief my traveling companion on what I'm up to, admitting that I've only recently been introduced to phenomenology. When I mention that I'm still not sure I have a handle on it, he purses his lips and suggests he might be able to help. "The essence is really simple," he says. "In history and society there are so many prejudices and theories. We see through these glasses, always with others' opinions. We are not willing to see what is happening in front of us. We have to let the phenomena speak . . . To let them speak, you must be silent. But it is difficult. I have so many opinions, but I try to get rid of them for a minute."

I ask him how this relates to the aurora, and he begins to laugh. His delight escalates and he leans his head back in a roaring chuckle, so dramatic I can see metallic fillings in his teeth. He says, "Phenomena decide what is fitting to them. We cannot know about the aurora before meeting it."

My impertinence inspires a history lesson. Hiro tells me about how Western imperialism changed things in Japan in the late 1800s. "Before then," he says, "people didn't always use literature. They knew how to behave in relation with other people and other objects." In Japan not so very long ago, the world itself—animals, humans, ocean waves, the winds—was an animated, sacred text. It's a worldview that Hiro's academic work seeks to revive.

"In Japan, physical and mental experience is still incorporated into everything," he says. "It is not separate. Take Shinto rituals. They are always located in gardens. To reach the shrine you have to experience nature. Almost all traditional religions in Japan try to give time apart from daily life. In Shinto, which people might call animism, every phenomenon has its own unique soul which we cannot help but admire."

Hiro tells me I am far too concerned with scientific theory. "It is not important if you want to experience the phenomenon," he says. "The rising sun in front of you is the only one on that morning, in that specific place. It is the only sun in history that will be experienced in that way. The earth is round? It doesn't matter. Not in that moment. Not to you."

Every culture in the aurora's viewshed has different myths to explain its origin, stories tied to their part of the world and how they perceive their place in it. The aurora borealis takes its name from the Roman goddess of dawn, Aurora. She was said to renew herself each morning with a flight across the sky, heralding the advance of the sun. In southern Sweden, the lights were historically talked about as the torches of Sámi reindeer herders searching for their animals in the north. In Norway, they were believed to be the reflection of fish swimming in the sky. In Sámi tradition, the lights were spirits in and of themselves—sentient and alive.

The plane's nose turns toward the earth. We're nearing the Kiruna airport, where dog-sled taxis await. Hiro says, as if closing a formal lecture: "I have learned, not as a philosopher but as a man, that we had better talk about concrete subject matter. That is what we base our interpretations on. You cannot divide physical and metaphysical. It is all one."

A few days later, I'm 200 kilometers inside the Arctic Circle at Sweden's ICEHOTEL, the largest snow-and-ice accommodation in the world. I incorporated the attraction into my itinerary after reading about it online. But, now that I'm here, all I really want to do is hang out with the housekeepers.

This is, I must admit, sort of characteristic. When I first started writing professionally, I created a column about people's jobs in a local newspaper. In those years of wandering my hometown, I found that almost

everyone—street sweepers, physicians, musicians—had something interesting to say about their work.

Instinct kicks in when I see two snow-gear-clad people walking
through the reindeer-skin-covered doors of the hotel. They're carrying
long brushes, brooms, and tools I've never seen before. Some visitors
might be interested to know the names of celebrities who've slept here.
But, though I'm no scrubbing bubble in my own house, I'm terribly interested in knowing how one might clean a room made of snow. So, I'm
going to find out.

Marinus Vroom and Marjolein Vonk are startled when I approach
them, but they agree to let me tag along. When we step into the sheltering hotel lobby—a room of packed snow—the loud squeaking of our
boots is immediately muffled, absorbed by a ceiling modeled after tree
trunks.

It takes a few minutes to establish that the cleaning crew I'm shadow-
ing is not, in fact, a cleaning crew. They are the two elite artists chosen
to create this year's deluxe luxury suite, which they happen to be touching up for a photo shoot. Their suite, Flamingo Blush, is the only one in
the hotel with a locked door, but it's opening. The suite features a platform that looks like a dance floor and a back-lit flamingo made of ice
blocks set into a snow wall. It was inspired by Ra, an Egyptian sun god
that was sometimes said to take earthly form as the sunset-colored bird
species.

Marjolein has been part of ICEHOTEL since 2001. In her day job,
she works as a stylist for high-fashion magazines like *Vogue*. Years ago,
while on a shoot at the ICEHOTEL, she saw someone build a chair of
ice and said to herself: "I have to do this! You want a chair? Carve one!
You want a chandelier? Make it!" At ICEHOTEL, she isn't stuck rear-
ranging the same old props. The possibilities are endless. Creativity.
Creation. Poof. Like magic. "Everyone turns into a child here," Mar-

jolein says, as she slips a metal planer across clear-as-glass ice slabs. "They want to laugh. They want to touch the ice."

They want to *feel*.

It's a tendency I've seen for myself. I spent my first hour here sitting on a bench near the entrance to the hotel, which is really more of a village of warm huts orbiting the main ice building. The path leading into the heart of the compound is lined with aquamarine ice columns. The one closest to the entrance has an edge that's melted. At first, I thought the indentation was due to its position in the sun. But then I watched a young boy run to it, rubbing his hand along its side. Then, I saw a grown man take off his glove to press his skin against it, and I realized that the hard edge had been worn away by the hands of hopeful pilgrims. It has become a point of connection like St. Peter's bronze foot in the Vatican, like the belly of a Buddha statue rubbed for luck. The ice here is no more miraculous than ice anywhere. But its status as a symbol serves to remind visitors that the elements and their mysteries are worthy of reverence.

"Something happened to me here," Marjolein says, slowing her work. "I live in the Netherlands and we have a lot of ice, but I don't know if I'd ever really seen it before. Now, I look at ice and see if it is soft or hard. I notice things."

Marjolein seems to feel about ice the way I'm starting to feel about almost everything. When I tell her I'm on a quest for wonder, that I'm mainly here to experience the northern lights, she says, without pause, as if there's no other way for me to succeed in this: "You need to talk to James."

She directs me to follow a path around the hotel to the back work area where forklifts and wooden crates are lined next to walls of snow, saying, "He'll be wearing an orange hard hat. He is here because of the aurora." Marjolein leaves it at that. But I have my instructions. Off I go. Past an outdoor ice sculpting class, past a row of red kick sleds, until, finally, I'm behind the hotel.

I find James McClean at the start of his coffee break, wearing the only orange hard hat in a sea of yellow ones. When I tell him Marjolein has sent me, he waves his coworkers on. They retreat into a small wooden shed, and we remain outdoors. James has a handkerchief knotted around his neck. It bears the symbolic colors of the Sámi flag, which is recognized here in Sápmi, the culture's traditional region. He's known among the ICEHOTEL artists as Mr. Aurora, though his job—officially titled Builder of Ice and Snow—has nothing to do with the sky and everything to do with sweat-inducing manual labor.

James is a U.S. citizen in his forties, here on a work visa, and he's spent most of the past decade working odd jobs that will keep him within the aurora oval. The stubble on his chin matches the dark bristle on his head, which is just peeking out from underneath his fleece-insulated hard hat. He is a stout guy—that's clear, even though he has on untold layers of gear—and he has the nose of a boxer. At forty-five, he resembles Bruce Willis in his younger, scruffier years.

James is an archeologist by training and—prior to his decision to live his life in accordance with the aurora—he hunted for Stone Age artifacts. His last gig was as a pool guy at a resort in Alaska, where he moonlighted as an apprentice to an ice carver in preparation for his current aurora-friendly job. But, despite his long-term dedication to the northern lights, he tells me that he's really more of an eclipse man.

He's traveled to Egypt, Easter Island, and all sorts of far-flung places to see the moon overtake the sun. But total solar eclipses only happen every few years, and, for a while, the in-between times left him feeling disconnected from the universe. That is, until he started spending his off-seasons within the aurora oval. James tells me that, outside of total solar eclipses, the aurora is as close to seeing the sun's corona—or outermost surface—as one can get.

James calls it the breath of God.

"The corona is the source of what you're seeing with an aurora," James says. It is the origin of sun flares, or coronal mass ejections, which spew the plasma that creates solar winds. "The corona is the breath of the sun itself. It's an exhale," he tells me. "The sun breathes just like we do. A coronal mass ejection is like a sneeze."

He explains: When those sun sneezes hit the earth's magnetic field—which is produced by the planet's Pele-churned core—they stretch it to its limit. When really strong solar storms hit, the outer section of the magnetic field is flung to the other side of the planet like a rubber band. Once the storm is gone and the field snaps back into its point of origin a few charged particles manage to slip in at the poles. Those particles collide with the earth's atmosphere to create visible light. When they hit oxygen, they turn green. When they run into nitrogen, they turn red. Voilà: the northern lights.

"It's actually pretty mundane when you look at it like that," James says. "But something happens when you see it. Because it's beyond the realm of ordinary human experience. When you see it, all the mundane stuff gets blown out of the water. You cease to be a lawyer or a banker or a builder or a cardiac surgeon. That's all gone. You become just a child of God staring at creation."

He believes this happens with auroras and eclipses. It's a realization he had in Egypt—home of Ra—in 2006, after he'd snuck onto a military base to ensure he was in the eclipse's narrow swath. He and a small group of fellow eclipse chasers had been approached by soldiers just before the eclipse, but when shadow overtook sun, the infantrymen put down their weapons and raised their hands in the air. James pumps his arms in the air to demonstrate what he saw, his palms open toward the sky. He jumps up and down ecstatically. A few hotel guests who've wandered to the frozen shore of the Torne River, just a few feet from where we stand, turn to stare. He must look like a wild man. He sort of is.

James grew up Protestant, but he got turned on to Buddhism when he was twelve. He also regularly goes out of his way to talk spirit shop with Hare Krishnas and Muslims. He likes to refer to God as "The Universal Being." He says, "Most people think in terms of you, and I, and that guy. They think of God as this separate entity, too. But the real truth is that it's a continuum of stuff. You can't separate yourself from it. You don't have to wait to go to heaven when you die. You're in heaven right now."

I survey the landscape around us—cloud-white as far as the eye can see—and I tell James that I was raised Lutheran, though I've developed a totally blurred-boundaries view of divinity. He gives a guttural chuckle and says, "Welcome home!"

As it turns out, northern Sweden is a hotbed of Lutheranism, though few people claim to be religious in this region where Christian missionaries simultaneously conducted revivals and horrific witch trials. Martin Luther himself saw Sápmi as the home of dark magic, evil. This was not in small part due to his view of the animistic and shamanistic power of the traditional Sámi drum. It seems terribly ironic that what Luther— founder of the institution I was raised in—saw as devilish is the very thing I have been drawn to as a sign of the sacred.

I'm the first American James has talked to in months, and he likes what I'm up to. My project is, in essence, a miniversion of the magical mystery tour that is his life. He's curious to know what phenomena I've chosen, and he listens carefully when I tell him. He's experienced all but coral spawning and the Catatumbo lightning.

He shoves gloved hands into the pockets of his work pants and asks:

"So, where's your eclipse? You're missing the most fantastic phenome-non known to man!"

James tells me officials are expecting 300,000 people—including 60,000 travelers—at the next eclipse viewing site. The idea of that many people from all over the world and all walks of life going to the imprac-tical effort and expense to see the moon overtake the sun is one of the craziest things I've ever heard. It is also, strangely, one of the most hopeful.

I've got friends who—upon hearing about these seekers—will say things like: "Must be nice." I've come to read this as an unintentional *Who do they think they are?* But my time on the road has made me think those pilgrims aren't necessarily any more privileged than anyone else. It might be nice, but it won't be easy. They'll be people who sold their houses to make the journey, people who duck the status quo in an effort to live the sorts of lives they want to lead. They'll be regular people try-ing to figure out a way to be true to the spirit within themselves—their innermost passions, their bliss. They'll be bound by the fact that they have been moved to pilgrimage for weeks, over thousands of miles, at great, impractical effort, in order to bear witness to a two-minute show of universal perfection.

That's right: two minutes. It is, according to reports across the scien-tific community, almost exactly how long the next total solar eclipse will last. And the whole thing has the potential to get rained out.

"So, from where, exactly, is the eclipse going to be visible?" I ask.

"Mostly over ocean. The only place it will touch land is around Cairns, Australia."

I start laughing. Cairns. Gateway to the Great Barrier Reef. Site of coral spawns that create reproductive egg slicks large enough to be seen from space. This is, and has always been, where I planned to end my phenomena tour.

"When?" I ask.

"November."

I can't laugh this time. "You're telling me that the next solar eclipse is going to be visible only on the other side of the earth, at the very spot I've been planning to visit in October?"

"You had the place right," James says. "You just had the time wrong. Now you know."

For the last year or so, my life has overtly revolved around the cycles of moon and tides. Not in an astrological way, but in a hey-this-phenomenon-usually-happens-eight-days-after-a-full-moon way. I've unintentionally started to read the universe like I read my calendar. This, maybe more than anything, has opened me to the idea of a divine pattern in seemingly random things. The universe is spontaneous, but—like the human body—the closer you look, the more it seems there's a loose, underlying pattern behind it all.

I'm in Sweden right now because it's an equinox month, and the equinox has historically proven to be a time of exceptional solar activity. I try to be diligent with my planning. But ocean temperatures and migration patterns are hard to perfectly balance in my brain, day-to-day, alongside concerns like: Does Archer, who's just started preschool, have a protein and vegetable in his lunch bag?

When I look into the specifics, I find that the full moon, used as a scientific indicator of the elusive spawning, might occur in October, but the eight-day window in which the coral spawn is expected pushes the phenomenon's annual appearance into the month of November.

It's when I was supposed to be there all along.

To catch the next total solar eclipse, I'll need to extend my already-planned stay in Australia by just one week. Really, my whole life has started to feel like a series of happy accidents, a wealth of synchronicity, defined by Swiss psychologist Carl Gustav Jung as "the coming together of inner and outer events in a way that cannot be explained by cause and effect and that is meaningful to the observer."

For something to be considered truly synchronistic by Jung, a convergence of events must have startling, staggering improbability strong enough to knock a person off her rational axis. It also has to have personal meaning. Running into someone you haven't seen in years: *coincidence*. Running into someone you haven't seen in years the day after you've had a dream about them: *synchronicity*.

Jung is best known for his interpretation of dreams as meaningful messages from an individual's subconscious, and he saw synchronicity as a sort of waking dream, a way of viewing life as a sacred text to be interpreted. It was a kind of road map presented by the convergence of consciousness and subconscious. Is synchronicity the result of selective perception, as a rationalist might offer, or is it a glimpse of an underlying universal wholeness, as others might suggest?

Maybe, to the individual, it doesn't matter much.

Jung saw synchronicity as an observable expression of a deeper order, *unus mundus*—one world, a unified reality. He viewed these moments as opportunities to marvel at connectivity, the realization that we all come from the same source and ultimately return to it. Moments of synchronicity, when recognized, are portals of transcendence, a chance to accept that there's something mysterious and larger than the individual at play. In some theologies, like Christianity, synchronicity is known as a blessing, or grace. In traditional Hawaiian culture and to many Buddhists, it's just the way life works. To me, even now, it's mainly an opportunity to blubber: *What are the chances?*

The classic example of synchronicity that Jung often used was one he witnessed during a session with a client, someone he thought of as über-rational. She gave stock answers to his probing questions and was resistant to opening up emotionally, but one day, she told him that she'd had a dream the night before in which someone gave her a golden scarab necklace, which is a symbol of rebirth in Egyptian culture. While she was talking, he heard something at the window. When he went to open it, he found a scarabaeid beetle. He gathered the insect—with wings appearing metallic in the light—and told her, "Here is your scarab." He wrote: "The experience punctured the desired hole in her rationalism and broke the ice of her intellectual resistance."

Isn't this what the sensation of wonder always does, in a sense? It punctures holes, makes stars in the domed roof-shell of what we know, and it makes us marvel about what's beyond. Physicist Erwin Schrödinger once wrote: "We are all in reality sides or aspects of one single being, which may perhaps in western terminology be called god." Science, in this way, harmonizes with the ancient religions of the world in finding connectivity.

One of James's coworkers pulls up on a forklift. Coffee break's over. James has to get back to work. He tells me that there's potential for the lights tonight. There was activity on the surface of the sun a few days ago, which is a good indication that a solar storm will be reaching earth soon, though scientists can't say exactly when or where the aurora will appear, or if local conditions will be clear enough to allow the light to reach us. But James has been watching the sky. He has a feeling that the night will be exceptionally clear. This is exciting, since the stars *and* the earth's atmosphere have to align if one wants to see the breath of God.

James was planning to spend a few hours waiting out the solar winds with his camera tonight, even before we met. "You're welcome to join me," he says. Then he slips me an unconventional business card, his contact information printed on a pair of fully functional eclipse glasses.

. . .

When we meet up later that evening in a wood-built, heated dining room, I tell James that as much as I'd like to see the northern lights, I'm also hoping to hear them. Every year, thousands of people report that they've heard the aurora. I've met nearly half a dozen witnesses myself, all in the space of a few days. What they claim to hear isn't the impossible-to-make-out waves of infrasound that have been recorded in the aurora at high altitudes. No, they claim to have been witness to the yet-to-be-recorded or scientifically explained, totally audible phenomenon that is the lights' signature song. There is ancient precedent for this. The Sámi word for the aurora is *guovssahs*, which roughly translates as "the lights that make noise."

James is skeptical. "I've spent thousands of hours with the aurora and I've never heard it before," he says, temporarily distracted by a young man who's come into the dining area. James watches as the guy whispers to a group of diners, who rise from their seats. Swedes aren't known for loud proclamations, and James knows what this might mean. Even when you're not outside, you have to be on alert if you want to catch the lights. He gets up and motions for me to follow. We're joined by an increasingly wide stream of people as we rush toward the doors. I have never felt more like a stereotypically loud American in my life, but I can't help but shout to a curious-looking couple as we pass their table: "Northern lights!"

We burst outside to find a crowd already gathered. Above, the aurora is tingling toward the bottom of its arc. The lower sections look like pink fingers dancing across an invisible piano. They extend down in various lengths. Pinky finger. Pointer. The upper stretch of the slender solar storm is somehow more delicate than I'd imagined it to be. It's a wisp of color. Stars are visible in the background as it slithers and twirls, shrinks and spreads. The arc it traces is, I realize, the curve of earth. This sky show is revealing the contours of the very planet on which we stand.

James shouts: "Look! Pink! That's about as good as it gets." The top of the aurora is glowing green, but the animate bottom of the arch is pink as Archer's nose after a day of playing in snow.

"Amazing!" someone shouts from the crowd that's gathered outside the restaurant's doors.

"I should get my camera out," James says, shivering in his fleece vest. In the rush, he couldn't find his outer jacket, but he knows the aurora doesn't wait. It can disappear as unexpectedly as it arrives. "This is the best I've seen in weeks and weeks," James tells me, the aurora fluttering like a glowing curtain in a celestial breeze.

The aurora's tingling pink energy dances, pounding out a visual song. The lamps around the restaurant can't compete with its power, its undeniable brightness. It is revealing the edge of our atmosphere. We are seeing the visceral meeting of space and earth, the bit of pure sunshine that has slipped through all protective measures to shine on our faces. It is, in essence, a visual reminder of life's tentative covenant with the universe. Like Alan said in Venezuela: If the sun changed its temperature, even a little, we'd be toast.

"The sky is bursting into pink flashes—I mean, when does that happen?" James says.

Well, now, for instance. I can't speak. I'm trying to focus, attempting to let the street lamps and crowds of the ICEHOTEL fall away. But just as I'm beginning to get a feel for the lights, just as I have gathered myself together so that I might be able to think about what I'm seeing—turning to explanations of nitrogen and oxygen instead of standing here, dazzled, in a stupefied gape—the lights disappear. They don't slip off stage left; no, they twirl themselves into nothingness as spontaneously as they appeared.

I turn to James and exclaim, "I need to see it again!"

He nods and says, "Yeah, that's it. You get it. Just imagine what it feels like with an eclipse. I've got to wait three years to see it again. See, you're spoiled with the aurora. Maybe it'll come back for dessert."

But we end up skipping the restaurant's sweet treats to wander the shores of the Torne, the best place to view the aurora in Jukkasjärvi, away from the hotel's lighting. We find a packed trail that will take us to the river. Above, stars flicker, pinpoints on a map.

I'm warm except for my hands, in too-thin gloves because it bothers me to lose dexterity. When I tell James that they're freezing, he looks a little concerned. "We better head back up," he says. "There's no way to know if it's going to come back tonight, anyway."

We start to slip-slide across the snow-covered river. I've been told that the Torne is beginning to groan, heralding the seasonal melt, but it's quiet tonight. There's no crackling from below or above. But suddenly, the sky stirs. Out of nowhere, the aurora appears as a slender branch of light, then it goes mad, all the heavens exploding into groves of green. I see pulsating, swirling, twirling figures drumming as they slip across the sky.

"You're just batting a thousand here," James says. "Look, it's twisting. Whoa!" He ducks a little. "Imagine if you saw that over your apple orchard in Normandy one year and didn't know what it was!"

The northern lights are not confined to the Arctic. Aristotle wrote of them. Julius Caesar once dispatched troops when he thought the lights were a raging town fire. They've been spied as far south as Mexico, pushed by particularly strong solar storms. In 1938, a rare appearance in England made Londoners think Windsor Castle was burning. Aurora drawings appear on the ceiling of the Rouffignac cave in France, where hunters recorded its appearance more than 10,000 years ago. And right now, at this very minute, the aurora is taking on the shape of an antler above my head. It breaks into horseshoe-shaped pieces that dance across the sky, prancing like the reindeer of Santa's sleigh.

It actually might not be coincidence that Santa's sleigh is pulled by reindeer, the animal Sámi have depended on for thousands of years. Or that the mythological elves of the North Pole wear replicas of traditional Sámi shoes, which are pointed at the tip to fit into skis. Or that this is really as close as humans can get to the North Pole without calling it an expedition. Some anthropologists believe Santa is actually an appropriated version of a Sámi shaman, a *noaide*, who used drums to navigate between worlds and consumed hallucinogenic red-and-white mushrooms that made them feel as though they could fly. The *noaide* are said to have been represented on some historic drums as being on a sledge— a small sleigh—being pulled through the air by reindeer.

When I looked for books on Sámi mythology and the aurora at the library of a local university before leaving for Sweden, nearly half of what I found was in the children's section. This seems awfully revealing of how we see myth. When someone is acting naïvely, foolishly, we say: *You might as well believe in Santa Claus.*

Myth and mystery, in a rational age, is something you're expected to grow out of, though, ironically, we tend to bemoan that loss of magic in the moment Santa's identity is revealed. We don't make room for adult-size fables. But some cultures believe we actually get closer to the mystery as we age.

I've noticed that the aurora seems to make talking about this sort of spirituality—even outside of established religious tradition—more acceptable than usual. When I announced my plans to see the aurora back home, I had friends—of all religious and nonreligious stripes—tell me that they imagined the aurora as some sort of mystical phenomenon.

The word mystical derives from mystery—from Greek *mystes*, initiate, and *mystos*, keeping silent. To have a spiritual experience doesn't require adopting a system of belief, a code of conduct, theory, or dogma of any sort—traditional or woo-woo. According to William James, mystical or spiritual experiences are—by definition—temporary, impossible to encapsulate in human language, and they transfer some sort of knowledge usually hidden from human understanding to an individual without conscious control.

R. M. Burke referred to them as moments of cosmic consciousness, believing that they were moments of joy and transcendence that brought individuals an enduring sense of order in the universe. Abraham Maslow called them "peak experiences" in an attempt to secularize them. Other researchers, interested in the psychology of spirit, refer to them as transpersonal experiences.

Whatever you want to call them: I'm totally having one.

James is whirling in the snow like a Sufi dervish, mirroring the now-swirling lights above in a ritualistic sort of dance, demonstrating a motion he's seen lots of people make on nights like this. "A lot of cultures up here believe the lights are the spirits of the dead. It's about realizing mortality and being initiated into an awareness of creation," James says, staggering to get his balance.

If so, James is more enlightened than most. But it hasn't come without cost. He tells me that he's sacrificed a lot for his life of continuous, celestial quest. He does not have a family or a permanent home. James follows employment notices to stay within the aurora oval, as the Sámi have followed the natural patterns of reindeer for more than 8,000 years. He lifts a gloved hand to the sky and says, "Human love is important, but cosmic love sustains."

James nods toward the heavens: "Right now, we're waking up. This blows the doors off of everything ordinary. It explodes the ego. It's about the death of ego. Ego death is when you stop thinking about yourself and you realize you're connected to the entire universe. It's the *us*. It's guys putting rifles down. It's powerful."

His voice gains octave. He's shouting now: "It's like something out of *Lord of the Rings*, but it's real! Real! Epi-phenomena!"

The lights curve into the hook of a J. It's almost as if they're writing out letters on a slate too large to see. James smiles and goes quiet. I realize it's the first time I've seen his stony-serious face soften since we met. The dark night washes us in waves of color. We are personally, viscerally, temporarily residing in the living, breathing realm of mythology.

James is shaking his head, as if, even after all these years—after all these magnificent ways the universe has revealed itself to him—he still has difficulty believing such beauty can exist. "It's a blessing," he says.

In this moment, we are realizing an experience that is—to tens of thousands of people—an I've-got-to-do-this-before-I-die sort of dream. We are standing on a winter-stilled river, being baptized by flowing, glowing streams overhead. Sheepishly, I admit: "Wanting to hear the lights as well as see them just seems greedy, doesn't it?"

"Yeah," he says, giving an under-his-breath humph, "that's what I was actually just thinking. You're wanting to hear something that's never been proven to exist. It's like you're asking for the impossible!" He's right. If the aurora is the breath of God, it's like I'm asking to hear the voice of God, too. Still, there's a sliver of hope in me, the afterglow of a lingering auroral storm inviting more light. As a totally yogied-out friend of mine recently said to me when I was having one of those pesky who-am-I-to ask-for-more moments: "You wouldn't ask for more if you didn't believe there was more to be had. You have faith in abundance, and that's not a bad thing."

James concedes, "You know, I do have friends that swear by the sounds. I have a theory that they're created by electrical discharges."

Many in the scientific community concur. The lights, roughly fifty miles above our heads, are in an area that is believed to have insufficient air to transmit audible sound waves. The varying speeds of light and sound also make this unlikely. Some scientists believe that if there is a physical source of the sounds, it can likely be attributed to tiny electrical discharges, a chorus of millions of microscopic lightning bolts firing off of all sorts of earthbound things.

There's also a theory that purports the noise is all in people's heads. Not in a you've-lost-your-mind way, but as a physiological reaction. Some researchers believe that the electromagnetic field produced during aurora actually has the potential to directly affect the bioelectricity of the human nervous system. Others think it might be an example of the brain mixing signals from the various senses. The sense of sight, if excited by a fast-moving aurora, might somehow be perceived as a sound detected by the ears. In other words, the aurora might be a visceral experience identified before our conscious minds can categorize it. As many a philosopher—and a particularly thoughtful chiropractor friend of mine—has noted: All human knowledge begins in the senses. The brain gets it secondhand.

My fingers are stinging from cold. I ball my hands into fists and pull them into the palms of my gloves, unwilling to move inside. The show isn't over, but it will likely dissolve as quickly as it came. When it does I somehow feel ill prepared. I hadn't expected the aurora to show itself so soon. I haven't had to chase the aurora as I thought I might. I just put myself in its path, and it came to me.

James paces a little, beyond an archway of ice, his work boots squeaking in the snow like rubber-soled sneakers on a basketball court. I can hear the hum of a far-off streetlight, the chatter of day visitors making their way from the hotel's ice bar, where alcohol is served in ice chalices carved from the river. But the sky isn't making a sound.

Still, visual whispers of sunlight are slipping into the coldest, darkest hour of night. I will never see these lights again. No one else will ever see exactly what I have seen. Though the lights follow eleven-year cycles of solar activity, there is no way of knowing exactly when or where the phenomenon will appear, or what form it will take.

When the aurora retreats—leaving the winter sky as hardened as it was before that first green sky-sprout began to stir—I have a hard time getting my bearings. James is sympathetic. "The aurora is the manifestation of light where darkness is expected," he says. "No matter how much you've read about it, you're never really prepared for that."

I just ran through a grand cathedral made of ice, its walls so sound-absorbing that I could not even hear my own footsteps, fast as they were. I am awake, and I'm on solid ground, but I feel as though I'm swimming through an icy sea. It's 3 a.m. I'm outside, under a still sky, wearing nothing but insulated underwear and a pair of boots in sub-zero weather. All this for a trip to the bathroom.

I forge through the snow-walled courtyard that gives overnight guests a private entrance to the heated reception area. There's one lone woman messing around at one of the lockers where I've stored my luggage, as have all ICEHOTEL guests. It would freeze if we took it into our quarters. She gives me a desperate look as I make my way to the front desk and ask if I might have a warm pillow. I took my sleeping bag in with me, but my pillow spent the day chilling on the reindeer skins that cover my ice accommodations. The cool side of my pillow is a wee bit too cold and I've developed a great fear that my drool-covered face is going to get stuck—like a tongue on a flagpole—to my sleeping bag's metal zipper.

The girl on duty hands me a small pillow with ICEHOTEL's icicle-shaped logo and says, "We give people whatever they want at this time of night."

I've already been told by an employee that it's not the cold that usually upsets guests, it's the quiet. She told me that it was possible here to listen to your own thoughts, to hear your subconscious. "It's actually pretty scary," she said, "to hear yourself think. You start to realize how much distraction you've had in your life—talking on the telephone while watching television, stuff like that."

I wonder, aloud, how many people end up dragging their sleeping bags into the lobby and am surprised to find that, out of the 200 guests at full capacity, usually only one or two don't make it through the night in their rooms. I have new determination.

When I finally crawl back into my sleeping bag, I can hear my heartbeat and nothing else. The sound is soothing and strong when amplified in my bag. I pull a woolen hood over my matted hair and drift, like a leaf falling in love with gravity, into the depths of sleep.

Soon, too soon, I'm awoken by a voice. "Warm lingonberry juice?" I shimmy toward the small hole of light at the top of my sleeping bag, my breathing hole, and I feel as though I'm emerging from a cocoon. When I peer out of the top of my bag, I see a woman wearing a silver cape. She's carrying some sort of tray that's hooked behind her neck, like that of an old-time cigarette girl.

I ask if I might have just a few more minutes of sleep. She's dubious, but she fills a white paper cup from a thermos contraption and puts it on my headboard, telling me she'll be back in a half hour. She returns in what seems three minutes.

"It's eight o'clock," she says. "We have to prepare for opening." Shortly, the entire hotel will be opened for tourists, who will pay a fee to wander through the rooms and take photos of themselves on the deerskin-covered ice beds. Including this one.

The morning light has given my room the blue-tinted opalescence of moonstone. Cold air is blowing through a vent hole that's been made in the domed ceiling. I close my eyes as a breeze hits my face. The lingonberry juice has gone cold. I drink it anyway.

This might not be the most comfortable place I've ever slept, but it very well may be the most serene I have ever known. As soon as I leave, the cleaning crew—the actual maintenance staff, of which James is officially a part—will push fresh snow down that ventilation hole. It will be spread on the floor like sand in a Zen garden. The only sign of my stay will be the ring my lingonberry cup made on the headboard, a circle interlinked with others. The pattern is as impermanent as a Tibetan sand mandala. Every year, the river provides material for a clean slate.

Nina Skarpa, manager of the Sámi-owned ecotourism company Nutti Sámi Siida, probably wouldn't flinch if I told her that I'd taken a drum as a sign that I was supposed to visit Sápmi. She is, herself, here because of a vision. She was living in Norway, working as a nurse in the trauma ward of a large hospital, when an image appeared in her consciousness. She was just going about her business and then there it was: a white, female reindeer. She couldn't stop thinking about it.

Now, if the image of a white reindeer suddenly popped into my mind, it wouldn't mean much. But to Nina, this was like a memo straight from the cosmos. She'd grown up among Sámi herders, and it was clearly a sign that some changes needed to be made in her life. "I had a strong sense that the reindeer was a sign telling me to go home," Nina says.

Just a week after that white reindeer made her feel called back to Sweden, she discovered a newspaper advertisement for a caretaker at Reindeer Lodge, Nutti Sámi Siida's base camp. When she called the owner of the company, they talked for hours, and she began to feel in her gut that moving was the right thing to do. But, still, it was a painful decision.

She left her eldest son in a Norwegian college. She finalized a divorce. She says, "In modern life, we tend to think the easy way is the best way. We want everything to be happening in the moment we wish for it, but life doesn't work like that all the time. Things are not always fun, but that doesn't mean we're unhappy. Good and bad are not black and white."

In neighboring countries, Sámi tour operators have taken to wearing the colorful stitched patterns of traditional clothing, but Nina—a strikingly beautiful woman, small-boned with black hair and glacier-blue eyes—is wearing sharp, modern ski gear. The only hint of Sámi fashion is a pointed hat made of goat skin and lined with colorful red wool. It's the handiwork of Johanna Huuva, a young herder who leads Nutti's reindeer outings. Tomorrow, I'll join her on one.

Working at Nutti has reminded Nina of all sorts of things she'd forgotten, things her aunt—the woman who raised her—used to impress on her, things like not picking flowers by their roots. Even reindeer, Nina says, know to leave enough lichen to ward against hunger in the coming, leaner years. "Nature will bring you what you need. It has taken me a long time to trust this Sámi saying—to trust life," Nina tells me. "You have to let go and look for little signs. You have to slow down your tempo in order to see them."

We follow the gentle curve of the camp's corral fencing, back toward the tiny communal kitchen hut where we first met. Nina says, "You know, taking this job, I didn't totally understand that first reindeer vision that came to my mind until I had one special calf that I cared for at the office, a white calf. It was a sign, a third sign, confirming that this is what's meant to be."

Meant to be. It's a difficult concept to take in, even when you're writing a book about natural phenomena and you find out that you've been unwittingly planning to visit the one point on earth where a fleeting eclipse is going to be visible. Yet it keeps coming up.

Jung explains that rationality demands the assumption that all things have a natural and perceptible cause. "We distinctly resent the idea of invisible and arbitrary forces," he wrote, "for it is not so long ago that we made our escape from that frightening world of dreams and superstitions, and constructed for ourselves a picture of the cosmos worthy of our rational consciousness." Yet the power of chance remains, as illustrated every time we utter: What are the chances?

In ancient Rome, if you tripped over your door frame, you wouldn't be teased as superstitious if you called off all events of the day. It would simply be seen as an accepted sign that you were off your game, with a lack of attention or clumsiness, in a world where even a minor injury could cost you your life. Seeing messages in daily life was as legitimate as reading a scientific study. Not so long ago—in generations as close as my great-grandparents'—an individual's powers of observation were still trusted.

Historically, nature has been seen as a sacred oracle, in part because individuals—everyday people—were fluent in its language. Laypeople, regular folk, were—by necessity—in constant conversation with all the world.

Nina isn't wearing a watch, but she suspects it's about time to start dinner. Locals often use natural cues to tell time—the reliable, patterned sounds of animals and the nuances of wind. Someone will arrive soon to cook for the camp, but after that there won't be an attendant on-site. She points to phone numbers tacked to the wooden wall of the hut, which has wooden walls lined with reindeer skins. It won't strike me until later, much later, that I am, in essence, going to be left alone in an Arctic wilderness with no food, no running water, and a phone connected to a source of electricity that I've been warned might not make it through the night.

Before she leaves, Nina directs me to a collection of books on Sámi traditional culture. The book sitting at the front of the shelf is, of course, *Drum-Time.* At the start of the eighteenth century, almost every Sámi house had drums. They were mostly used to divine the future. A bit of deer antler or a piece of brass was placed on a deerskin drumhead painted with Sámi symbols. The movement of the antler or brass would give the shaman an idea of where the deer might migrate when other natural-world signs could not be found.

When a Sámi shaman entered the drum-state—with vibrating reindeer skin pressed against his own—he navigated between the physical and spiritual worlds without regard to space and time. The shamans were, in a sense, medicine men. But their realm of expertise was not always nursing the body; it also included reconstructing fragmented souls.

The authors of *Drum-Time* acknowledge that Sámi culture still reveres the instrument. "We believe in the drum as a mirror of the soul," they explain. "The world of the drum is still in our dreams hidden in our language and in our way of thinking and acting. Hidden little islands inside of us."

This seems a very Jungian way of looking at things, given his belief that we all share predispositions in our collective unconscious. I savor all the information in *Drum-Time*, but I nearly stop breathing when the authors give an account of a traditional shaman's journey: "He began to speak of icy rains, fires, rainbows, boiling pools in the ground. All of this he had passed with the help of his protector. He had found the entrances, the doors to other worlds."

Storms. Lightning. Moon rings. Lava. This feels a little close.

"You too will see the one that rules the wind. Oh, yes, you will see the wind itself."

As in, the totally visible solar winds?

"Regardless of what you think, my drum will be your map to the other worlds . . . You too will be able to talk to he who controls the winds."

Oh, my.

It strikes me that synchronicity is not so different from reading the patterns of birds to learn about migratory routes. It's really just a term for carefully being on the lookout for signs in the context of one's own life. It's a way of deriving meaning from the unique and odd as the Sámi did when identifying *siejdde*, sacred places.

The *siejdde* were most often unusually shaped rocks. They were places of beauty where one might go to give thanks for good things. There were also dark *siejdde*, where small offerings would be made to ward off evil forces. But one of the most important roles of the *siejdde* was to provide a place to store the complexities of the human psyche, or soul. But when Lutheran missionaries smashed Sámi sacred sites and burned drums, this animated landscape was smothered, deadened. Earth went from life process to material product. And—if we're on page with Jung—this meant that all the good and bad that had once resided in the landscape retreated into the individual. Is this why I can't let the landscape hold some of my hope and fears, let some of my soul seep out of myself without somehow feeling like a flake?

"Man feels himself isolated in the cosmos, because he is no longer involved in nature and has lost his emotional unconscious identity with natural phenomena," Jung noted. Rationalism, he believed, has left us with a diminished capacity to respond to the numinous, or spiritual, symbols and ideas all around us. "Most of our difficulties come from losing contact with our instincts, the age-old forgotten wisdom stored up in us."

He called this the 400,000-year-old that lives in all of us.

I think I might actually be making contact with mine.

But how do I reconcile my iPhone-toting, e-mail-checking, thirty-something self with my 400,000-year-old one? How do I make peace with mainstream traditions so that I can move more freely along the individualistic path I'd prefer to tread? Sure, Pele's got my back, but I'm having some seriously mere-mortal moments down here in Alice's rabbit hole. I'm not sure what to make of all that's happening to me. I had no idea my little-ole-life had the potential to be so, I don't know . . . epic. I mean, I just read about a shaman's mystical, otherworldly experience and it sounded like a rundown of my travel itinerary.

It's nearly dark when I hear a strange sound coming from outside. I set my book down on a wooden table. Could it be the aurora? I start to rise from my chair, but—once I'm fully at attention—I realize it's just the frenzied cry of distant sled dogs at feeding time.

It is a bit of an oddity to be a woman traveling alone in the Arctic Circle, even on well-trod European tourist paths. I feel this sharply when, in a dining room the size of a large walk-in closet—where it's tough to pull out a chair without bumping into someone—I am seated by myself. There's a group of Germans who do not make eye contact with anyone outside of their party, a young, impossibly proper English couple—the woman has changed into riding pants and pearls in a camp that doesn't have running water—and another couple in their early seventies. The woman, who has an unruly cloud of gray hair, catches my eye and waves me over.

"Come and eat with us," she says. "There's no reason to go it alone!"

George and Yvonne Baker are also British, but they're still wearing their casual, Nutti-issued snowsuits. They have been in Sweden for several days. Yvonne is excited to share stories of their aurora sightings. She says seeing it last night, over the forest, was spectacular. "The angle made it look like the trees were lighting up." She cried at the sight of them, not an uncommon reaction.

As we settle into bowls of creamy soup, warm and comforting, I learn that George is a professional organist. This wouldn't be striking had I not just discovered, in Hawai'i, that organists are masters of infrasound. When I bring up the little-known phenomenon, Yvonne looks puzzled, but it inspires George to speak for the first time since I sat down. "To create infrasound," he says, "you need a big organ in a big building. It makes a very deep sound which really can't be heard. If you're playing a very quiet piece you add infrasound at the end."

Yvonne is confused. "Why would you play a note that you can't hear?"

"Because you can feel it," George says

He completed musical apprenticeship in Canterbury, England. He remembers it well. His instructor played a note and said, "Can you hear that, George?" He couldn't. His mentor told him to take a walk down the hall. The instructor played the note again, "Can you hear it now?" He still couldn't. But it was in his bones. "The floor was vibrating," George says. "The vibration was just barreling down the floorboards. For infrasound to be grand like that, you need a building that responds to that certain pitch."

He explains that, with many instruments, strings set the air vibrating. But there's a signature note unique to each instrument that sets the whole thing to tremor. It's called the wolf note. "You've got to be careful with the wolf note," George says. "It's almost overpowering."

Vibration and rhythm—both infrasonic and detectable—are fundamental to ritual across cultures. Neuroscientist Andrew Newberg believes that humans are biologically driven to act out myths, to bring the abstract into experiential form. He writes: "The fact that the unifying effects of ritual are generated by basic biological function explains the pervasiveness of ritual activity in virtually every culture . . . It also tells us why ritual ceremonies still have such power for so many, even in this rational age . . . Rosary group . . . prolonged ceremonial dancing . . . these unitary states . . . are triggered by the sensory effects of repetitive rhythmic behavior—that is, they begin with physical activity, and progress, in bottom-up fashion, to the mind."

Like, say, the instinctual knowledge of the *piko* rising to the intellect? It's what happens when shamans hit their wolf note and fall into a trancelike state, striking their nervous system, submitting to *unus mundus*. Our sense of spirit has always been evoked by dancers, shamans, musicians, and nature.

"So, do organists hold allegiances to any one denomination?" I ask George.

He shakes his head. "This one doesn't."

"You're sort of a freelance shaman, then?"

George gives a sly smile. "I suppose you could say that."

Remembering the first time he saw the aurora, George says, "I was in Shetland. It was like the spoke of a wheel circling above my head and I swear it was humming. People call them the Merry Dancers there."

"What did it sound like?" I ask, excitedly.

Johan Aldermam—a twenty-something Nutti representative with a handlebar moustache twisted at the tips—answers before George has a chance. "It sounds like this," he says, approaching our table. He extends his hand toward my face and wads a paper napkin in his hand to create white noise, static. "I've heard it plenty, and I've seen it a million times, but I still can't get tired of it. It's like looking into a fire. It's just hard to look away. I can't explain it. I can't try to describe it to someone else. It's almost impossible. The Sámi believed it was ancestors and gods looking down. The mythological part of the lights depends on what culture you're in, but it always goes back to spirit. It always comes back to something greater."

We return to our meals, picking at our plates until it's time to catch the night's sky show. The aurora is subdued. We watch it from the snow outside of the common hut, sprawled on fur-side-up reindeer hides. The low-lying arch of green disappears behind the trees without even a hint of pink. It isn't revealing itself as intimately as it did last night. We muse that it might be over Finland. Wherever it is, it seems far from here.

George and Yvonne go to bed early, retiring with mugs of spiral-steaming tea from the communal kitchen, and I'm left with Johan, who's begun preparing for breakfast the next day. He arranges cheese on a platter and slices red bell peppers, a Swedish morning mainstay.

Nina introduced Johan as Swedish, so I'm surprised when he tells me that his ancestors were reindeer herders, a traditionally Sámi occupation. His family was one of many that converted when missionaries began to burn Sámi drums. "At that time it was thought that being Sámi was somehow dirty," Johan tells me. "My family bought into that."

Unlike Nina, who self-identifies as more Sámi than Swedish, Johan isn't quite sure where he stands. All he knows is that he wants to live in accordance to the land, nature, the creativity of life itself. His great love, his passion, is making traditional Sámi-style jewelry of deer hide intertwined with tin and brass. "When you were born back in the day, the Sámi tradition was to give a baby a brass ring. Brass was considered protective. It followed that child through all of his life," Johan says. "You would wear it on your belt. It had a holiness to it, that metal." I notice for the first time he's wearing a traditional Sámi belt covered in tiny brass circles, spaced like the metallic studs of a biker belt.

Traditionally, Sámi used to mix brass fragments with soap to use on infected wounds. "It would heal them," Johan says. "For a long time, people tried to figure out why it worked, because it did." Not long ago, he explains, researchers found out that brass is a metal with antibacterial properties. Its protective powers were suddenly something that could be measured, and therefore—in a mechanical world—considered real.

He says, "I don't think things should be valued because of monetary worth. If something has healing power, that's beyond economic value. It's something I got from my grandfather. He doesn't worry about money. True riches are about what you surround yourself with."

I say, "Isn't that sort of a Sámi way of looking at things?"

Johan stops cutting. The kitchen knife hovers over the board. He exclaims, "You know what? It is! It is!"

I go back to scratching away at a notebook with my pen. Johan keeps cutting peppers. I start to feel a little awkward that I haven't gone back to my tiny sleeping hut like the other guests. "I hope it's okay for me to linger," I say. The hut is still warm from the oven, and it smells of caramelized onion. It's hard to think about returning to my own abode, with its sub-zero sleeping bag, until I'm ready to dream.

"It's good that you've stayed. You're part of everything here now," he says. "You aren't hiding in your cabin waiting to be served."

"But I'm not really doing anything," I protest. He's waved off my offer to help.

"Yes, you are. You're observing what goes into the making," Johan says. "You're paying attention. That's the important part."

When I wake the next morning it is already light outside. Accompanied by George and Yvonne, I find Johanna near the reindeer's enclosure. She's finishing up a feeding of store-bought lichen, which is stored in mesh bags. Her long white-blond hair has been pulled into braids, and she's wearing a red Sámi scarf tied intricately around the outside of her snow jacket.

The first thing I notice about the animals is their feet. They have onyx hooves that spread out like snowshoes when they rest their feet on the ground. But it's their ears that give them away. Johanna wrangles a nearby reindeer, hand-to-horn, and points at its ear, cut into slits that look like the torn wings of a monarch butterfly at the end of its migration. "We use knives to mark them when they are small," she says.

Every year, reindeer are born in May. All community members have their own unique symbols for marking the deer under their care, even children. Johanna says of her animals' pattern, as if it were on her own body: "My mother has nothing on her left ear. I have four marks."

She turns her attention to the group that's closest to us. These animals, considered well-suited for sledge work, roam freely in summer. "These deer are calm," she says. "But they are not tame."

We move the animals one by one to a line of sledges that are sitting along a fence line. I keep a steady pace, but my deer wants to snack on everything. He sniffs around at stray bits of lichen that fell during the morning feeding. He stops to chomp on snow. I get him to his sledge just as Johan arrives, bounding up on a snowmobile. He pops off the vehicle and sets about helping Johanna with the reindeer's gear. First comes the hand-whittled wooden harness. Then leather straps adorned with Sámi-colored wool.

Almost every local I've met wears an engraved, antler-handled knife on his or her hip. Johan pulls his from a sheath on his belt and begins to chip away at a patch of jagged ice that's formed on the top of my right sledge ski. "It's a beautiful way of transportation," he says, "but you really have to be firm with the animals. Use sharp sounds. Act crazy. They're still wild animals and they will do as they wish. When they look back, you've got to wave your arms to show them that you're active. Pay attention to what's going on with your reindeer; don't worry about any of the other animals."

We start out at a snowmobile crossing, which is as traversed as any major highway. Johanna takes off. I'm next in line. My guy doesn't budge. He's still crunching at a bank of ice like it's a giant snow cone.

I yell. I tap with my harness rope. I wave my hands. I jump around, putting my elbows on the back bar. I act crazy. Finally he moves. A few feet. I make it to a tiny snow bridge over a stream that has begun to melt. Then he stalls again.

Given the fact that I live with a wild two-year-old who takes twenty minutes to put on his shoes, I should be used to this sort of challenge. I should be patient. But I'm not.

My reindeer-sledge shouts become elongated screams. In desperation, my harness taps become pulls, which are counteractive. It's an action that tells the animal to stop. *Just. Go!* I can actually feel the tips of George's reindeer horns touching the outer layer of my clothing—like long, dull swords against my back. I'm at a loss about what to do next. I start to sweat.

Even though it is a warm, sunny day, perspiration is dangerous in the Arctic. I strip. My hat. My outer suit. *Leave it to me to freeze to death from sweat*, I think.

We've got hours of travel left. I get back on, though I'm not sure I want to.

Aye, aye, aye! I copy Johanna's calls to her reindeer. I jump and wave. My frustration becomes anger. This isn't going the way this was supposed to go. But how would I know how this animal is *supposed* to act any more than I know what the weather is *supposed* to be?

Johanna grinds the metal brake of her sledge into the trail we're following and walks back to see what is wrong. "What am I doing wrong?" I call out in desperation.

"Nothing," she says, shrugging. "Maybe he is tired."

It's only then that I realize how ridiculous it is to blame myself for this wild animal's behavior. Like it's about me. Like any of this is about me. But I suppose this is because I can't quite accept that—once I've done all I can do—I'm still at nature's whim. If I want to trust nature, to trust life, I can't always be trying to control it. Haven't I learned this by now? Isn't this, like, a main rule of parenting? Will I ever really be able to just do the best I can and then just *let go*?

"You should sit," Johanna says, her head cocked to the right.

"Is it easier that way?" I ask.

"You'll find out," she says.

Earlier this week, I asked a local how residents know when the Torne is thick enough to drive on for the season. I was thinking about municipal announcements, posted warnings, scientific confirmation. But the Jukkasjärvi resident just looked at me, like I was a complete idiot, and said: "You have to go out and test it for yourself."

How long is it going to take for me to get this?

Everyone is standing at attention, big and brave on their sledges now, except me. I'm embarrassingly laid out on the floor of mine like the queen of Sheba. This is, as it turns out, exactly what my deer needed. The disbursement of weight has somehow reminded him that I am here. It's as if he's just begun to recall what he's promised to do. He is moving.

The faster we go, the more fierce the day's wind. It hits my face, bursts blood vessels in my eyes. We break out of the tree line and onto the clean palette of the Torne.

When we stop to rest the animals at an embankment alongside the river, Johan hops off his snowmobile and walks over to say, sympathetically, "It's no piece of cake." He turns his attention to a traditional trading route in the distance and explains that winter, which is isolating from a modern view, has always been a particularly social time for the

Sámi. It is the season when impassable swamps and rivers freeze. The whole mucked up, muddy, isolating landscape becomes solid, concrete, passable again.

He gestures toward our reindeer. "These guys used to walk for thousands of kilometers. Back then, you didn't rush," he says. "You took it as it was." When we get back on our sledges I consider standing, but I don't. What do I have to prove? There is a Sámi saying that, left unheeded, is sometimes used to explain jet lag: Never travel faster than your soul.

We're off again. My reindeer goes from standing to full-speed in three steps. This time, the sledge is living up to its smooth-sailing promise. And, because I am sitting, I hear for the first time the crunch and clip of his feet against the ground. The song is made by a special bone on hind feet, a trait that allows the deer to hear each other when they cannot see each other, shrouded as they often are in snowstorms and mist. They provide a steady bass beat to the static hissing of the sledge runners.

Now that I'm not so concerned with controlling my reindeer, I can more fully witness his movement. And, because of the shifting of weight, what I'd seen as a sort of relinquished power, he can now fully sense me. I put my weight against the wooden slats of the sledge's backboard. The snow softens distant sounds so that all I can hear is my reindeer's tap dance. We're surrounded by unbroken sheets of ice, coated in snowfalls that glimmer like glass shards.

Johanna's animal momentarily loses focus and begins to snip at a patch of bark that's peeling away from a nearby tree. "*Aye, aye, aye,*" she shouts. "*Oye, oye, oye.*" That's all it takes. Yvonne, pulling up the rear, mimics all of Johanna's calls. But I just sit there. Silent.

Tiny tufts of lichen roll across unbroken snow like miniature tumbleweeds. In addition to digging for lichen, the reindeer also eat it off trees.

I can see it now, like a fragile version of Spanish moss swaying in the afternoon's mounting breeze. It's everywhere. On twigs, on bark. It looks like fur.

Suddenly—and I do mean suddenly—my reindeer breaks into a gallop. He senses what I don't have experience enough to know: We're close to camp. Reindeer legs, spindly as birch branches, crisscross in a pattern of perfection as he picks up speed, huffing and puffing as we fly across the remnants of a shattered sky. Behind us, his crystallized breath trails like the tail of a comet.

"If you play with the fire," Johanna says, "you will go blind." We're now in the camp's *lávvu*—a tipi-shaped, canvas-wrapped structure—and Johanna has just stoked the fire with the end of a stick. I cough a little as a spire of smoke lifts toward the small air vent above. Johanna heard this Sámi saying as a child. Even now that she's come of age, it reminds her to pay attention to the burning center of the *lávvu*. It doesn't instill fear as much as a deep sense of respect.

Historically, Sámi women were in charge of the hearth. Sárákkhá, goddess of childbirth, is traditionally said to reside here. Today, even Sámi who no longer find a real sense of numinosity in Sárákkhá consider it rude to walk behind the hearth. The goddess's place of residence was also a sanitary place for food. In Sápmi still, a reverence for fire is equated to a reverence for life.

The dirt floor of the structure is covered in a matrix of branches. They provide a layer of insulation under the deer hides that have been laid out for visitors. Johanna fills a sooty tin pot with water and pulls out a deerskin bag. The soft hide brushes my now-gloveless hand as she leans over to pour coffee grinds directly into the kettle.

She dumps a bag of raw deer meat into a pan, pushing it over the fire with a birch branch. Its bark curves and singes over the flames. When the meat is cooked, she folds it into traditional flatbread with spoonfuls of lumpy lingonberry jam. "I always eat this when I am in the mountains," she says.

Johanna's family is in the minority that still utilize *lávvu* tents. As recently as twenty years ago, some Sámi were living in traditional houses made of water-resistant birch bark and insulated with moss. And it's still possible to find elders who grew up in those. But now most Sámi live in wooden houses, with only a small minority of herders spending time in traditional structures.

In winter, Johanna's father tends the herds in the north but she and her brother stay busy closer to home, where they live in a wood-built home with their mother. But, come summer, they all travel north. For two months out of the year, they live in a *lávvu* as their ancestors did, hunting moose and elk as they trace the reindeer's path. Some anthropologists muse that it was the reindeer that domesticated Sámi herders rather than the other way around. After all, Johanna—like generations upon generations of those before her—does not lead the animals who wear her earmark. She follows them.

Johanna pours lingonberry juice in a small pot and places it on the fire. "If weather is bad, sometimes we have to stay in the *lávvu* when we're in the mountains. We sit like this and eat without telephone, computer, and TV." She rolls her eyes to indicate that this isn't always enjoyable. Sometimes, if she's really bored, she'll take her cell phone up to the top of a mountain where she gets spotty reception to check e-mail or call a friend. "But it's not fun to run for two hours just to go look at a telephone," she says. "I just leave it off."

The juice has begun to steam. She pulls the kettle from the fire and carefully fills a grouping of hand-carved wooden cups shaped like measuring spoons. Bits of reindeer hair float on the surface of my ruby-colored beverage. They look like surface-skimming spiders.

I've been told that, in Sápmi, people tend to walk more closely during winters, linger a little longer by fires, talk a little more than usual. The dark days seemed to usher in a certain sense of intimacy. The funneled interior of the smoking *lávvu* can serve to do the same. "I like it, the Sámi life," Johanna says. "It makes the best life I can have, I think."

Female Sámi herders were not unheard of historically, but modernity has ushered in an opportunity that might not have been available to a twenty-two-year-old Sámi woman a decade ago. Johanna—who is now flashing cell-phone images of herself in traditional dress, with the pride of a high schooler showing off prom photos—says: "Sometimes, when I'm out in the mountains, the men say, 'What are you doing out here?' But this isn't the old times, this is the new times."

The village of Jukkasjärvi pretty much consists of the ICEHOTEL, a convenience store, a gift shop, and the church, a tiny clapboard building painted bright red. When the Bakers and I arrive, the church is bustling with ski-gear-clad tourists who've made the long walk from ICE-HOTEL to see the place, famed as the oldest wooden building in the country, circa 1608. Its interior is lined with planks of whitewashed wood that have been pulling away from each other for years. Strings of paint hang between the separating boards like bread dough.

Its ceiling bears circles representing the moon in various stages, and the whole place smells like the yellowed pages of an antique book. George walks over to a wooden rack holding postcards. He takes one and slips a thick Swedish coin into a handmade donation box.

We turn to see Ann-Mari Hammarstedt Vilgats, local organist, walking down the aisle. She uncoils a scarf from her neck and begins to tell us the history of the artwork on the back wall. It is a 1950s-era wooden triptych meant to depict the revivals of Lars Levi Laestadius, a Lutheran minister who criticized the church's treatment of Sámi people. To the right, there is a snow-covered mountain in the background, the sky above adorned with two bright strips of yellow light meant to represent the northern lights. "People who come in here sometimes ask if that mountain is meant to be the ICEHOTEL," Ann-Mari says, her brow arched to show disapproval of this short view of history.

She skips over a bloodied, crown-of-thorns Christ in the artwork and points toward to a woman wearing a Sámi shawl, like the one Yvonne had tied around her shoulders. It is a depiction of Maria, the woman said to have inspired Laestadius's movement. The sun appears as an ethereal crown, a halo, the auroral oval behind Maria's head. "There were many churches built to mark the borders of Finland in Sweden's early history. There were no buildings before then, just forest and woods. They built the churches because they wanted to connect with the Sámi people," Ann-Mari says, "and they wanted to tax them, too."

Ann-Mari directs our attention to the organ. Where I've been expecting a creaky, sinewy sort of ancient artifact, I find a polished, magnificent work of modern art. The organ is inset with ivory reindeer horn, playing a role that's usually reserved for mother of pearl. Its center is shaped like the Sámi drum. "This is a Sámi organ, in a sense," Ann-Mari says. "It is made of wood, antler, and reindeer skin."

An image of the sun sits inside the drum's outline. I have read that when the missionaries first came to Sápmi, Sámi people started incorporating Christian symbols on their drums, a way of assimilating out of fear or reverence. The symbolism of this organ, to Ann-Mari, is more overt. "The organ says please forgive us," she says. "The Swedish were very harsh to the Sámi people. They burned the shaman drums." Sometimes, particularly pious shamans—those who refused to give up their sacred instruments during missionary-led witch trials—were burned at the stake.

When the Sámi artist Lars-Levi Sunna installed this organ in the 1990s, it marked the first introduction of Sámi symbols to a Lutheran church in Sweden. It is an institution that reputedly still involves people who believe traditional *yoiking*—the art of embodying phenomena through song as hula embodies them through dance—is a form of witchcraft, and he was afraid of what would happen to him. This, despite the fact that it was the church that had commissioned him to create the casing.

When he delivered it, Ann-Mari expressed confusion over how to approach the Sámi instrument as a Christian organist. The artist's advice still echoes in her memory: "Come as you are in front of God."

"You must know," she says, "that this is what the revival said to the Sámi people. It's a really lovely message if you strip away the terrible history. *Come as you are.* This is an instrument of healing. The spirit is there whether you want it or not." Then Ann-Mari, as Lutheran as a Lutheran can be, looks up at the organ and says: "This organ has many gods."

Ann-Mari's openness begins to open me. This is an organ that accepts mystery. It is a tangible admission of not having all the answers, of acknowledging that there are many different ways to find divinity. It is a skin-and-bone apology for historically using an abstract, institutionalized understanding of God to terrorize a visceral, sacred world. It is a symbolic attempt to make real the mystical, *unus mundus* heart of almost every world religion. It's a reconciliation of two traditions. And, just maybe, it's inspiring some sort of reconciliation within me.

"Are you ready to play?" she asks George, who simply nods.

Ann-Mari pulls a key from her pocket. The ancient wooden door to the organ loft shudders a little when she opens it to reveal a stairwell that is really more of a ladder. One by one we surface into the sunlight streaming from a high window. Ann-Mari cautions us to watch our step. The floor of the balcony is slanted so much that it's nearly enough to make one lose balance. But then again, so is the organ. It is magnificent.

What can be seen from the ground is nothing compared to what is held here, in the heart of the loft. Every stop-knob of the organ register is antler, etched like the handle of a Sámi knife, and on each one appears a scene of characters taken from traditional mythology. The carvings have been rubbed with birch shavings to give the recessed grooves a coppery hue. Each ivory of the piano is etched with a star, and its keys are not stark ebony, but rather the soft brown of burled wood.

Ann-Mari tugs on a few organ stops. "The symbols go along with the tone," she says. "There's a message behind every one. And the darker the horn, the darker the sound."

Ann-Mari has taken off her insulated boots. She's in her stockings. There are some dress shoes stored in her desk—shoes that would allow more mobility than her insulated gear—but she reports that a family of mice have taken them over. She pads around, increasingly eccentric. Her air of oddity is reinforced when she takes a paper cup of water and opens a wooden door to the back of the organ, saying, "The birds need water!"

"You keep *birds* in there?" Yvonne says, incredulously.

Ann-Mari laughs and walks back over to the organ. She plays a note. It sputters. It gargles. But then, a water-fed, metallic organ feature begins to chirp. The balcony, the entire church, is suddenly alive with birdsong. Twittery tweets bounce off the walls as if we're standing in an open-air tree house. "There are other organs in the world that have birds," she says, referring to the pipes that allow the instrument to tweet, "but not many."

Ann-Mari points to the organ pull that makes the birds sing, and she says, "The artist told me that this was symbolic. In the Bible it says all the tongues will disappear. All God's word will be the same." Creation as creator. *Let the phenomena speak.*

"Are the birds written into songs?" George asks.

"No," Ann-Mari says. "I have never seen a written note for the birds. I just use it when I feel it's needed."

"Are the stories of all the symbols written down?" I ask.

She shakes her head. "There is no written record," she says, "but I know many of the stories because the artist told them to me."

When I was a child, I don't remember it ever being brought to my attention that the Bible is full of mystical-minded phenomena: smoking volcanoes, swirling winds, lightning strikes. I didn't grow up in a cathedral full of saints' stories and visceral rituals involving cloud-evoking incense. My Protestant church was quiet. The air was still. The chosen sacred text was regarded as a destination rather than a travel guidebook. For me—and I know it's not so for everyone—this literal worldview was encouraged at the expense of the very thing I hoped to find: Enchantment in a disenchanted world.

But that's what I'm finding here.

Would it have been easier to be born into a religious tradition that spiritually felt right? Probably. But that doesn't mean I wouldn't have had to go through this spirit-seeking process anyway, to experience what Jung called individuation, the process of more fully becoming myself— the authentic me rather than the me I think I'm *supposed* to be.

Mysticism is the phenomenal essence of religion. It is direct observation of the divine. And the religions that came from the individual, phenomenal experiences of Buddha, Muhammad, Jesus, and Krishna purport through their more mystical traditions—and their most arduous rituals—that this sort of personal experience and relationship is possible for followers, too. They suggest that the individual, the self, has a direct line to divinity. But it's not a party line; the direction is different for everyone.

I started this phenomena chase of my own accord, yet I'm still not sure how I got here, how I've arrived at this very moment. I don't know how this pilgrimage to wonder has turned into such an intensely spiritual quest. What I do know is this: I'm beginning to see my own life as part of a magnificent, ever-unfolding story.

Ann-Mari pulls another stop, presses another key. "This is the Sámi wind god," she says. "The wind god is the tremor of the organ." It's a note that often jumps out in the song, creating a sense of surprise. "Who can say when the wind comes?" Ann-Mari says.

The voice of the wind god fills the church. Nature, life, is bringing me what I need—in its own time, in its own way. But, even after all that I've experienced, I'm still in the infancy of trusting this.

Ann-Mari—she who controls the winds—seems determined to help me make some pretty big leaps, though she couldn't possibly know the role she's playing. She raises her head from the organ and asks, as nonchalantly as anyone could, "Would you like to hear a Sámi drum?"

Is this selective perception? Coincidence? It doesn't matter. Not to me. Not in this moment. It's all I can do to nod my head to indicate that, yes, I would like to hear the said-to-be-nearly-extinct instrument. I have been told that surviving drums are held in locked cabinets. How could Ann-Mari have gotten her hands on one?

Ann-Mari points to two wooden pipes that are set away from the brass organ. They produce a note that mimics the echo of long-silenced Sámi drums. Ann-Mari plays it, and the entire church reverberates with a percussive sound. The walls shake. The floor itself begins to throb.

Her index finger wanders: "And here's the central sound. It is the

sun. The central sound gives life to the organ. This is meaningful because the sun gives life to us all." Then, of a particularly elaborate organ
pull, she says, "That's the frost man with his staff. He's beating down the
snow." She plays the note and the frost man beats the ground as if the
soil itself is a percussive instrument, making way for new growth: *Dun
da da dun.*

Even George and Yvonne—international organ connoisseurs seem
dumbfounded. This isn't any ordinary instrument. No, not by a long
shot. George clutches the sheet music he's brought close to his chest.
Yvonne has her hands clasped tightly at her chin. Ann-Mari continues:
"And here is the midwife, helping to give birth. This sound is warm and
calming." The organ pull for the note depicts Sárákkhá, midwife goddess of the *lávvu* hearth. She is, the artist has said, mother to us all.

Ann-Mari stops on an image of smoke rising from the tip of a
lávvu, which looks not unlike a volcano. "This is the quinta three," she
says. "The smoke, it carried us along between the mountains. It carried
us home."

The sultry note curves around rafters. It dances against the moon-
painted ceiling. It hits leaded windows, with their wavy patterns revealing a liquid past. The quinta's vibration travels over the frozen landscape
beyond, a scene that will—just months from now—completely transform with thaw. Come a warmer season, the sky will be as still as the
Torne is now, but the river's currents will be murmuring; the ground
itself will rumble with seeds breaking ground.

Ritual is important because it gives physical form to abstract ideas, as
Newberg's research indicates, but it was physical form—phenomena like
thunderbolts and auroras and cave-digging rivers—that gave way to
those abstractions in the first place. I'm starting to feel like I've been a
prisoner in Plato's cave—being taught that shadows are more real than

what casts them. But maybe all I need to do is turn around, not be so afraid to step outside, to forge my own spiritual path.

Symbols have the potential to conjure the sense of *unus mundus* that seems to reveal itself far too infrequently in day-to-day life, and I'm increasingly feeling emboldened to use symbols and signs as personal guideposts. But, despite their worth, symbols—hieroglyphs as well as words themselves—still seem, to me, fragile reminders of an overarching, visceral story greater than what will fit on the page, a spontaneous song of universal creativity that cannot be contained.

All religious rites are, at root, human interpretations of phenomena. They are most valuable to us when—for whatever reason—we're having difficulty experiencing the source of their original inspiration for ourselves. They're most dangerous when we forget that our culture is not the only one from which interpretations spring.

Increasingly, I believe mystery speaks to us each, directly, all the time. But only if we let it. This belief is partly born of the fact that my phenomenal journey is somehow singing me back to believing in the communicative, rhythmic, whole-world holiness to which I've always belonged.

Ann-Mari walks her fingers across the organ until they reach the cymbal star, a brass feature characteristic of European organs. "The cymbal star," she says," is actually a symbol here."

"A symbol of what?" I ask, but she's already struck the note. It sounds like razor-tipped snowflakes tumbling over each other in midair, like bells on a reindeer harness, the twinkling of a distant star, a crackling hearth, the fiery sun.

"I heard it once when I was a long way out of town," Ann-Mari says. "It sparkles, doesn't it?" Sure, it shimmers. But I'm confused. How could she have heard an organ note out in the Arctic wilds?

I lean in to study the Sámi-born symbol for the sound. The etching depicts a reindeer migrating toward mountains. A human figure on curve-tipped skis follows. Above them, as if the world's been turned up-side down, a river flows through the sky.

I ask you: What is a miracle if not the manifestation of light where darkness is expected? I am a child of God, many gods, and—with improbability that makes my beating heart ache—I just heard the north-ern lights.

CHAPTER 6

THE GREAT MIGRATION, TANZANIA

June 2012

I AM COCOONED IN A MOSQUITO NET. MY HEART IS BEATING rapidly, inconsistently. There is a monkey on the tin roof of my rented-for-the-night hut in Arusha, Tanzania, and I cannot sleep. I've spent the last week of my life obsessing over the preschool superbugs that invaded my house in the three months after I returned from Sweden. I've been worried about traveling, alone, in ill health, about navigating sub-Saharan Africa in search of the world's largest mammal migration by my little, lonesome self. And, as luck would have it, on my transatlantic flight from New York to Amsterdam, the woman sitting next to me vomited into a bag the whole way.

I do not want to be here.

I'm writing, pen mashed to paper, as if I'm trying to write my way home. I miss Archer. I miss Matt. I am too far from them. The journey to get here was arduous. It was awful, and I want to turn straight around and do it again.

I want to go home.

Was it a bad idea to drink that water hotel workers told me was safe? The bottled water I was given at the Kilimanjaro Airport tasted like chemicals. Was it full of chemicals? Is *that* why my heart is beating like this, or am I having some sort of panic attack?

My hut is lovely, but I don't really care. I want my family. I have spent twenty minutes weeping into my pillow from exhaustion and emotion. I have been awake for nearly three days straight, following a sleepless night in my house, where I rose—at 2 a.m. and 4 a.m.—because Archer was crying out.

But why am I not asleep now?

My bed is comfortable, though my nerves are being rattled by diesel trucks on the road beyond the hotel grounds, where, in morning light, women will filter by with barrels balanced on their heads and men will cart drying grass for cows that do not have room to graze. But tonight, it is dark. I am desperate for sleep. It reminds me of how I felt in Archer's first, nonsleeping year. But my baby is now nearly three. And I've just turned thirty-four. Yet I feel like a giant toddler myself, nervous and weepy. I'm crying for my son instead of my mommy. I am a middle-aged baby.

For my birthday a few months back, I told Matt I didn't want anything other than trees. It was a strange impulse, but he obliged. Our yard was historically forest, then a cabbage field, then pasture for horses. Now it's our home. And the only thing that would make it better, I told him, would be some native eastern white pine trees. He figured that, on our two acres, we could probably plant fifty. I agreed to the bulk, concerned about the fact that, when Archer walks through woods, he sometimes pretends he has a saw, influenced by Matt's occupation. Guilty because, in the chaos of my kitchen, I sometimes use paper towels.

For every tree that's cut down, I tell Archer, we have to plant a young one. But each time I've uttered the words, I've been reminded that—in order for him to really get this—I have to show him. Those birthday trees were an admittedly ambitious way to do it, and the gesture was made even more ambitious by a confused worker at a nearby nursery. When Matt went to pick up the celebratory trees, he was given a bag of 500 seedlings. He protested, but he was told that, because of the confusion, he could have them for the same price as 50. The trees were already giving.

Matt dug holes in our land, first with a shovel, then with an auger. Archer and I went behind him, wrangling roots. When we were done, we had exactly 450 left. We mentioned our abundance to our next-door neighbors, who said they'd love a few. This went on and on, neighbor to neighbor, until it became clear that Archer's beloved pine forest would soon be a lot bigger. And I want nothing more than to sit and watch it grow. Starting tomorrow.

In my can't-sleep discomfort, I start scheming about how I might go home to do just that. But, even in my desperation, I cannot begin to imagine trying to rebook my flights. And, what—I'm going to abandon a week in the Serengeti chasing wildebeest because I miss my family? Because I had a gross plane ride? Because I'm alone, and I can't sleep, and any minute now I might actually have a monkey on my back?

Buck up, camper! I tell myself. I hardly ever get homesick. But my last two trips have been too close together. I am tired. I want to go back to my comfortable little house, with my comfortable little bed, and my happily snoring husband. But I've got eight nights before I can sleep in a familiar place. *Game face.*

I pull out a notebook and string words together like pearls on the page. I craft sentence after sentence. I begin to calm myself with the rhythms of writing. Pen up. Pen down.

Outside, traffic slows.

I have looked forward to this trip for a long time. But my discomfort here has been amplified by the realization that the people in the group that rode from the airport with me this evening, also here on safari, were not of my tribe. They made jokes about suing our transport driver over lost airline luggage. They told me they were here to get away from the real world. I am here to find it.

There are dying flowers on the table next to my bed. In the corner of my room sits a broom ready to clean wooden floors streaked with gold. The whole place is constructed of exotic wood Matt would know by name. If only he were here.

Tomorrow, I will try to see it all with new eyes. I will resume faith in the journey. Ever since I conjured the idea of this phenomenal pilgrimage, it has felt like something beyond me, bigger than me, something I am supposed to do. And I am doing it. Nature will bring me what I need. *Won't it?*

The next day, I am charged by an elephant. *Nature, this isn't exactly what I had in mind.* But here it is, a giant bull's head barreling toward me. My safari guide, David Barisa, has maneuvered past a line of elephants skirting this red-dirt road. He started out slowly, testing boundaries, and the animals seemed comfortable. But then, out of nowhere, this guy bolted from behind.

The bull's face is fully framed in the huge open windows of our Land Cruiser. He's coming close. Fast. I watch until all I can see are his tusks, and then I turn forward, as if doing so might push us along. I grab my seat, bracing for impact. I am sure the animal is going to roll our vehicle. But then, suddenly, we lurch forward. The elephant steps back.

David is shaking. I am, too.

"I had not engaged the gear," he says, falling into a fit of nervous laughter.

"Has that ever happened to you before?" I ask. I've been in the Serengeti National Park for all of an hour.

"No," he says, "but it makes me wonder what people have been doing here lately."

Elephants, as it turns out, really do have long memories. David says, "Their families have been killed and they are wary. They remember human beings are not always friendly. They know about poachers. You have to have an escape road."

When we're farther out, he pulls over to inspect the vehicle. "The trouble is when they give you a warning—with a swinging trunk and flapping ears—and you don't move quickly enough." David's fingers find an indentation near the roof. "There is a tiny mark here," he says, running his hand across metal. "He pulled back."

The secret language of elephant-produced infrasound has been detected ten kilometers from where the emitting animals stand, and, when sent through the earth, it has the potential to travel much farther. If the bull's infrasonic capacities are sensitive enough to allow him to experience cries of his kin from miles away, it must be awful to feel a motor running thirty feet from his face.

"Elephants are gentle unless they're provoked," David says as we ride along. This seems a reasonable philosophy. I'm upset I've unwittingly done any provoking, but what I can't stop thinking about is this: That irate, 25,000-pound, possibly grieving animal pulled back. What a show of mighty restraint.

I tense as we approach another herd, but David remains calm. He's going to be more cautious this time. Unfortunately, he cannot control the cries of the wildebeest. These are the bearded, ever-migrating, famously unattractive animals I've mainly come to see. And there are thousands of them between us and the elephants.

Each year, roughly 1.3 million wildebeest make a circular trek around the Serengeti in what's known as the Great Migration. They are joined by roughly 200,000 zebra and 350,000 gazelle. It's a fine orchestration, with the zebra eating the hardest grasses, the wildebeest following to consume nutrient-rich leftovers, and the gazelle dining on the fresh sprouts that rise from fertilized plains. This composes the largest remaining mammal migration on earth, and it is loud.

The wildebeest sound like they're all simultaneously squeezing comical clown noses: *Honk, honk!* It's a strange sort of snort-laugh, and it's dorkishly endearing. "They do that to find each other," David says. "The babies are calling the mother, and mother calls back."

Behind them, an elephant lifts her trunk. Her baby has somehow ended up on the opposite side of the road. The mother begins to wave her head and flap her ears frantically. It looks like she might pick off a few wildebeest. We'd be next.

"Let's leave them," David says. "You don't ever want to get between a mother elephant and her baby."

No, I don't. But the scene is introducing me to the notion that the migration isn't just about the three core species that compose it. Elephants and giraffe do not migrate, but they do travel to be close to the migration when it comes around because it means there are plenty of wildebeest—i.e., easy prey—which means a safer scene for them. Predators hang around because it's like an all-you-can-eat buffet. Bugs and birds like the prolific poop. It's a system refined by evolution. But it is changing. Even David, who has been here for only two years, can see it. "The pattern, it is different. It is delayed because the wildebeest stayed longer in the south. There were rains there. The storms, they did not move ahead."

There's a lot that scientists don't know about the migration—exactly why it happens or how it's sparked—but they generally believe it is related to the weather. Studies have shown that wildebeest can anticipate grass-growing storms from miles away, possibly drawn by lightning. It's an instinct that has led to the peculiar migratory tradition of backtracking at times, following rains. These animals are not focused on a destination or goal; they are simply, always—no matter what direction it takes them—headed toward life, greenery, steadily enough to ultimately move them forward, toward wherever they seasonally need to be.

David and I come across yet another herd of elephants, their hairline-fractured tusks caked with mud from mineral digs. Their walking is surprisingly quiet. Two of them greet each other, their trunks twisting in embrace. David cuts off the engine and I hear the delicate *whish whish* of grass parting as they walk. Their harvesting of grass bouquets makes a surprisingly loud noise. The ripping oats sound like cotton sheets being cut with dull shears.

"Look over there," David says, pointing toward an open field. "You can't see the end of it. Some people call the Serengeti an endless plain, but I call it a sea of grass."

In surrounding countries, where violence often erupts, there are usually a few major tribes struggling for power, David tells me. But, in Tanzania, there are 120 tribes, with Chagga being one of the largest and Maasai—famed for their beautiful beadwork—one of the most visible. Though David's family walked away from the traditions of their Chagga ancestors two generations ago, he still knows what the animals meant to his ancestral tribe. "Chagga chiefs," he tells me, "used to wear leopard skin to represent intelligence. A leopard can read your mind. It knows things, because it sits and watches."

Wearing animal skin is a way of inhabiting other species, of gaining their strength and knowledge. It is something that Johanna and her Sámi ancestors have always done, loving, wearing, and eating reindeer not as products to consume, but as soulful extensions of themselves. Art critic John Berger has suggested that the first paint was likely animal blood, and that the first painting was of animals. "Animals first entered the imagination as messengers and promises," he writes. "Everywhere animals offered explanations, or more precisely, lent their name or character to a quality, which like all qualities, was in its essence mysterious. What distinguished man from animals was the human capacity for symbolic thought, the capacity which was inseparable from the development of language in which words were not mere signals, but signifiers of something other than themselves. Yet the first symbols were animals."

It's a tendency we have not given up in a secular sense.

"There are some animals they use to represent countries," David says. "Kenya uses the lion in their emblem. It is fierce, but you can tame it. In Tanzania, you have the giraffe. It is calm and peaceful. In Uganda, they use the crane."

David peers over his sunglasses to ask: "Why is it that your country uses a bird of prey?"

"The bald eagle? I think it's meant to represent power."

David nods, as if this makes complete sense.

Animal behaviors ultimately, always, remind David of human ones.

I ask him if there's an animal he gravitates toward. He does not hesitate: he favors the lions. And it's not because he wants to seem macho. It's because, recently engaged, he's thinking about fatherhood. "The lions make a good family," he says. "The lions stay together. Their social structure revolves around females. Young ones can suckle from any of the mothers. The males also participate. They share parental care so more of their young survive. It's the female lions that hunt. The males are built more for defense. I think this is like African culture, too. In some communities, like the Maasai, women build the huts, they milk the cows, they take care of the young ones. The man does nothing but take the cows to graze and then come home to eat. But they are also protectors."

To our left, we see another lion family sleeping in an acacia tree. There are six cubs. One raises its leg to lick its foot. Two momma lions are asleep in the tree. But there is one standing out on a limb, a lookout.

David says, "I also like that lions are very curious. The young ones especially." He points to the lioness watching us. "See the black tip on her tail? That's so when the mother is in the high grass, the cubs can still see it. They use that as a follow-me sign." As we pull away, he adds, "Some days, you can drive all day and see nothing, and sometimes, you go out and see everything in just a few minutes."

Luckily, it's one of those days.

In front of us, wildebeest herds appear as dark spots on the horizon, shadows of passing clouds. Some are making their way across the plains at a steady rate, heads at attention rather than sloped into grass. Like the zebra, wildebeest travel in lines. It's a behavior that gives them an advantage over predators. If they always moved in big groups, it would be easy to pick out the weakest of the herd since they would always be at the back. But, by traveling single file, everyone is given a fighting chance.

"When they move like that, they look like soldiers," David says.

There are, among these herds, a lot of babies. All of them are roughly six months old. Female wildebeests synchronize their births each year in the Ngorongoro Crater area, south of here. No one is really sure why the animals come full circle from their northernmost migratory locale to give birth, but they suspect it has something to do with proteins in grasses or minerals in the Ngorongoro soil that provide for lactating mothers.

"There are so many wildebeest born during that time," David says, "the lions won't be able to finish them."

A pair of Fischer's lovebirds take flight, clearing our path. They appear green as emeralds glittering in sunlight, jewels tossed up by the earth itself. David points to open plains in the distance. "That's where the wildebeest are headed."

We're moving toward a mobile tented camp run by &Beyond, an Arusha-based outfitter, when we come across a film crew that's parked in the middle of the savanna, cameras erected on the roof of their vehicle. They're filming an especially large herd.

I am in a nature documentary. Only, I'm not. The film in progress is going to capture the herds' great numbers, but here's what it will surely miss: The sound of the wildebeests' crying is carrying from left to right. Then, right to left. It moves like tides. The air seems to tremble when the animals move. The ground actually shakes. Even IMAX theatres can only go so far.

The cameras are fixed on the herd in front of us. But behind us there is another. I can hear them—thousands of them—going about their business without a single set of human eyes witnessing their movements. And then there is that motionless plain to the east, as beautiful as hard lines of poetry punctuated with dark acacia, but lacking the action that makes for great television.

"People come all the time and ask why are the wildebeest not crossing the river," David says, referring to the iconic images of wildebeest fording waterways full of hungry crocodiles. "They don't understand that the film crews are not showing the migration—they're showing part of it. The crossing is the most recognizable moment, but it's only a part of what is happening. Here, we have the lions waiting instead of crocodiles. Here, the young wildebeest have not been tested. They have only just begun. They are just starting their lives. It's their first time to move, to take that risk. Here, they are initiated."

It's early June. Last year, by this time, the herds were farther north. David looks out over the writhing mass of brown and black. The animals are kicking up dust, volcanic soil so fine it has gathered in the corners of my eyes. David sneezes. Last week, he was sick from extraordinary amounts of inhaled earth.

He looks at the herd the crew is filming and says, "The real question of the migration is this: Will the animals make it to the other side of Kenya? Will they be able to make it back here next year to do it all again?"

Wildebeest can live for twenty years, which means there are animals here that have been in migration since 1992. A few will die here, on these plains, tonight. But an overwhelming majority will make it through the Seronera area. They will find their way back, reliably, again and again.

We follow the road into a stand of trees. "We're in the tsetse fly zone now," he says, handing me a beaded, wooden stick with long strands of dark hair sprouting from one end. I follow his lead, letting the swatter slap my shoulder, like a bullwhip, to push the biting flies away.

When I accidentally slap myself in the face, it stings nearly as much as the skin-slicing mandibles of the tsetse. "What is this made out of?" I ask, fingering the coarse, iron-like strands of the swatter.

"Wildebeest tail," he says.

The &Beyond campsite is surprisingly plain. There is a wooden post bearing a bleached bull skull. Beyond that, there's a communal tent with plush couches and chairs. The entire place has only ten guest accommodations—tents hidden in small clearings separated by pools of tall grass. "This is Osman," a camp manager tells me in greeting, gesturing toward a mocha-skinned man wearing an &Beyond-issued khaki fleece. "He'll be attending you."

"I've never been attended in my life," I say, trying to make light of how uncomfortable this sort of attention is making me.

The manager smiles. "We will do everything we can to make your stay here a good one."

"And I'll do everything I can to be a good guest," I say.

This provokes a huge eruption of laughter from a group of loitering porters and butlers, but I wasn't trying to be funny. "I see you will fit with the &Beyond way of doing things. We take care of each other," the manager says.

This I believe to be true, but I am on my own for dinner. And, if I thought it was uncomfortable sitting at a table by myself in the Arctic Circle, it's only because I'd never had the pleasure of being seated at a candle-lit table with only distance, easily measurable in feet, between me and a lion who is roaring at the sky. It doesn't help that David has told me that night is the best time for hunting because the air is denser. Smells and even sounds travel much farther at night.

I eat quickly to join the camp's roughly fifteen other guests in the tented lounge. They fall into talk of bank mergers and clothing lines, the cuteness of Lacoste's alligator logo. Bored beyond measure, I excuse myself and walk over to the campfire—which is in safe solo walking range, as no guest is allowed to wander alone at night—where Osman is sitting with another butler.

There, I have the unsettling realization that Osman is waiting to escort me to my tent. But the awkwardness of this fades after it becomes clear he doesn't have anywhere else to go, other than the small tent he shares with several other butlers. I believe him when he assures me that he'd rather be here.

The young employee sitting next to Osman has been staring at me since I sat down, in a way that tells me guests joining butlers by the fire isn't a commonplace thing. Solo travelers are rare. Finally, he asks me, "Is this place very famous in the United States?"

"Yes," I tell him. "There are people that have never heard of Tanzania that know about the Serengeti." It is, I explain, one of the most famous places in all of Africa.

"No. *Really?*" The butler settles more deeply into his canvas folding chair. Beyond us, the silhouettes of flat-top trees are visible in moonlight. "So," he says, "this place is to you like New York City is to me. That's where I would like to go in your country," he says. "It is the most famous place in the United States. There is also Las Vegas. I'd like to go to Las Vegas."

He lowers his voice to a whisper and leans in to me, as if sharing a secret: "They say people there marry at night and divorce in the morning!"

Osman says, "They also say what you do in Vegas stays in Vegas. That means if you marry in Vegas, it's like you never got married!"

His friend laughs. "Oh, I'd love to go. I'd love to see big movement of cars! Big buildings!" As he speaks, the fire stirs. A log falls to the ground. Flames spit and hiss like snakes.

Osman tells me he grew up in the shadow of Kilimanjaro, so I ask if he's ever climbed it.

"Yeah," he says, "I've climbed it fifteen times."

I stumble to share my bewildered admiration—*fifteen times*—but Osman just shrugs. He has been a porter on Kilimanjaro. Now he's a butler in the bush. Around here, those jobs have the wow factor of saying you once worked a summer at Applebee's.

Earlier, when we met, Osman told me he'd like to become a business-man. But now he is feeling open. He tells me that his real dream, his big dream, is to become a pilot. "But I am embarrassed of this," he says, "because I gave up on it. A friend told me it was hard. And now, I am too old to try."

He is twenty-six.

When we reach my tent, Osman loiters for a minute and says, "I like the idea of your book."

"Thanks, the book—just being here—is me living out *my* dream."

He's quiet for a minute. "Can I ask you something?"

"Of course."

"Why did you come alone?"

I want to cry, again. Traveling alone is one thing. Traveling alone when you're sleeping solo in the heart of the Serengeti—within the scent-space of lions—is another. In my comparative wealth, I am embarrassed to admit the truth, that I am the only member my family could afford to send, and just barely, because of a professional opportunity and windfall discount. But I do.

He nods. This he understands. His cycle is to work six weeks on, two weeks off. When he goes home to Arusha, he lives in a one-room apartment shared with several friends. When he can, he visits his mother's house so he can help care for his younger siblings.

"I feel like I am always struggling," he says. And he doesn't mean struggling to be able to go to the grocery store without having to use his credit card. He means struggling to make sure his brother has adequate protection so he will not die from malaria. That his mother has access to water that will not lead to dysentery.

I don't know what to say, but I feel like I should say something. Before I can, Osman turns to me and says, "I want to tell you, my name isn't really Osman. It's Athman." He pronounces the *Ath* by putting his tongue hard against his teeth. I strain to make out his plastic name tag in the dark.

He pinches the slender piece of plastic between his fingers, as if he'd momentarily forgotten he was wearing it. "It was guests that gave me my name, mostly Americans." During his time as a porter on Kilimanjaro, he found that Americans had trouble pronouncing Athman. "They always said Osman," he tells me. "So that is who I became."

"But Athman is a nice name," I say, uneasy about the appropriation.

"Please, call me Osman," he says. "It's how everyone knows me here. If you asked for Athman, no one would know who you were talking about. I'm Athman only to my family. I don't know why I'm telling you this. I do not tell this to anyone."

I'm touched by his sharing of ideas and quiet, complicated identities. I think of the Naval Academy student I sat next to on my connecting flight from Amsterdam to Arusha. The cadet was coming to Tanzania because he had received a $100,000 grant from the U.S. government so he and a group of fellow Navy SEAL hopefuls could climb Kilimanjaro. It was considered elite military training. They would be accompanied by local porters.

"You know, Osman," I say, "there are people who make it their life goal to climb Kilimanjaro. They train for months, they buy fancy outdoor outfits, they travel for days to get here. And do you know what most of them are probably thinking when they land at the airport?"

Osman shakes his head. It's something he's been mystified about for years. All those seekers, focused on the top of the mountain. He's always thought them foolhardy for making such a calculated struggle in a world already so difficult to manage.

"They're thinking: If I can climb Kilimanjaro I can do anything I set my mind to. They return home feeling bold, courageous. You've climbed that mountain fifteen times, and you did it carrying everybody else's stuff on your back. That's amazing!"

"You are right," he says quietly.

"I don't know what will happen in your life, but you have climbed Kilimanjaro *fifteen times*! I bet every time you went up that mountain, you were helping someone else realize *their* dream. That makes me believe you're going to be okay. Maybe you will even fly one day."

"You are right!" he says, louder now. "What you say is important for me. I will remember this!" Osman puts a hand to his heart. "I think God gave you a secret," he says. "It is a beautiful thing."

. . .

When the sun rises, I shower in river water that's been warmed over a wood fire, delivered in a bag. I dress in DEET-soaked clothing and follow lampposts back to the main lounge tent. Their metal rods are bent like the hind legs of leaping gazelle. The sky blushes pink.

"There are lions close to the tents," David says when he arrives.

He brings the Land Cruiser around and points to an impression in the grass. "A male and a female were lying here," he says.

The grass is so high it's poking into my arm, which I have been resting on the vehicle's edge. I pull it to my torso when David points to a low-lying bush ten feet from where I sit and says: "The lions are hiding in there. They are kind of afraid."

The lions. Are afraid. Of us.

"We will find more lions," David says, afraid of disappointing me. "They are everywhere." He points to our left. "Vultures. That means there is a lion near. They are waiting for their turn to eat. We will go there."

We take a left onto a road that consists of two tire tracks of beaten grass. "I can smell wildebeest," he says. "They were here yesterday." I inhale deeply, and I'm pleasantly surprised when the scent reminds me of my maternal grandfather's barn, which was always full of goats and sweet hay.

As we cross a small creek, tires splash mud onto the vehicle. There, on the other side, in a lion-colored field, stands a huge male. I'm surprised by the greeting, and I can't imagine how the wildebeest must have felt encountering the same scene yesterday. But David hardly notices, because there are two more large lions—a male and a female—right in front of us. They're lying in the middle of the road, using the slight, car-pressed indentions as ready-made beds.

The lioness's tail flicks. The male puts his head down. In the distance, I hear the honking of a wildebeest herd that talked to me in the night. But the lions don't budge. Their bellies are still swollen from their last meal.

David maneuvers the vehicle around them and switches the engine off. The male opens his eyes. They lock with mine. I don't move. He doesn't move. David has a gun somewhere in the vehicle, but I don't imagine he could get to it if something were to go wrong. We are coexisting, in a tentative agreement. The air is cool, dry, light. I keep my voice low; I do not move except to breathe.

Until now, the only lions I've ever seen in my life have been in zoos. John Berger proposes that there is a certain sort of distancing in this view. In zoos, people look at animals, but animals rarely look at people. He writes, "At the most, the animal's gaze flickers and passes on. They look sideways. They look blindly beyond. They scan mechanically. They have been immunized to encounter . . . That look between animal and man, which may have played a crucial role in the development of human society . . . has been extinguished."

But has it?

The first time I ever found myself in wilderness with a large mammal, I was in northern Maine, standing on the opposite side of a pond from a full-grown moose. I remember thinking then how amazing it was that this creature could exist. That there was enough wilderness left in the world so that—even in the seemingly done-over continental United States—an animal as big as that could conceivably roam its whole life without seeing a human. And maybe this is, in a way, what Berger was talking about: seeing *and* being seen.

It startles me to realize that I came because I wanted to see animals, but what has moved me is the realization that *I* am being seen. I can look all I want, but it wasn't until these eyes-of-the-wild saw me that I felt truly absorbed into the landscape. This lion's witnessing of me is sending an electric current through my spine. It's not a bolt of adrenaline, it's the realization that—right now, in this very moment—I am as much a part of this place as he.

"It's rare to have two males this close," David says. "Maybe they are brothers." The field lion is ambling toward us now, mouth open, jowls jiggling like those of a slobbering St. Bernard. "I think he's headed toward that tree," David says, pointing. He's right. The lion ultimately dissolves into a dark puddle of shade.

I whisper in amazement, "How did you know?"

He says, "You must know the habitat and behavior of animals to understand them. It makes you a very good observer. I can say, most of the animals, you can read their body language. You can see them express, communicate without words."

The entire landscape, in fact, seems to speak here. Each species, animal and plant, sings out its yearnings and desires, attracting and seeking the other living beings that will help it grow. Each and every living thing communicating, at once, with all the world. David says, "After being out here, when I go back to the city, I start to read people's expressions more. Humans communicate in a lot of the same ways as these animals. They talk with their faces."

The lion opens his eyes again. We're staring directly at each other. Right now, I have to focus on the moment—not my abstract understanding of what *could* happen—if I want to keep cool. "Whereas in animals fear is a response to signal," Berger writes, "in man, it is endemic."

I'm working on this.

The wind through the grass sounds like the shush of elephants walking. I do not break my gaze. It feels like we're playing a game of sudden death. And—because of the flies swarming his amber eyes, flies I'm close enough to see—the lion is the first to blink.

In this moment, the entire world is green and gold and blue. The entire world is here, in this field, this moment. I start to think of the field as my field. This lion as my lion. Maybe the human impulse for ownership is really a show of our yearning for connectivity, a way to fill an emptiness left by the modern view that we do not all share equally in wilderness, in all the world. Maybe it is this sense of belonging, not ownership, that we incessantly hunger for, somehow—in the mechanized view of modernity—confusing the two. All I really know is this: In this moment, I feel less like a skittish house cat, more like a self-assured lion.

When we finally leave, David gets a little turned around. Briefly, we are lost. Though the park has changed over the years due to all sorts of factors, human included, being here can make one forget time. There are no manmade symbols. Only rocks and hills and trees, and the symbolic significance we give them. "See that mountain?" he finally asks, pointing to a hill with the hard slope of an elephant's forehead. "That's the one that tells me where camp is."

This is the sort of landmark awareness I've been trying to teach Archer lately, awakening him to using plants, and landmarks, and symbols to make his way in the world. If I were not having phenomenal experience after phenomenal experience, I would not be parenting in this way. If I were not being led by wonder, it is not the source from which I would teach. I know this because I sometimes catch myself saying things that do not line up with the experience I've gained.

Less than a week ago, on a morning car ride, I asked Archer if he knew where we were going. "To school!" he said. Then he looked out the window and asked, "Where is school? I can't see it." I laughed a little, hiding my amusement in the crook of my shoulder, and told him that, later, we'd look at a map, saying, "It's located to the west." And then I realized how odd it was that I was explaining this abstractly. To my still-viscerally-connected child, the word "west" meant nothing.

"Look at the sun," I finally said. "The sun rises in the east, behind our house. It sets in the west. When you see the sun go down in the afternoon, you will know where your school is." Archer went quiet. He has seen the point on the horizon where the sun sets. This, he understood.

Later that day, I told him about how moss grows on the north side of trees. I took him onto a neighbor's land and asked him to lead us home by listening to the sounds of roosters and river currents. If we lived in a city, the sounds might have been those of a neighborhood dog, the winged flap of pigeons in a park, the beep and clank of a garbage truck, the cellist that leaves her window open during practice. Though the exercise didn't go very well in terms of leading us home, it seemed to awaken him to a certain, phenomenal, order of things. It taught him, and reminded me, that there are a million different ways to map the world that have nothing to do with global positioning units, or even pens.

During our time with the lions, the wildebeest herds have somehow disappeared. David says, "I've had guests ask: 'How can more than a million wildebeest just vanish?' But it is a possibility. They move into areas that are not accessed. They have that instinct. They know when it's time to migrate. We just don't know exactly *how* they know."

David's guiding powers are similarly mysterious. Within twenty minutes, we're staring into another gyrating field of flesh. The females move slowly, fluidly, but several males run wild, raising and bowing their heads. David points them out and says, "So much wasted energy!" It is the action of rutting season, with males trying to maintain territories. Their hooves kick up dust, tinting the whole scene sepia.

Another safari vehicle passes. David and the driver have a quick conversation in Swahili. He turns to me: "That guide told me there's a fresh wildebeest kill ahead. Let's go."

I can't help but feel a little uneasy about the fact that we're headed to see a corpse. It doesn't help when we pull up behind a vehicle of heavy-metal tourists in a car with "Predator Safaris" plastered across the spare-tire cover. Are we here to ogle a dead body, to stare at death? Or are we here to stare at life, energy repositioning, the circle actually cycling?

"Smell the blood and guts?" David asks. I do. It's a disturbingly strong scent, unfolding wax paper in a butcher shop. "The food is plenti-ful now because of the migration," David says. "When there's not so much there's a scrambling. Everyone trying to get a piece of the kill."

The smell of blood iron will not leave me. Even when I breathe through my mouth, the air tastes rusty. If this were television, I could turn the channel. But I am in the bush, and I cannot—will not—look away.

This lioness is lying with the carcass of her prey, its fingerprint-distinctive stripes visible beneath a raw pink blossom of peeled-away skin. The two bodies appear to be sleeping together under a sheet of churning flies, haloed by the thorns of acacia limbs, in a loving embrace. David takes a deep breath. "This is a fresh kill. She probably pulled it there, into the shade." The flies keep eating away. Laying eggs. Coaxing life from death, light from darkness.

A hyena appears, as if pulled by its nose. It circles our vehicle, search-ing. It comes three feet from where I'm sitting by an open picture win-dow. It smells the kill, but when it sees the lion, the hyena retreats into high grasses. "It will come back to eat what the lion has left," David says. "Nature does not waste."

He sometimes has guests who turn their heads from carcasses. Some-times, visitors will not even look at a lion because of the role it plays. He reasons: "I think for most guests it's just a gross factor or mortality fear. Some people are just not used to facing reality."

It's a perspective that David, who has spent the last few years of his life studying biology and living in the bush, does not understand. What we've witnessed is necessary. It is, in the end, what supports cycles of life that span generations and species. "If it were not for the lions, the predators, how many wildebeest would there be?" David asks. "What would that do to the habitat? It would vanish. And then, *all* the animals would vanish."

We leave the crowds and drive, without seeing any other vehicles, for a long time. David goes quiet. I cannot see his eyes—he only removes his signature shades after sunset—but his brow is furrowed. Finally, he says, "The way that it all works together is an ecosystem. The things we cannot know outside of science, I call that God. But there are people that say of all the mysteries, we will find out in time."

"But new mysteries are born every day," I say.

David chuckles.

"Muslims, Christians, everyone has different names for God," he says. "But outside the institutions, I think people are almost always talking about the same thing."

"Yeah," I say, "me, too."

I'm coming to believe we're collectively yearning for what Jung called the *Anima Mundi*. It's a term borrowed from ancient alchemists who searched for the spiritual radiance of God, not as a somewhere-out-there abstraction, but rather in the physical, phenomenal world. They sought to turn commonplace metals into gold, holy light embodied.

According to my dear college friend Aaron—fluent in Greek and Latin—*Anima Mundi* basically translates as "Soul of the World." Not long ago, still reeling from my bout of synchronicity in Sweden, I told Aaron—son of a Catholic mother and Jewish father, scholar of ancient Greek myth—that instead of choosing my religion, I feel like I'm creating my own, piecemeal, as I stumble through the wilds.

At this, he laughed. And he laughed. And then he said: "Aren't we all?"

· · ·

When David and I arrive at camp, Osman meets us with drinks and white towels that turn copper when we wipe our hands. The campsite, surrounded by thorn bushes, is alive with ratcheting, sawing sounds. "What's making that noise?" I ask David, who has already downed most of his hand-squeezed lemonade. "It sounds like cicadas."

"It is cicadas."

I'd been expecting an exotic answer. This is, after all, a place where one should—upon hearing the beat of hooves—think zebras, not horses. But, despite the fact that cicadas have long been part of the summer soundtrack of my life, I'd never before considered them. Probably because I've never heard a cicada sing quite as loudly as this.

I turn my head so that my right ear is pointed toward a nearby bush. My eardrum begins to throb and pulsate inside of my head. The entire landscape seems to echo in my skull. The sound of the insects—which can reach 120 decibels, causing human hearing loss—is so loud it burns.

I go back to my tent, where fiber mats that smell of sea grass are rough underfoot. I wash my hands in rainwater from a brass container. When the tinkling against metal ceases, I hear comic snorting outside. I unzip my tent to see a line of wildebeest moving through. I'm part of something ancient and uninterrupted. But then again—even though I've long neglected to acknowledge it—I always have been.

I wander through camp, noticing cracked trees for the first time. When I find Ivan, a round-faced camp manager, lingering by the campfire, he tells me the downed trees are the result of elephant visits. The animals come through periodically, rubbing against the acacia. Ivan says, "When they move, nothing can really stop the elephant. It is a symbol of a king."

Tembo is the Swahili word for elephant. Ivan, father of three boys, tells me some parents name their children Tembo, which would indicate that their child was wise. *Punda* means Zebra. "If you were named Punda, you might be beautiful and sensitive, healthy," Ivan explains. "You might be graceful, quite agile." A daughter named Cicada might be a high-pitched crier, a natural-born singer.

"The Maasai, they have clan names—Hyena, Lion," Ivan says. "Even other tribes, no matter where you go, name after animals. Tribes in the highlands name their children after things like rain. You can name with nature—how nature behaved when you were born or how your mother acted when she was pregnant." If you were born during a full moon, for example, you might be called Shining Moonlight. "You grow into a name," Ivan says. "A name is also a story. It tells people who you are. Sometimes the name doesn't fit, but it is to keep a memory. It's an identity. It's who you are and where you're from."

"Ivan is an interesting name," I say.

"Yeah, my uncle, he went to Russia just before I was born and he brought back the name Ivan. My favorite traditional name means waterfall. But almost always children are given English names now."

"Why?" I ask.

He says, "I think it's globalization. Everyone watches television and people are going to church more. They start reading the names written in the holy book. You call somebody an animal name, but when you take them in to get baptized the pastor will say: 'No. You can't do this. You can't name your child *Hyena*. You should give them the name of a disciple, someone important.'"

"Are there really people named Hyena?"

"Yes," Ivan says. "I have a friend named Fisi, Hyena."

Ivan's own children were baptized Tony, Adrian, and Austin. Out of the three, Austin's name has gotten the most backlash. "It's very hard to pronounce for people that speak Swahili," Ivan says. "My family is Lu-

theran. They go to church, but then they go home and pray under trees."
He shakes his head. "I didn't get taught the old ways. You cannot do it
partially. And there has to be a training. You're chosen to learn the sacred ways when you're young. There is no documentary to teach me the
old ways of my tribe, but I can read the Bible and it teaches me what I
need to know A to Z."

I find it terribly strange—this notion that Ivan has turned to Christianity because there's no documentation of his own tribe's spiritual
tradition—but I have come to believe that the general leaning of the
modern world, everywhere, is like this. We value academic degrees more
than experience, trust professional documentaries more than family stories. We believe in the alphabet, that what's written down is the gospel
truth. It is the great boon of literature that it is available to everyone—
not just a chosen few—but the movement from oral to literary traditions
seems to have given us horse blinders in a world where everything we
encounter is telling us something, where all we see and hear and feel is
invested with its own soulful authority.

He glances at me shyly. "Are you religious?"

"I was raised Lutheran," I tell him, "but I'm not conventionally
religious."

"Why not?" he asks, cocking his head to more intently study my face.

"In part, because of the baptism story you just told."

Ivan sighs and turns to the fire. He says, "There really *is* something
nice to the old names, the ways of this place. When someone uses a
name of an animal or a thing in nature, we see that it means something
to that family. But it is hard to have that kind of name here now. Children named after nature are sometimes picked on. They ask their parents, 'Why don't I have an English name?'"

English name. The term makes me think of names like Baker and
Porter and Miller, all names that came from the occupations of ances-

tors. Historically—in many cultures, not just those of Africa—names were part of the phenomenal world. Identities were no less complicated, but the stories given at birth were, for better or worse, chosen because they represented something directly observable and life-world connecting. My own son is named in homage to my paternal grandfather, a highly adventurous wildcard who used to carve bows from wood, fletch feathers onto arrows. Historically, Archer was a surname in the trade-naming tradition. I have unconsciously—though maybe, I realize now, not unintentionally—taken it back.

"Hey, Ivan, what's your last name?" I ask.

"Moshi."

The irony is so obvious, so thick, so immediate, we both begin to laugh until we're cackling like hyenas, animals that sometimes switch up their *woo-ee* calls for trembling giggles. Moshi is the name of Ivan's home village, the birthplace of Chagga tribal culture. It is where his son, Austin Moshi, will learn to navigate between the abstraction of a Texas city he sees on television and the ancestral village that rose from the very land on which he stands.

The next afternoon, tsetse flies follow David's Land Cruiser into camp. Swarming. I step away from the vehicle and linger to watch other safari-goers come into range. The flies force everyone who disembarks to do a dance with their hands. Swatting. Ivan comes up behind me. "You know why this is a national park?" he asks. "You know why the Serengeti, the migration, still exists? It's because of the tsetse fly!"

"What do you mean?"

"This land is good for livestock, it's good for farming. But a long time ago people didn't come here because of the flies. They didn't settle because of the tsetse. So these little insects helped this place. They protected it. They became soldiers of the Serengeti. Things have value that we don't know and cannot see," he says. "Nature serves as a reminder of how we fit into all this. We think we're smarter than animals. We think we can see things coming. We talk about globalization, but we cannot know the big picture."

But we do know a little, and it isn't good. Climate change has badly affected Ivan's family's farm, where generations have grown coffee and bananas. Droughts, nearly unanimously accepted in the scientific community as the result of human-caused climate change, have pushed him to work here. "We protect this area, but other areas also get benefit," he says of the Serengeti. The same goes for degradation. When one thing is destroyed, everything—and everyone—suffers. "It is all connected," he says, putting his hands out, palms up to represent scales.

His right hand goes down, "Somebody will value the animals."

His left hand goes down. "Somebody else will value the minerals. It is always like this."

Not long ago, the Tanzanian government came close to building thirty-three miles of commercial highway across the northern section of the Serengeti. The highway would have linked isolated villages outside park boundaries with larger cities and central African nations, and it would have severed habitat. "The animals are used to the dirt roads, but they have never seen a tarmac," Ivan says. "They might not have crossed it. What would have happened then?"

Likely, scientists predicted, an eventual collapse of the wildebeest population. The road would present a barrier between forage and water, as well as increase poaching and traffic accidents. "They stopped that road, but there are always those forces at work," Ivan says. "It's a few people who have power. They don't think about benefit to the whole community."

Ivan points to a guest who is waving away tsetse flies. I recognize him as someone who complained about the insects at dinner last night.

Ivan says, "If they kill all the tsetse flies, they might destroy something else, too. The outcome, nobody really knows."

Next week, this camp is scheduled to move. The very tent I sleep in will be folded up and driven north, to be set up in anticipation of the migration. Ivan's life, like those of all the men working here, consists of minimigrations of their own. Monthly, these men support their families by traveling with the herds in their seasonal search for food. And—in the process—they make smaller circles, traveling to and from their own home places. Ivan, like Osman, is here for six weeks, then he goes home for two.

Ivan misses his children, but he brings his wild lessons back to them. "I become a better parent by being out here," he says. "You watch the hyena with the baby. You see the lion, the wildebeest. You see them teach: You have not positioned yourself. You need cover. You need this or that. The survival starts like training sessions, hunting and survival skills. Out here, if you have one mistake, it is all over."

I accompany Ivan to the camp's office tent. A laptop is set up on a folding table. I can see his bunk peeking out from an inner canvas wall in the back. He takes a seat on a military-style wooden trunk. "When I first get home," he says, "I watch my children. I've been away for a long time. The first week is training. I make sure they're becoming good citizens. I watch them like I've been watching the lions and elephants. Am I raising this kid the right way? Then, in time, we become friends. Every parent wants their kid to be successful, and to be successful, you need to watch in order to understand. If you are hunted, or hunting, you have to see out of the sides of your eyes, open your ears. It is like this for humans, too."

Especially in places like this.

By the time I make my way back down to the hearth fire—senses on alert for four-legged camp intruders—the sky has darkened. Tonight's fire is hearty, whole logs have bent the metallic band meant to hold flames in. I take a seat next to a tall guide with a kindly smile. He's wearing khaki. Like me. Like everyone around us. The stereotypical colors of safari are not for style; they're intended to keep the tsetse at bay.

When I ask Antony Kivuyo—a Maasai ranger with broad shoulders and a cleanly shaven head—how he ended up working at the camp, he tells me, like a wildebeest incarnate: "I was seeking greener pastures."

Antony is fluent in English, Swahili, and local dialects. As a trained Maasai warrior, he is also versed in the language of the wind, the stars. He speaks nature, which he believes holds the wisdom of god—by all of god's names. Antony says: "Where someone else may use the word God, I prefer the word Nature."

He asks about my daily wildlife sightings, and when I bring up huge herds of wildebeest, Antony says: "Nature gives the wildebeest an offer. When the lion is born its eyes are closed for one week. In three months, maybe, it starts to walk. But a baby wildebeest can stand fifteen minutes after it is born. Nature gives it what is needed. And it needs to be able to run. Nature offers you the way, and you follow it to survive."

And this doesn't just apply to wildebeest.

The origins of the Great Migration are a mystery, but it's generally believed that it began around the same time modern humans began to evolve here. East Africa, often called the Cradle of Humankind, is widely believed to be our species's evolutionary birthplace. It is from this very point on earth that modern humans likely emerged, evolving into who we are today.

Early on, our African ancestors were probably stationary. But, over time, maybe after learning of the abundance of food connected to the Great Migration, humans evolved bipedal ability. This allowed them to do something other predators could not: pick up their offspring to follow herds. The Out of Africa theory—considered the most likely creation story by many scientists, archeologists, and anthropologists—maintains that all *Homo sapiens* on earth come from a small group that trekked out of the African continent to populate the world after marrying visceral skill with a newly developed ability to think abstractly.

"The Maasai are allowed to go with their cattle across the borders of Kenya and Tanzania because Nature favors them to be pastoralists and grazers," Antony says. "I live to be Maasai, but life is changing. First of all is this global warming. We have short rains. You can't plant and harvest, you need to migrate, following precious weather. Now, because of the climate, a lot of Maasai send their children to school." His father was one of them.

Antony became a warrior at nineteen. When he was initiated into the Maasai warrior class, his attitudes toward school changed. He says, "I was like: *I am special.* I thought, *I am a warrior and nothing else matters.* In a traditional way, we treat other people like they are not warriors. No one could tell me what to do, not even the principal of my school."

One day, Antony's attitude got him suspended. When he went home, his father saw that his son was at a loss for direction. He said to Antony, "Do you want to continue with school? Or do you want to live in the village and be a warrior, matting your hair and drinking milk from everyone else's house?" It was not an easy question to answer. Antony had grown up dreaming of being a warrior, idolizing them and their characteristic hair, slicked back with rust-colored iron ore and cow fat.

As a boy, he had been given a stick to help his father herd cattle. Now, his stick had become a spear. But he wasn't sure of what to do with it. Africa was changing. He would have to change, too.

"When I finally decided to go back to school," Antony says, "when I first left my village, my father told me: 'You are a warrior forever, but school can make your life better.'"

"I think I'm here because I've had too much schooling and not enough bush," I say. Antony nods in understanding. For the next generation, here too, abstract forms of knowledge might become overbearing.

"To learn from Nature, it is amazing!" he says. "When you become a warrior, you get a spirit in your heart. That's why Maasai can cross in front of a lion. You don't worry about what the lion is going to do because you are a warrior. The elders tell you some words when you become a warrior. They tell you: *No one will be special like you. Never fear anything in your life.* This becomes your way of living."

Like all warriors, Antony was circumcised when he was initiated. This came after he had already learned how to walk in the bush, after he'd learned the traditions of his forefathers, who constructed a culture that reveres cattle and does not kill them often for meat—choosing instead to subsist off of their milk and draws of their blood. "We do circumcision *without pain killers*," Antony tells me, slowing his speech to emphasize the bravery this takes. "Becoming a warrior is like a wall you are crossing. You have to be ready."

He's looking at me gravely, but all I can think of are the women in his village—women all over the world—who give birth, under the threat of death, without even the mention of an epidural. As if he can tell what I'm thinking, Antony says: "After I went back to school, I realized, I am a warrior on my side. But maybe you are a warrior on your side. Maybe you are a warrior in your tradition."

Now, I'm not sure about that, but I would say parents are a certain sort of warrior class, regardless of gender or culture. No one I've ever met has felt smart enough, diligent enough, ready to fully accept the tasks of parenting without fear—but still, they move forward. Unfortunately, where I come from, there are not many elders putting the don't-be-afraid of anything spirit into the hearts of wayfaring warrior-parents.

Parenting advice, where I come from—really, advice about nearly everything—seems to fall more along the lines of: *Dr. Phil says you shouldn't do it like that.*

But in Maasai culture, there are all sorts of safeguards for the burgeoning individual warrior-soul, all sorts of *piko*-pumping gifts bestowed. Every child is given a guardian spirit at birth. Babies are also given a signature sound in addition to their names, a vibration that transcends language like the strange sing-song beauty of a hyena call, the winsome moo of a cow. It is a sound used as a form of announcement, to be used when approaching villages in the dark. Cattle are, conversely, given human names, and they are grouped into families. Often, it is by calling their names that the herder confirms everyone has made it home.

Antony says, "When I go back to my family, I do ceremonies. I do singing. I keep the tradition. I keep it well. But I will not follow in the tradition of marrying more than one wife." His father has six wives. He has none, and he only wants one. It's not so much cultural factors that have made up his mind; it's what nature is dictating.

"Life is changing," he says. "It's complicated and expensive. Even if you have one hundred cattle, there's no room to graze. The rains are not dependable. Land is small now because of human settlement. If you can't have one hundred cattle, you can't have three wives." He will take what feels right in his tradition—what works in the context of his life and environment—and he will leave the rest. Of other traditions—including those of the missionaries who ran his school—he will do the same.

Another camp employee walks by and gives Antony a small wave. I know from earlier conversations that he is also Maasai. He ended up working for &Beyond after he came by the mobile camp to make good on a drought-induced loan delivered in the form of goat. When Antony raises his arm, I can see that he's wearing a Maasai-beaded belt, a tourist-driven supplement to a cattle-based economy.

Antony turns to me and says, "Nature is giving me the offer to live in the bush like this, and I am taking it. Nature is still supporting my life. I am doing this job to survive. That is why I am here."

He braids his stout fingers together and rests his elbows on his knees, leaning into the fire. "Sometimes, things come to you. You wonder: How did this happen? Who brought this to me?" he says. "It was Nature. It is always Nature!"

I laugh. "I'm here because I'm writing a book about *natural* phenomena."

"See," he says, knowingly. "Nature gave you that."

In Antony's village, life-sustaining blessings are often credited, by name, to Engai Narok, or Black God. He says, "Black God is not a person, not a tree." Engai, he tells me, is the force of life itself. Black God is said to live in a hiding place—no one knows exactly where—which, of course, means that Black God potentially lives everywhere.

"Maasai believe that, if you need rain, burning something in sacrifice will remind Black God to bring it. I have seen this ceremony," Antony says, shaking his head in disbelief. "Two days later, I swear, it always rains!"

Around us, lanterns come to life like giant fireflies. Guests are gathering beyond our chairs. We'll soon be swept into the crowd as dinner commences. Antony walks me over to a huge collective table set up under a thorn acacia.

"I do not really know much about Black God," he says. "But I do know this: When I see the rains coming, *that* is Nature."

The hippopotamus is widely considered one of most dangerous animals in Africa. And the staff of &Beyond's Grumeti River Camp—where I've arrived for the remainder of my stay in Tanzania—tells me that there's one that loves to stand in front of my tent. "You must be careful when the hippo comes out of the water," a camp manager advises. "It will take down anything in its path."

When I express concern about this quirk of my accommodation, known as tent number seven—or, as a fellow guest referred to it, *the one sort of out there by itself*—the manager says, "It's okay. The hippo has not harmed a guest yet." *Yet!*

As if this isn't enough, there are also vervet monkeys to worry about. They come begging for food, habituated by guests who bribe them so they can snap photos. "You have to keep your eyes open," he says. "You have to make sure the monkeys know you mean business. Otherwise, they are going to steal your bread."

At this mention of monkey business, I laugh. He doesn't. I do not like this.

I arranged to come to Grumeti months ago, when I thought the migration might have already traveled this far north. It's a gamble that hasn't paid off in a traditional sense. Animal movements now indicate that it will be weeks before wildebeest reach this place. I will not see large herds here, pushing their way across the Grumeti River, but I might find a few trailblazing zebra.

The camp likes to mix things up with dinner in various locations, and, this afternoon, they've erected a makeshift bar in a field of short grass. It's flanked by two park rangers with AK-47s.

"What are they doing here?" I ask my assigned guide, Humphrey, a bubbly man with a wide smile and painfully crooked teeth.

"They follow us around. To make sure nothing happens. There are poachers."

We're interrupted by someone in the distance: "Where's Leigh Ann? I hear her voice." Even though I have a pretty characteristic voice—one that inspires telemarketers to ask for my mom—this recognition is surprising.

As it turns out, the tourists who rode with me into Arusha from the airport have made their way to Grumeti. The whole group appears more relaxed now, especially the lawyer among them, Fred, who—during our initial meeting outside of Kilimanjaro airport—was seriously miffed about his lost luggage. He's clad in a mismatch of clothing from the variety of lodges he's stayed at since we last saw each other. Despite the tastefulness of the logos, the hodgepodge makes him look like a khaki-clad, safari-going version of a sponsored NASCAR driver.

Fred's wife greets me and nods toward guards. "Wonder what they're here for."

"Poachers," I say.

"They think we're poachers?"

"No, they're here to protect us from poachers."

Her face softens. Into a smile. "You're kidding, right?" she says.

"No, I'm serious."

At this, she begins to break down. Into laughter.

"For a minute," she says, waving me off, "I almost bought into your bullshit!"

I decide it best not to push the issue.

The woman, finally done laughing at my perceived tease, points toward Fred, gold bracelets jingling. "I think he's actually having fun. You know, he didn't even want to come!"

Fred notices that she's looking at him, so he wanders over. It's true. "This has become one of the top experiences of my life," he says, "and I didn't want to be here because it was inconvenient! I didn't want to get the shots. Didn't want to take malaria pills. I was nervous about doing something different. I can't believe I almost missed this! There's no way to explain what it's like being here. It's like being back in your birth-place! Unless you're here, you can't get it!"

Fred absentmindedly adjusts his sun hat. "Here, I'm an observer," he says. "At home, I'm an actor. I try to control my environment, but here, I have no control. I have no control over an elephant or a lion. Nature is what's important!"

He takes a sip of the Kilimanjaro-brand beer he's toting in his left hand. He is in his fifties, but he has taken on the relaxed air of a college kid at a lawn party, albeit a lawn party with AK-47s. He opens his arms to the savanna and says, "The magic is back. This is my world! I'm no longer a lawyer. There is so much more to it all than that!"

He is uttering, nearly down to the phrase, what eclipse-chasing James—whom I'm now planning to rendezvous with in Australia—has seen happening to people during cosmic phenomena. I do believe Fred is having a mystical experience. "Think you'll be able to keep this magic with you when you go home?" I ask, imagining wildebeest calls replaced by the honk-honk of L.A. traffic.

His back slumps a little as he holds out his arms. "When I go home, it will be like a dream. It will seem like I dreamt all of this. But, I am here. I am living it! We're part of this place!"

The rest of his group seems unmoved by their time here, but I feel it, too. It's an inexplicably high comfort level in a place that seems like it should be the most nervous-making landscape on earth. And, of course, it does have its high-drama moments. But the sense of belonging is over-whelming. This is Eden. And—despite ecological decline—it has not fallen. *Yet*.

We've got the whole world in our hands.

A few rangers ramble over to join the small cluster of guests. "Tell us a story of your most dangerous encounter with an animal," someone prods them.

One ranger tells the story of a hippo that charged him from behind a bush one morning as he was on his way to the office. "Luckily," he says, "I had a cell phone." He didn't use it to call for help—of course not, what good would that have done out here? No, he popped that hippo in the face with it and took off.

"What about you?" Fred asks a quiet ranger that's standing beyond the circle. "What animal do you fear the most?"

The ranger looks Fred in the eye. He does not blink.

"Humans," he says.

Outside our vehicle, the landscape moves as if we're on a carousel. Humphrey is a much slower driver than David. But still, it's hard to read what's out there. I see a wildebeest that turns out to be a termite mound. When I apologize for the false sighting, Humphrey says, "I call those ALTs. Animal-Looking Things. But, if you don't look, you don't know what you've got! You could think it's an anthill and it could turn out to be a cheetah."

It's just that kind of place.

In the distance, a gazelle leaps over lion-colored grass, high enough for me to see the bottom of its hooves. "He's showing us that we cannot catch him," Humphrey says, laughing so hard that he throws his head back. "He is flirting with us!" Humphrey's cackle softens to a giggle. "I am the Bogart of the bush!" he says. "I show the romance of the animals!"

Only recently did Humphrey learn from an American guest that there's an old movie star who shares his name. He slaps the steering wheel playfully, giving his characteristic near-wildebeest, honk-like laugh. "Seriously," he says, "I don't know why my parents chose this English name. But what I like about it is how people say it in Swahili. If you tell anyone in Swahili my name, they will always say: Amfree. I Amfree! And I am free because I meet people and we get to share days! It's not like I'm in an office. I am free! I can go anywhere I want and look for things. I can move! There's no stress—not that kind of stress when you are confined. I am never bored. To me, that's what freedom means."

When we stop to check out a pride of lions, all females, I ask Humphrey if there are age limits for safaris. He nods toward a lioness who appears to be lovingly nudging her cub. "When female lions hear children cry in the vehicle, they might think you've taken their cub," Humphrey tells me. "They will attack if they think that."

Enough said. Even though I'm still homesick—even though, yesterday, a fellow guest made my face burn when she said to her husband: "Can you believe her son is with her husband, alone, for over a week?"— I'm glad my little critter is in the clear.

Humphrey has a young son, too, a newborn he dreams of bringing into the bush someday. He says, "I'm working for my son to go to school, to have good opportunities, but sometimes I feel very sad to be away from him. But this is a chance to find what is good in life so you can tell him about it. Maybe someday you will bring your son back here. People who don't understand what you're doing here might think you're a bad mother, but they don't know what your plans are for your son."

Humphrey has told me that his favorite animal is the honeyguide, a bird known to lead bushmen to honey. The wild birds fly along— watching and waiting for humans as a family dog might—and, when they get to a store of honey, they do a special dance to let their human partner know where the sweets are. The bushmen then break through honeycomb that the bird is not strong enough to access on its own, and together, they share the spoils.

"Maybe we're like the honeyguides," I tell him. "We go out so that we can show our children where the sweetest things can be found!"

Humphrey seems thrilled by this. "Yes! I like the good life. A good life means good stories. Stories are important for anyone to be fulfilled. When you fulfill your own goals you have to be happy. When you're happy, when you are experiencing, it's good for the family. You are becoming strong. Like a warrior!"

I'm sort of reveling in this continually surfacing notion that I could be considered a warrior not in spite of my role as a mother but because of it, when I notice a notebook on the dashboard. It's covered in magazine photos and the mismatched letters of a ransom note. It reads: "Sixth Sense."

Humphrey notices me looking at the collage-covered notebook, the size of a back pocket. "I did that during my training," he says. "They told us we could make the book look nice."

"Why Sixth Sense?" I ask.

"Because I think most animals have more than human senses. Animals have a sixth sense, though they might not know about it. They respect each other. They know their responsibilities. They don't fight for no reason like some humans do. They care for each other. They know what's supposed to be done. Imagine if we could live like animals—not caring about how many things we have. They only take what they need. Nothing more. To us, it looks like the animals are lacking some things. But they have their own ways."

There is a herd of elephants in the distance. We watch for a few minutes as they ramble across grassland. "They look healthy," Humphrey says, relieved. Yesterday, an &Beyond ranger came across one that had been wounded, in the foot, by a poacher's bullet, creating a general atmosphere of sadness and unease among staff and guests alike. Tensions have grown around the park over the years, with wealthy international tourists and operators and conservation groups demanding precious land, cutting down areas locals depend on for farming and grazing. The human communities around the park are not often included as part of the Serengeti ecosystem. Ivan's scales are not balancing out.

"This country is very poor and there are people who live in, how can I say, an under land," Humphrey says. "They don't have basic needs. They eat one meal a day. They do not have good shelter. They become poachers to provide protein for their families. But others poach for bush meat trade and trophies," he says. "Those are people who do not pay attention to their animal instincts."

Humphrey slides his notebook back onto the dashboard. He says, "There are businessmen that have everything and, still, they want even more. They don't think about how they are affecting everyone else. But if they had the sixth sense, they wouldn't do this. The animals, they don't have education, but still everything is equal for them. They know what they need and that's all they take. It's like with the wildebeest. Sometimes the eldest wildebeest know the way. But the young ones, they use their instincts to move around. They still know what's right. They get lost sometimes, but they find their way. It's instinct. It's in you. It's in me."

There's a certain inversion to this sort of thinking. A challenging of what it means to be human. But animals are always doing that.

When Jane Goodall first went into a Tanzanian forest to begin her now-famous work with chimpanzees, a human was defined by tool-making abilities. When she reported to her mentor, Louis Leakey, that she had seen a chimp craft a tool from a leaf to fish insects out of the ground, he famously declared that this would require changing the definition of tool, the definition of man, or lead to an acceptance of chimpanzees as part of the human race.

Since I've been here, I've had a ranger tell me he's seen a hippo nudge a drowning baby wildebeest to shore. Another once watched a lion lead a lost young elephant back to its herd. These animals have had no formal education. They have no church-learned morals. There seems to be no immediate personal gain for their risk. Given this, Humphrey is introducing the idea that animals might be more humane than humans.

This sort of acting-faster-than-intellect occurs in humans, too. People jump in front of buses to save strangers, into lakes to rescue children they've never seen before. In 1990, at the Detroit Zoo, a chimpanzee was pushed into water during a fight with fellow captives. His keeper did not try to save him. But a thirty-three-year-old truck driver from Cement City, Michigan, was there with his family. When he saw the chimp go down, he jumped into the water to save the animal, despite cries from the zookeeper that he would be killed. But the man was not killed. And the chimpanzee was saved.

Jane Goodall often tells this story in speeches. And she recounts that when the man, Rick Swope, was asked why he did such a dangerous thing, he said: "I happened to look into his eyes, and it was like looking into the eyes of a man. And the message was *Won't anybody help me?*"

We seem to have accepted that self-preservation is a principle of human nature, yet there are moments when it dissolves in favor of spontaneous instincts that make one act in the interest of another's life at the risk of one's own. German philosopher Arthur Schopenhauer believed moments like the one at the Detroit Zoo were moments of transcendence that gave a departure from the rational, returning individuals to the experience of *unus mundus* by inducing a temporary, visceral realization that you, and I, and the other are one.

My guides' stories indicate that all sorts of species have this inexplicable, irrational sixth sense Humphrey's been talking about. If animals do not have the ability to think in symbols and abstraction—considered to be what makes humans unique among animals—then the hippo cannot know that the wildebeest preserve the health of the grasses both species feed on. The lion cannot understand that it is genetically connected to the elephant.

But, still, they act.

Last week, if someone had told me that I was acting like an animal, I probably wouldn't have taken it as a compliment. Today, I'm not so sure.

On my way to breakfast the next morning, my burgeoning courage is put to the test. When I step out of my tent, I encounter a family of baboons. These animals can run up to 40 mph. I have not jogged a day in my life.

One of the twenty or so baboons has a baby clinging to the fur of her back. At the sight of me, the infant swings downward, disappearing into the thick fur of the mother's belly. A father jumps out of a bush fifteen feet from where I'm standing. Slowly, I back up, until I'm behind the banana-leaf structure sheltering my tent. Obscured. The family goes back to their business.

I wait. I wait until I'm too hungry to wait anymore. Monkeys might steal my bread and these baboons could take my very life, but I don't want to be trapped. I hear a bird that sounds improbably like a wildcat above me. Something moves in the bush to my right. I am afraid. But no matter what happens, I cannot run.

Here, fear isn't abstraction, like worries about mortgage payments and pesticides on produce. It's tangible, observable, snarls and bared teeth. Here, fear leads to bloodshed. And fighting fear only creates more of it. Panic spreads. So, I let my unease settle into my bones. I take the marrow of it into my heart and imagine it stronger. I need not fear these animals if they do not give me a sign that I should, and I have to trust myself animal enough to read their signals.

I know I'm having a pretty plush experience out here—tracing the steps of many a tourist before me while wiping my hands with moist towelettes—but I'm suddenly feeling pretty adventurous. The nonhuman world has become the more-than-human world. And I'm feeling somehow more connected to my gut instincts. When there are no bars, glass, how-to guides, or helpful bush guides at hand, all that's left is individual, internal instinct responding to external signal.

I move forward slowly, steps measured and slow. A few baboons notice and move along. Others stay. They are all less than ten feet away. Two steps back. One step forward. It's the motion of the migration, how a bow is drawn to send forth an arrow. I make this motion repeatedly, for fifteen minutes, until a porter passes on a parallel trail—unaware or unshaken—and the remaining baboons scatter.

On the camp's main deck, I'm joined by Humphrey and a group of middle-aged South Africans speaking Afrikaans and toting cameras the size of an Olympian's calves. The two men in the group, trucker magnates, have pot bellies peeking from under their T-shirts. Their wives' fingers drip with jewels.

"Why are they doing that?" the taller of the two women, Hestermarie, asks Humphrey of the hippo pod beyond camp. She's pointing to a hippo flipping its tail like a helicopter blade, spraying water. Hestermarie and her husband, Johan, own their own wildlife preserve—as do the couple they're traveling with. They've amassed quite a bit of knowledge along with land over the years. But they've never really spent much time with hippos. They've never noticed this behavior before.

"There is a story about why they do that," says Humphrey. "They made a deal with the lion."

"A lion?"

Humphrey confirms with a nod. The story explains that, long ago, a hippo wanted to spend its days in the water. So, it asked a lion if that would be all right. The lion was not sure, saying, "If you are in the water, you will eat all the fish and take from others." The hippo promised that—in order to prove it was not eating fish—it would swish its tail whenever it put dung in the water so the lion could see there were no fish bones. Over the years, hippos have abided by this promise, using their honorable sixth sense to not take more than they need. So, in cool, baptismal waters they have been allowed to stay.

"Are there stories like that about wildebeest?" I ask. "Do you know any myths connected to the migration?"

"I only know of one," says Humphrey. "A grandfather told it to me. The wildebeest was the last animal to be created by God. And when the wildebeest was created, it was made from the spare parts of other animals. The different parts that remained after the rest of the world was made. It has the flat face of the grasshopper, the stripes of the zebra, the tail of the horse, the horns of the buffalo. And the wildebeest has hind legs that are shorter than the front, like a hyena. That lets them leap. Because they were created last, all these parts were just joined together."

"Nothing left for waste," I say.

"Yes," Humphrey says. "This story is not written up. It is only told around the campfire."

When we approach the safari vehicle—which is completely open on the sides—I notice its canvas roof has been removed at the request of my safari mates. When we're in, they point to the vehicle's fixed windshield and bemoan that it can't be lowered in this model. They'd prefer to have nothing between them and the bush. Still, the glass doesn't stop Humphrey from a sighting. He points excitedly.

"What is it?" Hestermarie asks.

"You don't see the zebra?" he says. "Open your eyes very wide and you will see them. It's really a very big dazzle. There is a lone wildebeest among them. He's using them for their eyes."

We stop in front of the dazzle. It is a sign from nature, telling this lone wildebeest that the rest of his family is coming. He is, Humphrey suspects, one of the few stragglers from last year's migration. "Sometimes," he says, "there are animals that get sick and have to stay. Some others go off on their own and they get left behind."

"Will this wildebeest rejoin the herds on their way back through?" I ask Humphrey.

"Probably," he says. "He might have just needed a rest."

Unexpectedly, the wildebeest sticks out its tongue and blows: *Thh, thh.*

I must be eyeing the animal suspiciously, because Johan says: "You know, he's just saying hello." Then, Johan sticks out his tongue and blows it like a kazoo, spittle spraying all over me.

Thh. Thh. The wildebeest responds, unexpectedly.

"You're talking to him!" I say.

Johan expands his eyes, curious about my surprise. "You can talk to him, too," he says, with a gentleness that catches me off guard. "It's okay."

I've heard stories of people getting out of their cars in national parks trying to pet elk, and I don't want to be taken for an elk petter. I don't want to interfere with the natural order of things. But to pretend that I am not here, that I'm not part of this, seems wrong, too.

I twist in my seat. I stick my tongue out. *Thh.*

I feel silly, like a jester. The zebra do not lift their heads—as if they know I'm not talking to them in their dog-bark-braying language—but the wildebeest looks.

Thh, he calls.

We have a little conversation—rounded vowels and tongue-in-cheek—and the exchange thrills me beyond measure, even though it has the cadence of two whoopee cushions deflating in turn. Johan turns back around in his seat to ask Humphrey: "What do you call the cheetah in your language?"

"*Duma*," Humphrey says. "In yours?"

"*Jagluiperd*," Johan says. "I think it's amazing. You can take one animal—the same animal—and there are all these names in all the different languages!" In Tanzania alone, the wildebeest has multiple monikers—the most common being wildebeest, gnu, and *nyumbu*.

The wildebeest spits as we leave. The rumbling of our animated engine inspires a jacana to take to the sky. "See how much better it is to see the birds with the top off," Johan says, turning to me. "When you don't have a roof over your head, you can see everything!"

"When we see a jacana," Humphrey says, "we begin to look for the buffalo. We move the opposite direction. Buffalo are dangerous and aggressive."

"We follow it when we are hunting buffalo," says Johan. "It leads us to the animal we're looking for. We call the jacana the Jesus bird because it can walk on water."

"I've never heard that before," Humphrey says, amazed.

This group of South African guests camps in the bush almost every weekend. But, for all their adventures, they've never seen the migration. It's why they came. And, unless they travel to the region I've just left, they're going to miss it. The bush is like that. And they know it. And they accept it. They trust that, with a little effort, they, too, will ultimately be able to bear witness to the honk-and-walk of the migration that—as far as human history can see—has no clear beginning and, if humans wise up to their sixth sense, no end.

But, for now, their main concern is having a cocktail.

We disembark in an area of short grass chosen for safety, and Humphrey unpacks liquor bottles and tins of dried fruit. As he works, Johan comes up to ask about a picture of a religious leader he saw hanging among reigning politicians in an office back in Arusha.

"A lot of missionaries come into Tanzania," Humphrey says. "They start to put churches all over the areas. There are people born here that will die of old age without ever seeing the city. The world is one village now, but still, there are people living here that only believe in the sun and the trees."

According to theologian Thomas Berry, ancient Christianity believed in the sun and trees, too. The church once accepted that there were two valid texts available to followers—the scripture of the natural world and the scripture of the Bible. Berry writes: "The Psalms do indeed tell us that the mountains and the birds praise God. But do we have to read the Scriptures to experience that? Why are we not getting our religious insight from our experience of the trees, our experience of the mountains, our experience of the rivers, of the sea and the winds? Why are we not responding religiously to these realities?"

But some people are. I don't know what Lutheran bishop Frederick Shoo, known as Tanzania's "Tree Bishop," would say about someone naming their child Hyena, but—in his own way—he's trying to reconcile the text of his holy book and the scripture of nature. Within the last hundred years, 92 percent of Kilimanjaro's glaciers have disappeared. The snows of Kilimanjaro—which I've glimpsed through clouds—may be memories by the time Archer turns ten. And, if they are, meltwater rivers relied upon by millions of people for their very lives will be gone.

So, the Tree Bishop is mobilizing congregants by including tree-planting ceremonies in funerals, baptisms, and weddings. He is connecting the nondogmatic, sustaining scripture of nature and the respected literature of his tradition through visceral, earthly ritual. These actions clear the very air, cool streams with shade, give soil roots to hold fast to.

They help people, once again, believe in trees.

On the ride back to camp, the women start to reminisce about their weekend adventures. I listen from the backseat, clutching the metal bar in front of me as we hop over unseen termite mounds, earthen speed bumps hiding in the grass.

"Remember that time the hyena stole our fruit salad?"

"Oh, we were so looking forward to that fresh fruit! And he spilled everything on the ground! What a disappointment. None of us, not even the hyena, got to eat any of it!"

"And remember when that elephant charged a vehicle in South Africa?"

"Yes! The elephant's tusk ended up just inches from that man's chest!"

"What about when that lion mauled the tent next to ours?"

"Well, that was irresponsible how they left their food lying around."

Tsetse flies might mistake my mouth for an airplane hangar, gaped as it is. Hestermarie notices. "Everyone was fine," she assures me of the lion mauling, "but the place was a mess!"

I sputter: "How do you go out weekend after weekend knowing these are the stories you might—or might not—come back with?"

Hestermarie's friend says, "The experience! The experience is worth everything! This is the bush. It is the spirit of Africa! It's not as though it's easy to be here, but you go out expecting these things to happen!"

And that's when we hit a mud hole.

Within seconds, our back tire plants into the ground, sealed in muck.

"Should we get out?" Hestermarie calmly asks Humphrey, who surveys the high grass surrounding the vehicle.

"Not here," he says.

Even in the road, grass is high. There are likely unseen dangers lying in wait. I haven't had ranger training, but even my limited time observing wildlife out here has taught me that. But the two pot-bellied men are already on the ground, wearing flip-flops and mesh water shoes. They are outdoorsmen who have walked through herds of elephants, directly feeling their infrasonic rumbles. Humphrey's protests prove futile. The guests are many, our guide is one. And the reality is: We need to work together to get out of this.

I scoot to the left, following my fellow safari goers. We hang off the frame of the vehicle, trying to loosen its tires, to no avail. It will not budge. The vehicle is so off-kilter now it is in real danger of flipping. And it's not my imagination or greenhorn safari nerves telling me we're in trouble—it's nature.

The sun will soon hit the horizon, signaling to all of the Serengeti's animals—human and otherwise—that it's time to hunt. I know this due to a trick I learned early on in my time here, aligning my fingers with the horizon, my body with the earth. Each finger that fits between the sun and the horizon represents five minutes.

Pointer. Middle. Ring. We're running out of time.

I look at the ground below. In a small, exposed patch of mud, I see the unmistakable rounded print of hippo tracks. They're sunk as deep as our wheels in the mud. We're close to camp—it's almost visible from here—but we're also in the animals' path.

"It's like I said," the spirit-of-Africa lady tells me gleefully, "we just expect things like this to happen! This is what we do on our weekends!"

Hestermarie adds, "*Now* you've had a real African experience!"

The men are trying to help Humphrey with the vehicle, but they report that something is wrong. "I'm afraid it's going to flip," one of them warns Humphrey. But they decide to give the engine one more go.

I slip back into my seat. The women tell me to brace myself, and I wrap my fingers around a steel bar, knees against the seat in front of me. It's almost full dark now. The group is silent. The vehicle's engine throbs, surely annoying elephants for miles around.

"Did you radio the camp?" one of the men asks, his adventurous tone somewhat faded now that he's realized something is wrong with the vehicle's mechanics. He looks at the roof, maybe rethinking his request that the canvas be removed for bird watching. If nervous predators visit in the night, he told me earlier—as a hypothetical—the smartest thing to do is to climb up there. But there's nothing to hold us.

Finally, we see a light ahead. Most of the time safari vehicles leave lights off at night since grass reflects. They're letting us know they're coming. When they are close, we shout for them to stop, lest we all get stuck. What would we do then? They heed our warnings and pull up alongside. But when they reveal the cord they've brought for towing, it's obvious that it is not long enough to get us out of our mess.

Early attempts make our vehicle sputter and it's agreed that there are too many people in the vehicle. But we cannot be left standing outside. The air has grown cooler. I can almost see our scent swirling on the thickening air, slipping into the noses of hungry predators.

Finally, the guides decide we should switch vehicles. So we jump out. I use the attached steel ladder to get down. When my feet touch ground, they find the muddy precipice of a hippo track. The cruisers are circled like metal beasts attempting to protect our small human herd.

Humphrey grabs my arm and I pull myself into the rescue vehicle. As soon as we are all in, the driver flips on his lights, and we see five hippos staggering out of the river onto land. When their eyes catch our headlights, they appear to glow like neon signs. "Predators' eyes reflect red and herbivores' reflect green," he tells us.

One of the South Africans shines a flashlight into the darkness. The beam finds a line of hippos, water glistening like diamonds encrusted on their skin. "Put that away!" the driver says. "You will blind them!" With dramatic emphasis, he turns off the headlights and we inch forward, hippos crossing our path, appearing as shadows wading through milky moonlight.

Back at Grumeti, a night watchman escorts me to my room. I lie awake, listening to twigs cracking under the weight of something walk-

ing around the sides of my tent. Finally, I fall asleep. I dream until Matt
calls for me to wake up, rhythmically saying my name, which my parents picked from a book because they liked the sound of it. The vibration
of Matt's voice almost feels like it's shaking me: *Leigh Ann. Leigh Ann.*

Is it morning? I sit up, caught in the fluid terrain of dreams and
reality.

Is Matt *here*? Why can I not see his face? How can his voice possibly
be reaching me?

Slowly, I continue to solidify consciousness. I feel the breeze kicking
up through the mesh vent holes at the top of my tent. I see dancing slips
of moonlight on canvas. I smell the river. My fingers trace the uneven
edge of a hand-woven throw. I open my eyes.

I am not in my house. I am not with my family. So why, how, is Matt
still talking?

Leigh Ann. Leigh Ann.

Then, as if in slow motion—as if in a movie—the words begin to
morph.

Rarrraaann. Rarrraaann.

It's not my husband; it's the hippos.

When I recognize the animals' voices, I laugh out loud. The hippos
respond with snort-cackles. I can hear them jump—one to three tons at
a time—into the river a few yards from my front tent flap. Their belly
flops are followed by vigorous thrashing and splashing that makes the
river roil. After a few minutes, they settle in, and I fall asleep to a watery
chorus.

On my final day in Tanzania, I have an eight-hour layover in Arusha. A
kindly shuttle driver suggests I pass some time visiting the local cultural
center, a sleek, modern building designed to look like a Maasai warrior's

shield. I expect to find a tourist trap. And I do. But, with time to spare, I wander behind the building, where I discover a thatched-roof hut. Fraying burlap has been hung in its open eaves for shade. Half the structure is a kitchen used by workers of the cultural center. The other half is a woodworking shop where men create handicrafts for its souvenir store. The workshop is strewn with shoe-polish-stained rags. It feels comfortable. Familiar for obvious reasons as the Serengeti did for mysterious ones. It reminds me of my husband's basement work space, my paternal grandfather's kitchen, my maternal grandfather's barn—places where they all, respectively, whittled wood.

The resident carvers are finishing lunch. One is still eating, scooping the white paste of traditional, corn-based *ugali* with his bare hands. We introduce ourselves and learn there are nearly as many tribes represented under this roof as there are people: Kamba, Chagga, and me—cultural product of A Tribe Called Quest.

The two most talkative men—John Ndambuki and Jeremiah Kimeu—are sitting under a lifesize ebony carving of Jesus, his slender arms outstretched. Around his head is a crown of acacia thorns. His hair is close to his scalp, tight as wool. Below him is a collection of wooden, dark-skinned men in khaki suits and white hats I recognize as Colonial-era British pith helmets.

I tell the men that my husband is a carpenter, and that both of my grandfathers were woodcarvers, and they're genuinely thrilled. They want to know what sorts of woods my husband uses for his work. I talk of pine and walnut and cherry, the difference between North American soft- and hardwoods, a little surprised to realize how much I have learned by association over the years.

Jeremiah pulls out a coaster-shaped piece of ebony to show me its coal-colored heartwood. He knocks on it with worn knuckles and suggests I do the same. John pulls a small scrap shaped like the top of a Maasai talking stick—a ceremonial object that gives its possessor a turn to speak—from a pile behind him and holds it up for me to examine.

"It is like pine?" John asks.

I nod, excitedly, to confirm he is right.

"Sit," Jeremiah prods. "Join us."

He pulls up a low-lying stool like the ones they're sitting on. It reveals its age in a stone-smooth concave seat. There is a large crack on its right side. When I sit, I can feel it against my thigh, making it seem as though I'm inside a nearly-opened egg. Jeremiah takes down a flimsy plastic bag full of crumpled newsprint. He slowly twists the paper loose until an ebony animal falls out.

It's a wildebeest.

The animal's right leg is out. Its grasshopper face has a small goatee. Its beard seems to drip from under its chin. Flank muscles catch light, giving the animal a sense of muscular movement. "Why did you choose to carve a wildebeest?" I ask. "It isn't exactly known for its beauty."

Jeremiah shrugs. "I like the walking of this animal. The migration is good because you have to move forward. You have to learn together. You have to play together. The wildebeest show us this."

No matter what is happening, no matter how busy he gets or how hard things are, Jeremiah tells me, he can think of the wildebeest making their way and feel calmed. "Always," he says, "always, they are moving."

He places the wildebeest in my hands. It is as cool and smooth as river stone. I rub its abdomen with my pointer finger. He pulls another animal from his bag, a zebra carved of light wood and painted with stripes. "I like the zebra, too," he says. "All one family."

Jeremiah learned to carve from his father, who learned from his father. Now, here in this shelter, he is teaching two teenagers the craft, alongside John, who—with whitening hair and a stained blue work suit—is the eldest of the group.

Next door, the grill steams. The smell of coffee floats over a partition, along with the indecipherable chatter of men eating at the counter. Tanzanian hip-hop blares from a stereo covered with a dirty washcloth meant to protect it from sunlight. I move my head to the beat, and the youngest apprentice—maybe sixteen—pauses from his polishing to laugh at my goofy antics.

"You like?" he asks of the music.

"*Ndiyo!*" I answer "yes" in Swahili. This seems to please him.

"What is your name?"

"Leigh Ann. But people here have been calling me Leone."

It's a name I've actually started answering to. At first, I didn't correct my hosts because I didn't want to hurt anyone's feelings. I figured Leone must be easier to say for Swahili speakers than Leigh Ann. And, really, it didn't feel like a big deal—ironic given my reaction to Osman's name change, I know. But I've come to like being called Leone in the way Humphrey has taken to the Swahili mispronunciation of his English name.

"It is a local name, a good name," the carver tells me.

Leone, he explains, means lion.

His hand disappears into a basket of rags and emerges holding a male lion with a sleek, subdued mane, ebony tail curved up along its back. It is one of John's carvings that the apprentice has been asked to polish. The young carver holds it in a shaft of sunlight to show me its detail, and then he begins to rub it with shoeshine from a dented tin.

Jeremiah hits a chunk of rosewood with his machete, a tool of poachers turned to an instrument of art. The torso of an endangered rhino begins to emerge. John is still holding the scrap of cypress wood he's picked up to illustrate the weight and shade of my native eastern white pine, and—after sharpening his tools, metal on wood—he, too, begins to work.

"What are you making?" I ask.

He gives me a shy smile and says: "I am making you."

At first, I think this might be some sort of three-dimensional interpretation of the caricatures drawn for passersby at fairs and festivals. "You've done this before?" I ask.

"Never!" John exclaims, laughing. The other men join in the good humor, entertained by this spontaneous, artistic impulse. One end of John's stick is mottled with pock marks, as if it were, at some point, filled with nails. He saws it off and lets it drop to the hut's cement floor, keeping only the unblemished section for the task at hand. Wood shards fly across cement. He takes up a file with a leather handle, rounds my wooden head. Then, he pauses to blow dust from my emerging face.

John slips his creation into the crook of his big toe to brace it against the stump he's using as a chopping block, each action resonating through the cement pad under our feet. His bare ankles are darkened with scars. Violent hatchet chopping gives way to more intricate cuts with a small knife. He raises his eyes to study my cheekbones, the contour of my forehead.

Word spreads that John is doing something unusual. The lunch crowd has gone, so the women from the kitchen, heads wrapped in bold-print *kanga* cloth, come over to watch. Under their supervision, John looks at me, he looks at the wood, and he giggles a little to himself. This is the first time he's ever used a live model. And the first time he's ever used soft cypress for a human form. It is the color of almond meat, the shade of my skin.

One of the cooks looks at me, shakes her head, and exclaims she has never seen anything like this. She motions for John to hand over his work-in-progress, and he complies. The wood darkens under her fingers, still wet from washing dishes. She looks at me, looks at the wood, and then nods approvingly.

"I have been carving for forty years. It is my heart," John says.

He gives his handiwork one last look. Then, he hands me myself.

"A gift," he says.

I stare at the cypress with the sort of concentrated awe I had when I looked at my son in the months after he was born—his skin somehow my skin, his eyes somehow my eyes. Through John's hands, I have received a sharp nose, deep-set eyes, a long forehead. Lips that appear puckered. One eyebrow is slightly raised, as if I'm getting ready to ask a question. For my hair, he has used the straight lines he usually reserves for a lion's mane. The indentations run down to the middle of my back.

My voice joins those of the cooing cooks, praising his work. John smiles demurely at all the attention, but he remains humble. He reminds us all that the figure is still only a scrap, a discard of his larger works—lions, elephants, wildebeest, cheetahs, the animal armies that come marching out of this hut.

Humans and chimpanzees share 98 percent of the same DNA. We're 79 percent the same stuff as whales and hippos. Despite our superficial differences, humans—here, there, everywhere—are, by genetic design, 99.9 percent the same. And you, and I, and everyone we know, share a substantial amount of DNA with any given oak tree.

There is a Maasai creation story that addresses this sort of interconnectivity, an only-told-by-the-fire narrative of cross-species creation. In the beginning, man found himself alone. But, unlike biblical Adam, he did not wait for an unseen god to get to work. Out of loneliness, in hope, he did all he knew to do: He started to create.

That first man on earth carved the first woman out of wood, and set her by his front door. In the morning, when the sun rose, the figure came to life and became his wife. In this cosmology, man and mystery were partners. It was from a tree—not a man's rib—that woman was born. And in the soft flesh of cypress, I have been born again.

Polepole, it is said in Swahili, like a mantra, on nearly every climb of Kilimanjaro. *Slowly, slowly.* This is the pace of evolution, the movement of these woodcarvers' hands, the way of the migration. It is how I will make my way home, back to Matt and Archer.

Jeremiah gestures toward the fragile human form cupped in my palm. "You can show this to your son," he tells me. "You can say to him: 'Look! This is your mother. Your mother that comes to you from Africa!'"

CHAPTER 7

TOTAL SOLAR ECLIPSE, AUSTRALIA

November 2012

ARCHER HAS BEEN TELLING PEOPLE I'M IN AUSTRAFRICA. THIS is actually a pretty good description of the lingering, confusion-laced jet lag I'm experiencing in Cairns, Australia. The headline of today's local paper reads: ECLIPSE FEVER GRIPS REGION. It's no exaggeration. The November 14 event is nearly a week away, but roads are already packed. Since I'm coming off a needed travel hiatus, this trip has arrived at just the right time—for me, if not for coral spawning.

I've spent the last couple of days with James, my Arctic Circle buddy, and his friend Kate Russo, an eclipse-chasing psychologist. They ended up joining me on my ill-fated quest to see the spawning. At some point, hundreds of coral species will synchronize the release of their eggs on the Great Barrier Reef in a confetti-style celebration of new life. But not yet. Spawning predictions, a local biologist explained, are not an exact science. The moon was—as per usual—right on time, but water temperatures were still too cold. The general word among dive operators is that the event will occur a few weeks from now in a rare split spawning, with two smaller episodes rather than one big explosion.

But, really, no one knows for sure.

The failed attempt—which required night swimming with sharks— was somewhat disheartening, but I knew the projected dates were ambiguous. So did James. When I bemoaned, preflight, that I might be traveling around the globe for something that wasn't going to happen, he responded via e-mail: "Perhaps you won't see the great coral spawn. Such is the nature of Nature. Do not neglect the aspect of being denied . . . The hunter sometimes comes home empty-handed, yet each time learns some valuable insight to improve his hunting skills."

I suppose this way of thinking helps when your primary focus in life is chasing two-minute phenomena. Weather predictions for the eclipse have, so far, been bleak. There's a chance James and I are going to miss not one but two wonders here in the Southern Hemisphere.

Saying good-bye to James before the eclipse feels premature, but—in the uncertain months leading up to this trip—we made our own plans. His include a few days of what he calls "reconnaissance," which entails comparing Google maps to in-person coordinates. Mine include heading up the coastline to wait out the eclipse, which isn't as simple as it might sound.

When I stumbled onto the fever-gripped state of Queensland, I was already late when it came to accommodations. Hotels had been booked years in advance. Luckily, a sympathetic biologist connected me to John "Harry" Harrington, a Quicksilver Cruises boat captain who lives in Oak Beach, just outside of the resort town of Port Douglas. He has a room off his garage intended to shelter friends and family, and he's offered to take me in.

The Harringtons live on three acres of rain forest that were once cane plantation. Their driveway appears at the end of a suburban-style development, then it disappears. The land was barren when they bought it, and their neighbors still live in open fields. But, over their two decades of residence, the Harrington family has planted 4,000 native trees on their acreage, making my fifty pines seem meager.

A coil of mosquito incense burns on the porch outside their traditional Queenslander home, drifting in and out of cranked-open windows. Harry's wife, Tina, comes out to greet me. The corrugated metal outbuilding I'm being lent isn't fancy, but it has wraparound windows that look out over gardens.

"I've put some bits and pieces in here for you," Tina says. Most precious are three perfect tomatoes and several lady finger bananas from a neighbor's yard. Her dog, Marley, leans against my leg. A phone rings in the main house. She jets off to answer it.

This is not my first time in Australia. I turned sixteen at the southern end of this country, while visiting as an exchange student. In a way, it is the place where I came of age—found independence, first ventured out on my own. Now, I'm back, half a lifetime later, and I'm pleased to find myself feeling like a thirty-four-year-old exchange student.

Marley takes up residence by my front door. He moves only when Harry—whom I've been corresponding with for months—returns home from a day on the nonspawning reef. He calls my name before approaching the backyard hut. I rise, greeted by the luxuriously sweet smell of lilies that have been placed in a vase by my sink.

Harry is a fit man with graying hair. I tell him of my immediate love of his place, and he says, "This region has the most prolific life on the planet. I like to live where there's life, because I like to observe."

He is trailed by his elder son, Jack, a preteen with skater bangs that fall over his left eye like a pirate patch. Something moves in the understory of a small stand of palms and Jack leans in to whisper, "There's an emerald-winged dove!"

I'm shocked by his knowledge. It must show. "I believe you don't just say, 'That's a bird' when you're showing your child the world," Harry says.

"You might also see sunbirds with yellow chests," says Harry's younger son, Daniel, a little freckle-faced blond. "There are a lot of them around."

The family graciously invites me over for dinner, bowls of homemade pasta served on a rough-hewn table. It is a welcome change from the culinary scene I'd been part of in Cairns: Me, subsisting on peanut butter; James, gnawing on salami every time I saw him, seeking out McDonald's milk shakes, which he called "the cheapest nine hundred calories money can buy."

The Harrington family already has their eclipse glasses ready. Tina bought them after seeing the transit of Venus earlier in the year, driving nearly two hours to procure them. The four glasses she delivered to the boys' school ended up being used by nearly 200 children, who had previously had access only via a computer.

Harry walks me out with a flashlight while the boys hustle through their bedtime routines. As we dodge a walkway full of cane toads, Harry says, "The aboriginal people have been coming here for forty thousand years, to Oak Beach." He has heard that one clan, from down near Cairns, used to travel through his very yard. "To me," he says, "that gives a perspective of reality. It gives an overview, just like the sunrise or an eclipse."

Before Harry says good-bye, Jack runs out of the house with two books on Australian birds. Because I've also expressed an interest in native trees, Daniel trails with a book on flora. As they approach, a bunch of loudly squawking birds flies overhead. The flock is obscured by palms, but the boys know them by their song.

"Sulphur-crested cockatoos," Daniel tells me.

In nearby Port Douglas, I meet up with Kate, who has a girlish charm, not in small part due to dimples. She's originally from Queensland, but she lives in Belfast, Ireland, now. She's taken a six-month leave from her job as a clinical psychologist to be here for her eighth total eclipse. As it just so happens, she recently published a study about the psychology of eclipse chasing. She's come up the coast to do some promotion for the book, *Total Addiction: The Life of an Eclipse Chaser.* James is one of the nine enthusiasts featured.

Her book signing table is set up in front of a posh restaurant facing a park, where an eclipse festival is set to rage. There are dozens of books that need to be inscribed this afternoon. She decides it might be best if we chat while she works.

I'm especially interested to hear what she has to say about eclipses as great cosmic coincidences. Because that is how people often refer to the phenomenon. Why? Well, the sun is 400 times larger than the moon. But, because the sun is exactly 400 times farther away from earth, the moon is able to cover its surface exactly. This perfection is so overwhelming, I've found that even the most pragmatic chasers have trouble dealing with it.

"I'm not a religious person," Kate says, "but I find myself asking: *How can this alignment be a coincidence?* When people say that, they're trying to find an answer for things that can't be explained. This comes from a very core level. With religion, you're entering from within an adopted framework. Spirituality, you're trying to make sense of it for yourself. People draw upon Buddhist beliefs, Muslim teachings. It's hard to put a language to it, and the language we have is within a religious framework."

In her clinical work, Kate works with grieving families. She's seen that being with a loved one on the edge of life and death—or experiencing it for yourself—can bring into focus the idea of life as something precious. In those moments, there's a shift in perspective that makes trivial concerns fall away. The eclipse, she thinks, has the capacity to do the same thing in a nontraumatic way.

She says, "Suddenly it's not just the sun rising. It's the sun in a universe that's so much bigger. It allows you to feel it so powerfully, so quickly, so unexpectedly . . . The eclipse comes and goes. Life comes and goes, and you have to do what's important and make choices for what you want to do, whether it's eclipse chasing or something else . . . It's not lucky that things fall into your lap, it's lucky that you take advantage of opportunities."

This is one of the key linkages between the dozens of eclipse chasers Kate interviewed for her book, which—through a phenomenological approach—explores the psychology of chasing by recording anecdotal experiences. All of the chasers have told her they are really lucky. But, according to Kate, this means they've made choices that allowed them to be in the right place at the right time.

To her dismay, it seems everywhere she goes on her eclipse-chasing book bonanza, she hears people saying things like *If I had lots of money I'd do this, too.* "But it's *so* not about money," she says. "I think people put restrictions on their lives. They perceive: I can't do this because I don't have the money. I can't do this because of *whatever* . . . But if you've got that passion, if you've made that choice, it will happen."

I think of how, at every stage of this phenomenal project, it has seemed impossible.

Yet, I am here. So is Kate. So is James.

"The real issue," Kate says, "is that people don't feel free. They feel they have to live according to this script that's there for everybody. And when they come across people who aren't living according to that script, they think: 'Oh that's exciting,' or 'That person's got lots of money.' But it's really just living in a different way . . . Ultimately, it's about freedom of choice, when you feel free to live your life. It's a decision you make."

"And you think eclipses can give people a greater sense of freedom?" I ask.

"Yeah," Kate says. "I think certain people are primed for it. They're curious about things."

Kate, like me, falls into the terribly ambiguous category of spiritual but not religious, and she finds eclipse viewing has a lot in common with mindfulness, a way of seeing the world that's based on Buddhist principles. It is a practice of living in the moment, allowing yourself to experience things as they occur. She says, "Rather than living in our minds, it allows us to live in our bodies."

"There's a therapeutic aspect to observation, especially when it comes to anxiety, don't you think?" I ask.

Kate has always enjoyed giving people perspective through counseling, and she thinks the eclipse has the potential to similarly change lives for the better. It's a connection she's never actually considered before. She says of eclipse evangelizing, midrevelation: "It's really important to me to help them gain perspective through experience instead of through talking about things!"

With eclipses—with direct experience of all dazzling natural phenomena—transformation happens without a mediator. It's therapy with no therapist. Religion with no leader. Spirit felt without the influence of a human hand. "Just let it happen! It's technically a shortcut!" Kate says. "The experience is the thing!"

. . .

The day before the eclipse, I join Australian astronomer Fred Watson and a handful of other professionals who are leading a tour group inland. Clouds have already begun to threaten views along the coast. Halfway to our viewing spot at Maitland Downs—a cattle station chosen by tour manager Marnie Ogg because of its characteristic dryness—we stop off at a coffee plantation.

Immediately, I start cruising name tags.

Back in Port Douglas, when I told Kate about my plans, she realized two of her friends—Chris and Miranda Pigott—were going to be in my small group. I was pleased until I remembered that Miranda had been cited as a weather jinx in Kate's book. I recounted the last line of the relevant chapter from memory: "[Chris] is anxiously awaiting to see whether Miranda is indeed a bad omen, as she will be accompanying him for the next total eclipse in November 2012."

When I brought it up, Kate laughed. "You'll find out too!"

I find Chris, a Scottish film producer, wearing a small gold chain and a spotless white shirt. Long gray hair splays at the nape of his neck like an Elizabethan collar. He has isolated himself from the group with a Sudoku puzzle. I introduce myself as a friend of Kate's. Chris has attempted to bear witness to five total eclipses, starting in 2001 with Madagascar, and he's seen more than half of them alongside Kate. Tenderly, I bring up the jinx. Chris turns to see where his wife, Miranda, is standing. Assured that she's safely out of hearing range, he says: "Miranda is still a little sore about that. Jolly bad luck," he says. The missed eclipse was in Shanghai, where clouds prevented catching even a glimpse. It was the only trip Miranda has accompanied him on, until now.

He turns in his seat to look around at the group, nearly everyone wearing matching tour shirts and snacking on precut squares of lemon cake. "Some people like collecting eclipses," Chris says. "It's like a badge. I thought I was nothing with six, but I've probably got more than all of these people. The more you've got, the bigger the swagger you have: *Well, I went to the Antarctic!* That sort of thing."

"Are you going to try to see the next one?" I ask, thinking of the upcoming eclipse over the Faroe Islands.

"Well, unless I'm dead," he says. "We might get northern lights and eclipse at the same time. That would be divine! Awesome is a word that is overrated, but that would be the correct usage. A T-shirt is not awesome. A song is not awesome. A volcano is awesome! An eclipse is awesome! Awesome means very powerful phenomena. It means something bigger than everything else! The night sky is awesome, but certainly a solar eclipse is awesome . . . We're lucky to live on this planet. None of the moons around Saturn ever eclipse."

He's also wowed by this: The phenomenon of an eclipse will not last forever. The moon's orbit increases roughly a centimeter per year. About one billion years from now, the moon will be smaller than the sun's disc and total solar eclipses will—as viewed from earth—no longer exist.

We're alive at just the right time to bear witness.

"I like the predictability very much," Chris says. "You know where they're going to be a hundred years ahead of time!"

"But what about the weather," I say. "That's not really predictable."

"Yeah," he says quietly, "I suppose it's not."

Miranda approaches, her arms covered with woven bracelets. "It's refreshing, really," she says. "We're not in control."

"I don't like not being in control," Chris says.

The jinx gives her husband a weary look and says, "No one can control the weather, dear."

· · ·

I soon realize that I have unintentionally arranged to spend the final hours of my great spiritual pilgrimage with an international collection of self-proclaimed, somewhat famous atheists. They include my British-born seatmate, David Malin, the astrophotographer who took the first color photographs of space.

He is in his seventies, but he's dressed like a schoolchild today, wearing shorts and a navy-and-white gingham shirt neatly tucked in. His thin white hair is covered by a floppy-rimmed sun hat. We settle in for a four-hour drive inland, and I explain what I'm doing in Australia, musing aloud about the interconnectivity of nature. He says, "I think the sense of wonder is what makes us human. When you're less than ten, you don't link things together. But as you get older, the complex linking of things into a whole can re-create your curiosity. If you get good at it, that's where wonder can be found."

This is, I realize, what has happened to me, each phenomenal experience compounding the wonder of the last. It is through patterns—complex and simple, big and small, personal and universal—that a sense of wonder has been revived deep within me. It is an awakened awareness of interconnected mysteries. And David thinks that sort of wonder can be relayed, to some degree, through scientific imagery. "Imagine," David says, "if every parent took their child on their knee and told them that they were made of stardust! They would never forget that."

David's photographs appear in galleries as well as observatories. He says, "I think art and science come from the same part of the mind. But art doesn't have the same framework. Artists are curious, like scientists, but they can be messy."

He shoots me an apologetic look.

Before David became an astrophotographer, he was a chemist. "You want to know something in chemistry, you boil it," he says. "You do experiments. In almost all science, you can do experiments. You can change conditions, add new ingredients. But with astronomy, all you can do is experience what the universe sends. You have to interpret it the best you can. There's information everywhere!"

Hearing this astronomer talk about *experiencing what the universe sends* is like listening to myself struggle with what to call the great mystery of being. When I ask him what he thinks about people using the term "universe" in a spiritual way, the way some people use the word God, he gives me an uh-oh-you're-one-of-those looks and says: "I think that's unfortunate."

I try to balance my woo-woo by quoting Einstein's bit about cosmic religious feeling.

David seems unmoved.

"I'm familiar with the quote," he says. "But I have no religious feeling."

For a long, silent minute, it seems that I've alienated my friendly, wonder-loving companion. But then David says, "I understand spiritual feeling. When I go into nature, when I'm standing before a great sunset, I get a lump in my throat. That's difficult to experience in a rational way of living. We always seek explanations to things. In the modern world, you do it seeking science. In the world before, you saw something in the sky, you evoked a reason for it. The Greeks evoked the movement of planets in the sky. It's reasonable to think that planetary movement affected our daily lives, because we invent things even though we don't understand. Rituals are a good example. They're bred into you. Yesterday, a lady came into a room where I was sitting and I stood up and shook her hand. It's a ritual. It's a nice ritual, but there's no good reason for it."

Well, there is a reason, albeit a symbolic one. Handshakes are thought to have originated as a gesture of peace. They were intended to give

those encountered the opportunity to feel—with his or her own hand—
that the newcomer was not carrying a weapon. It was intended as an
outward, phenomenal sign of an inward, intangible peaceful intent. It
still is.

Meeting David is—in terms of astrophotography—sort of like meeting the wizard behind the curtain. Among fellow scientists, he is known
as the man who colored the stars. "When light levels are very low, you
don't see color," he says. "If you live by the color of the moon, you live in
a gray universe."

It was through David's photographic techniques that mankind
gained access to the privilege of documenting purple and blood-colored
nebulas. These days, he spends most of his time taking photos of his
grandchildren with the small handheld camera he has packed for eclipse
morning. But he still has a special interest in the way we see the wind.
As in, the winds of an eclipse, shadow bands.

"They're very subtle," he says of the thin shadows visible on the
ground before and after an eclipse. "There's the theory that they exist,
but we need tangible evidence," he tells me. "They're hard to photograph well."

"But haven't you seen them?" I ask, remembering a speech he gave
earlier about watching shadow bands on beach sands. David is the only
expert astronomer onboard who has actually seen an eclipse. Even
Fred—touted by the news show *60 Minutes* as the lead astronomer in
Australia—has never witnessed one, though he's been giving television
and radio interviews about the eclipse all morning. I would be more
surprised by this if I hadn't already talked to lightning experts who
seemed indifferent about the Catatumbo and marine biologists who
don't know how it feels to swim among coral eggs.

David shrugs off his phenomenal experience with shadow bands,
saying, "That's anecdotal." He wants photographic proof.

The thin-lined trees blurring outside our windows grow denser as we move toward Maitland Downs. With each mile, we come across increasing numbers of cars and camper vans parked alongside the road. Soon, there is little space between vehicles. "Gosh," David says. "There are hundreds!"

But his mood dampens when he looks up, toward clouds that are forming to the east. "Oh, dear," he says of the coming weather. "It's something we can't predict. Science has no way to control it. You just have to pick a spot and see what happens."

Australian aboriginals were the world's first astronomers. At least, that's what one of guest speaker Ray Norris's colleagues suggested in an article. When the round-bellied astrophysicist read the claim, he was skeptical. He remembers thinking: *I'm going to look into this and disprove her in no time.*

We've gathered under a tarp-topped dining area surrounded by rows of canvas tents. "I had two objectives," he tells my dinner group, which includes Australian television personality Jennifer Byrne and her eighteen-year-old son, Connor. Ray says, "Were they really doing astronomy and how long had they been doing it? The culture is 50,000 years old . . . How far back does it go?"

The answer, years into Ray's research, is: *We really don't know.*

Ray is one of the main reasons I chose Fred's tour, intrigued by the way his work marries science and mythology, oral and literate knowledge. Ray says, "We can't date the stories. As far as I can tell, aboriginals could not predict eclipses, but they understood how they worked."

Most early accounts of aboriginal astronomy were written by Europeans. They are varied and often culturally insensitive accounts, but there's one in particular Ray likes to talk about. It's the story of Daisy Bates, an

Irishwoman who lived in the desert in the 1920s. She heard word of a coming eclipse and began to warn locals. She did not want them to be alarmed. But, when she told the Wirangu people working for her about the phenomenon, they were nonchalant. They told her that the eclipse was just a visible embracing of the Moon-man and the Sun-woman.

"But that's just creating deities," Connor says, raising his eyebrows.

"It's not just making up stories," Ray protests.

Take, for instance, myths explaining the association between the moon and the tides. Modern astronomers explain the connection by talking about abstract gravity. The Yolngu of Arnhem Land traditionally explain it through a narrative, sensory approach. When the tides are high, water rises through the sky to fill the moon. When the water runs out of the moon—leaving a dark sky—the tides are low. An emptying and refilling of the moon reflects the planet's waxing and waning.

"They've come up with the correct answer in their own cultural way," Ray says. "The story explains this in every important respect." This lunar connection to tidal movement was protested by Galileo. Ray says, "Someone suggested to him that the tides might have something to do with the moon and he said, 'Oh, no.' He got it wrong, but this story had it right!" Galileo, it seems, thought a connection between the moon and tides sounded too magical to be true.

Cilla, Ray's wife, scolds, "Ray, I think you're being rude to Galileo."

Ray shrugs. "If he'd just gone to the sea and looked, he would have realized it was right." The mechanics are different from modern understandings, but the observed connection is there. "I think this is what we call science," he says.

"But where do we draw the line between science and art?" Connor asks.

Ray shakes his head. It's a question he spends a lot of his life thinking about. His work with indigenous groups has made him think of story-telling a little differently than he used to. He's a skeptic, but he's become more open to the ideas of mythology and symbolism in recent years. He can see them unfurling all around him, even in the halls of academia.

"Okay," he says, "think about this: dark energy. We know the universe is accelerating, that there's a real object. But we have no idea what it is."

According to NASA, 70 percent of the universe is made up of dark energy. Dark matter makes up about 25 percent of the place. Everything ever observed, which is known as normal matter, adds up to less than 5 percent of the universe.

Ray says, "First we ask: Okay, what's doing this? So, in order to be able to talk about it, we give it a name, dark energy. The first thing you do is give it a label. It's like terra incognito!"

Dark energy is, in cosmological terms, the margins of the map.

"There are pictorial symbols and there are linguistic symbols," I say. "The words *dark energy* are symbols for the unknown. All words are just symbols."

"I agree," Ray says.

"But is this really science?" Jennifer asks of aboriginal astronomy.

"Yeah," says Connor. "Where's the proof?"

But it's not so much about proof as it is perspective.

"Okay," I say. "I'm going to bring up a dirty word."

This gets everyone's attention. Jennifer leans into her elbows. I turn to address Ray: "In order to be a scientist, don't you have to have faith that there's something out there to be discovered?"

Faith is, of course, the dirty word among this group.

They're unified in their tailspin. There are round-robin shouts of "No!" Jennifer throws up her hands. Ray shakes his head. I've committed a faux pas. I knew it was a risky question.

"It's curiosity, not faith!" Jennifer says.

"Yes, curiosity!" Ray shouts. "Faith is something altogether different."

"But don't you have to believe there's something to be curious about in order to move forward?" I ask.

I'm a little afraid these skeptics are going to see me as some sort of astrology-loving nut or religious fundamentalist. But I'm neither. I reside in the hinterlands of spiritual, but not religious, terra incognito.

Ray says, "I don't believe in anything. I have hypotheses."

In time, I let the conversation migrate. But, later, out of curiosity, I look up the actual definition of faith. It's hard not to laugh out loud when I read the entry on Dictionary.com.

The definition of faith: Belief that is not based on proof.

The sample sentence given: *He had faith that the hypothesis would be substantiated by fact.*

I have, over the past few years, begun to revere ambiguity and mystery nearly as much as I fear it. But it's not a popular view. "To form a culture like ours, a culture predicated on the avoidance of disarray," psychologist Kirk Schneider reasons, "we need to cultivate intricate defenses against mystery, and to acquire sophisticated strategies that enable us to skirt the complexities of being. Hence, much of our speech is geared not to acknowledge our humility before life, but our control, coordination, and management."

Writer Alain de Botton suggests that this worldview has led to a subsequent shift in what awes us. "For thousands of years," he writes, "it had been nature . . . that had a monopoly on awe. It had been the ice caps, the deserts, the volcanoes and the glaciers that had given us . . . a strangely pleasing feeling of humility." It is what philosophers of the eighteenth century referred to as the sublime. But its axis has shifted. He writes: "We were now deep in the era of the technological sublime, when awe could . . . be invoked not by forests or icebergs but by supercomputers, rockets and particle accelerators. We were now almost exclusively amazed by ourselves."

When Marnie announces that it's time for Ray's talk to begin, he nervously stands up. He doesn't much like speaking in front of crowds, and he's anxious about giving his talk without his standard PowerPoint presentation. His fears don't subside until it's pointed out that he'll be speaking directly under the actual constellations those photographs represent.

Around 3 a.m., I start to regret that I supported Chris when he said he'd stay up all night if it would ensure clear skies. Sleep is, to me, sacred. And our tents are too close to one another.

I have a cot. It came with a mint and a tiny pillow, but the tent reminds me of the ones I slept in as a teenager trekking across Australia. The desert air was so dry that breaking down camp always left me with bloody knuckles. One night, during that long-ago adventure, a pack of dingoes brushed up against my tent. Tonight, I would trade this cacophony of snorers for a lion pride.

I lie awake for the next few hours, listening to cars move down a nearby paved road searching for the right spot to witness the eclipse. With them, my mind races to last night, when I was standing in line for bush fare. I'd been chattering away to Jennifer about the effect of my great adventures on Archer, when she turned to me and said: "You're not doing it for him, you know, you're doing it for you. You're doing it to become a fully realized person. There is no guilt in that."

She's right, of course. When we follow curiosity, when we admit to faith in something greater than ourselves—whatever that might be—we are not closing doors for others, we're opening them. I've been fanning Archer's sense of wonder by giving oxygen to my own.

Jennifer was a foreign correspondent until Connor was eight. "I have no guilt," she told me. Her schedule changed when her husband revealed that he needed her to be around more. "It was his turn," she said, "and that was okay. It's give and take."

In her life, this meant career mobility for her husband, who other tour goers have breathlessly explained is an equally famous broadcaster in Australia. In mine, it means it will soon be time for a puppy, basketball goal, an upgrade to our basement home brewery.

From somewhere in the blue morning, a lone bird screams: *whohohe*.

I watch light creep on the horizon. There is an ochre-orange cloud on the line between land and earth. In the growing light, a whole river of stars presses against the horizon like an earthen dam. The camp generator begins to grind. I hear footsteps.

Cahoo, another, singular, bird sings.

The limbs of surrounding eucalyptus trees look like lace held against the coming light. I leave my canvas cocoon and wait with a growing number of campers clustered around a silver hot water dispenser. When I have my turn, I balance tea in a rattling porcelain cup and saucer and head up to the lookout area.

Behind me, a bus-horn-turned-bush-alarm-clock blares.

Jennifer and Connor are already on the hill, stationed in chairs. I join them, and we all leisurely put on our eclipse shades.

The entire coastline—visible beyond a distant range of hills—is covered in froth. But the sky in front of us is crystalline. Well, except for that impending dark, circular thing.

"Is that a cloud?" Jennifer asks.

"It's happening!" I scream.

The moon's advance is turning the sun—which has taken on a sherbet hue through our glasses—into an orange slice. This shape is obvious, expected, but there is no anticipating what it feels like to see a crescent sun. The sky—our understanding of day and night—has been turned inside out.

"It is just so bright! It is just so good!" Jennifer exclaims.

"Just wait till the diamond ring stage!" Connor says.

"Don't jump to the destination," Jennifer warns, never breaking her gaze. She shakes her head: "It just eats away."

It does look as if the entire sky—which is increasingly dark—is chomping at the sun with perfect teeth. Each minute, a little more of the morning light is devoured. It is clear why, in China, eclipses have traditionally been viewed as a dragon eating the sun.

"It's going to be very weird," Connor says.

"It already is!" I exclaim.

"I was told the birds would be quiet, and I expect them to be quiet. If they're not, I will complain!" Jennifer jokes. But the birds have already stopped their morning chattering. It's as if a gray satin sheet is being pulled over our shared cage.

Jennifer walks over to talk to Fred, who has set up a telescope, leaving Connor and me alone. The teenager is well-versed in eclipse mythology. He tells me that, historically, eclipses tended to wreak havoc. "Under every light soul there is a heart of darkness," he says. "But, in modern times, eclipses don't cause panic. They unite people. We're here for a common cause. Civil wars also unite people, but they have a destructive outcome. Uniting people can be very beneficial or very detrimental."

Together, he purports, we can make the light brighter, or turn the darkness darker.

"Eclipses could have brought out the worst in humans. When people believe they're going to die, that's when they reveal who they truly are. But there is hope in it, too. Some people are natural Machiavellis. Some don't choose to be benevolent and caring, but so many do. There is an ability to be destructive, but they chose to make a concerted effort to create the best in their own worlds and in other peoples'. The hope is that, even though it's there in every one of us, in most people, darkness is locked away."

Though he has an academic bent to his speech, a beyond-his-years intellectualism to his demeanor, he's thinking of taking a year off before heading to college. He says he'd really like to explore the philosophical balance of light and dark. But how will he do this outside of the academy? It's a path laid by the stories of his mother, former international correspondent, world wanderer.

"I think I'd like to travel," he tells me.

In the blue-lined journal I filled during my youthful adventures in Australia, I wrote: "So many of the things I've seen here seem unreal, like they're in a movie." This tendency to feel removed from the most splendid parts of what I'm experiencing is something I have battled—and observed in the comments of other travelers—again and again.

I think of this when Connor and I join Jennifer to take turns looking at the sun through Fred's filtered telescope. When I hover above the eyepiece, I can see what looks like a force field around the sun. When it's Connor's turn, he says, "It looks like it's alive!"

Fred interjects to let us know that what we're actually seeing is the atmosphere shimmering. But it appears, to our very eyes, that the sun itself is quivering like living coral. "It's seriously cool, anyway," Connor says. "It's like the eclipse: I've read about it, but it's just *surreal* when you're seeing it."

I know what he means. Surreal: *unbelievable, dreamlike, fantastical.*

It is a word I have used, in the face of wonder, over and over. Because, in Western culture, we tend to keep nature at arm's length. Nature is not only new life, it is decay. And to us mortals that is, well, scary. When we experience nature's greatest mysteries with our own senses—when we actually bear witness—we tend to say *It's like we're in a movie.*

When experiencing the messy emotions of awe and wonder, we retreat to the symbols we've been taught to trust. We see the documentary as more reliable than the real thing. The symbol more consistent than the scene. This reliance on controlled understanding tends to get in the way of wonder, by tricking us into thinking that life is something outside of what we are—at any moment—viscerally feeling. But films and charts and diagrams are only there as intermediaries. They are only storylines that might serve to show us where we actually need to be. Sure, we can sometimes fall prey to illusions, but most of the time, is there anything more real than what we are—with all our senses firing at full speed—actually experiencing?

Above us, the moon continues to chomp away. Connor adjusts his squared eclipse glasses, and says, "In most societies the sun is the service of life. The Incans and the Egyptians, they were all for the sun god. The Greeks had Helios."

There's a coolness to the air now. The breath of life is being taken away.

"It's just irresistible!" Jennifer exclaims, snapping a photo. "Look at all this color!"

I prop my eclipse glasses on my head to look around, careful to keep my eyes lowered. We have a 360-degree view of the horizon, and it is entirely filled with the varied shades of Australia's ochre. In the clouds, earth and sky are meeting to stoke a wildfire that seems to be burning brighter as the dome above us darkens.

Suddenly, a wind rushes toward us from the direction of the moon. It is strong and sudden, as if a planet-size blanket has just been unfurled to disturb the air. I pull my arms close in an attempt to warm myself against the eclipse-born breeze.

It looks like twilight now. The reds are muting to pink, and there are hints of the blue dawn returning. Behind me, someone shouts, "Keep an eye on the time!"

The irony of this, of course, is that clocks are just approximations of the sun's location. Standardized time is just a construct that was created to regulate the cycles of trains. High noon is different for every spot on earth. Totality is to occur here at 6:38 a.m. But there's no need to keep an eye on the time. *We are staring at its source.*

Below us, down toward the coast, clouds are gathering. They look like sea foam pushed against mountains by an unseen tide. There is barely a sliver of orange rind left in the sky when Fred shouts: "Shadow bands!"

I turn to look at a white sheet that's been hung from the roof of a four-wheel-drive vehicle to provide a canvas. And there they are, shadow bands, lines running horizontal to the horizon, dark, shimmering shadows surrounded by fainter ones. They look like heat rising from the hood of a hot car in summer, the wavy air that hovers over a raging barbecue.

Fred explains the bands as a rippling of the earth's atmosphere, visible turbulence. This is the latest in a string of theories that have arisen since shadow bands first appeared in the lines of ancient Norse poetry. Earlier theories suggested that the bands were a diffraction of the sun's rays around the moon. And there are still other ideas. Astrophysicist Stuart Eves thinks they might actually be the result of infrasound that's been—in the supersonic shadow of the moon—transformed into a visible shock wave.

This sounds too fantastical to be true, but it wouldn't surprise me. After all, nature has all sorts of players in its silent symphony. Throughout my journey, infrasound has reminded me that no matter how far I travel—like Mark Twain standing on the edge of Halema'uma'u—I can see only the tip of things. But, when I'm deeply witnessing, I'm able to sense more.

When I look around, I notice that the light has taken on a silvery quality. Even my own shadow has a soft edge, like I'm standing in the midst of a still-being-developed black-and-white silver gelatin photographic print.

"It's freezing!" I say, my shadow somehow a reminder of the morning's lost warmth.

A nearby astronomer explains, "The temperature is dropping faster than the light. Infrared still comes through at sunset. But here, the whole lot's been chopped off!"

Everything around us has dulled to gray. The sun above is only a sliver of color, fading fast. The left side of the moon overhangs, bleeding into darkness. And so it goes that I'm standing on a mountaintop—on the edge of light and dark, life and death—when the sun finally turns to a thin-lipped smile.

Just as it seems all light will be lost, an eclipse feature known as a diamond ring appears as a brilliant flash of light shining through a valley of the moon. I can see the features of its face, backlit and fine-featured as shadow art, craggy and cool. Also visible are bits of the sneezing sun, bright solar flares erupting and curving. It is absolutely spark-of-life dazzling. Then, it's not.

The moon slips into place with a visible *click*.

The light is suddenly and completely gone.

For reasons I cannot explain, I hold my breath. I can't see anything through my paper shades.

Instinctively, immediately, I take them off.

I am flinging myself on the mercy of the universe. I am fully exposed, totally and completely open to whatever is to come. We have reached the moment of totality, the only time when it is possible to see the sun with naked eyes.

Slowly, the plasma that has been hidden in the sun's harshest rays begins to push out from the center of the moon, like iridescent petals blooming in darkness. Before me, the corona cries out in streamers of light. The face of the sun is white as stars, lilies, snow. It expands until it is a ring of pure light pulsating in the sky. Its edges have the same twinkling as those pale fingers that play music in the solar winds.

I am part of a pin-point perfect cosmic alignment.

The mountaintop is as quiet as a forest in winter, and it appears to be covered in metallic ash. In the sun's sudden absence, time has stopped. I have a strange sensation of the ground disappearing beneath my feet. I am suspended in a sea of silver, ethereal light.

It's not unusual to hear people referring to a total eclipse as "The Eye of God." And it does look like an eye, the deep black of a pupil, the radiant lines that appear in an iris. It's as if the universe has taken me aloft, naked-eyed as I am, to stare into its soul.

Everything is silent and still. I can feel the heat of realization rising from my gut: Nothing is a given. Not the regularity of the sun rising and setting. Not even gravity. I am right side up. I am upside down. Without permission, my throat pushes out a guttural, not-quite-screaming sound.

My heart *thum-thum-thumps*, trying to escape the prison of my chest. I am not afraid. I am inconceivably alive. I am wholly present in this perfect moment. And this moment is all there is.

My eyes well with tears, born of something beyond my conscious mind. I release the pen I've been holding and press its barrel against a notebook. There is nothing to add. I unabashedly bask in the magnified glory of all my sensory gifts. I laugh. I cry. I am a madwoman in love with the universe.

I am also, of course, a mother. And a martyr. But not in the socially expected way. No, a while back I decided that if I was going to hear and talk about motherhood as martyrdom, I'd better look into it.

As it turns out, the word martyr comes from the Greek *martys*.

It means "to witness."

It was originally used in secular as well as religious spheres, in the way a notary public might be used today. Being a martyr, as the term was originally intended, did not require sacrificing one's life. It was the term for a professional-grade observer. Some martyrs were given golden crowns for their service as witnesses. This practice is thought to be a possible origin for the religious iconography of halos.

And I think it might be time to take the term back.

It has taken some serious legwork for me to recognize the personal fallout of living in a culture that values the data and images of the abstract theoretical over sensory, direct, visceral witnessing. This sort of symbolic thinking has led to many fine, life-bettering, life-sustaining inventions and discoveries that I wouldn't want to give up. It is, in fact, the sort of thinking that allows for the precise eclipse predictions that have brought me here. But it almost had me tricked into thinking that my sense of wonder could somehow survive without my fully alert, physical presence. That it could live—as if on life support—through gizmos and gadgets and nature videos on YouTube.

But it can't.

I have to be the on-site, expert witness of my own life.

Even so, I'm not necessarily very good when it comes to relaying what I've seen when put on the stand, questioned by friends and family. When I attempt to share this primal experience a few weeks from now, on request, I will bungle my words. Ultimately, I'll do an odd little hula-style dance that ends with me pushing my hands—fingers spread like rays—into the air. And when I get to that embodied moment of totality, when I get to the part where I see the face of the sun for the first time in my life, I will spontaneously make an *ahhhh* sound.

It will be operatic, the sound of revelation, the last syllable of alo*ha*. And, from this day forward, the white-gold glow of this eclipse's halo will be the image that arises in my mind whenever I hear someone singing: *Hallelujah*. Because to experience totality is to viscerally witness the grand privilege of being alive. To even attempt to experience it is to exhibit body and soul gratitude for the lucky opportunity that is life's light. And I can see how it could become addictive.

In Kate's book, when asked about what drives him to chase eclipses, James explains: "To witness for ourselves the splendor of the corona, that solar wind made manifest to our sense for those few moments . . . is like witnessing your own birth, the birth of our species, the birth of planets, the birth of physics and time, the birth of all that is knowable and unknowable. This is a powerful revelation of the true nature of the universe compacted into a few minutes that might otherwise take a lifetime of searching and study to realize."

Interestingly, my compacted minutes of revelation are being spent with people who *have* spent a lifetime studying the sky. Along with tens of thousands of other onlookers—transfixed, with possibly retina-burned eyes—we are channeling our attention to a white-gold ring in the sky. But—whereas I've gotten lost in the sensory magnitude of the experience—some of my companions appear to have kept a focus on known names and numbers.

"Venus!" David says, spontaneously appearing to my left as my dream-state meeting with the universe dissolves under his voice. He points to the morning star, which is vibrating like the head of a muffled drum. "Look at it!"

A woman's voice calls: "Thirty seconds!" Is this intended as a warning? A subconscious, failed attempt to slow down the oh-so-temporary phenomenon?

I, for one, am reveling in this rare privilege of witnessing beauty powerful enough to inspire entire armies to retreat from war. So, I'm startled when another, somewhat trembling voice behind me vocalizes something I didn't even realize I'd been struggling with somewhere deep within: "It's real!"

It's real.

The stories have come to pass.

It's all there. The sun. The moon. The alignment. It's not just an abstract theory. It's not an experiment, or a picture in a book, or the dangling of a Styrofoam solar system set. The universe is real. Totality is one of the realest things I have ever experienced. Today, the breath of life—the origin of solar winds, the whispers of the Greek god Helios, of all the sun gods and goddesses of cultures around the world—is a tangible, visible thing.

What I'm witnessing *seems* impossible. What I'm witnessing *feels* real.

The moon is a marble gliding through space. And it does glide—smoothly, serenely, and faster than I would have guessed. I don't just *know* this, I have *seen* this. I don't have to *imagine* where I am in the universe, I can *sense* it.

I am a voyager in the inconceivable grandeur of the cosmos. The sublime—greatness beyond measure, calculation, imitation—is immersive during an eclipse. And two minutes of treading in it is a very long time.

We fumble to get our glasses back on as another diamond ring appears, on the opposite side from the last, the moon's crater-pocked face once again revealed through streams of light, as brilliant as a carbon-pressed gem. Within seconds of this gasp-producing sight, the corona is gone, its ever-flowering glory masked by its own brilliance.

The group begins to clap. Life will go on. The cycle will continue. The moon's movements will pull the tides. The sun will continue to coax seeds to life, promising light to those willing to travel through the depth of soil's darkness.

We draw deep breaths of relief. Tears of joy mingle with those of sorrow, and not just on my own tear-tattooed face. It is frozen in a wild expression that Kate calls "awe face." Fred looks similarly stunned. I walk over to him. "What did you think of it?" I ask.

"It' s an astonishing event, really," he says. "The symmetry! Suddenly, the universe has a third dimension! It's a three-dimensional experience! It was a perfect eclipse, wasn't it? I was moved as a scientist. I find the whole thing about eclipses really special. We have this phenomenal, incredible coincidence."

"So, you were moved as a scientist," I say. "But what about personally, as a human? Do you really believe that was a coincidence?"

I'm sort of pressing him. Maybe it's because he's here with his son—an exceptionally tall child who once, in a storm, asked his father to make the lightning strike again, as if he had the power of clouds in his hands. Maybe it's because I want to know how it feels to become acquainted—for the very first time—with something you've been considered an expert on for all your adult life.

Finally, Fred lets down his guard. His arms, which have been crossed, fall to his sides like tree limbs loosened by strong wind. "I think the universe is telling us something, but I don't know what it is," he says. "I think it's the providence of science to try to figure it out."

I suppose this is, in the end, what it comes down to: Some people think it's the providence of science. Some, the providence of religion. Some don't think that there's anything to be unraveled. Some have faith that there is. There are also, of course, a few people who have never given a thought to this kind of thing in their lives. But who among us has not experienced fleeting, extraordinary glimpses of something that left us groping for rational explanations in the quicksand of all-encompassing wonder, muttering: *What are the chances?*

So, what *are* the chances for what we've just experienced?

Herein lies the eclipse's great kicker: *Its probability cannot be calculated.*

No one has the information necessary to figure out the chances of earth being privy to what we've just witnessed. Because no one knows how many universes there are. Subsequently, no one knows how many planets have suns. It is absolutely beyond our reach to calculate probability.

Still, because we come from a culture of control, we call it a coincidence. Because, in a mechanical way of looking at the world, mystery doesn't easily compute. We live according to a mythology based on predictions, data, statistics. And, when it comes to the probability of eclipses—which seem, on the surface, to be so very well understood—these metaphors melt down.

But, today, instead of cowering in the face of the unknown, we're celebrating it. The cattle station has erupted with the delicate clinking of circulated champagne glasses. Marnie is elated. Everyone around her is shouting, "Congratulations!" It's as if she is a wedding planner and we've just witnessed the bride and groom—the sun and moon—having their first dance.

She pulls a couple from the back of the crowd and calls for everyone's attention. The man is wearing a woolen hat and a shirt with unbuttoned pocket flaps. The woman is dressed nearly the same, the front of her pants covered in dirt. They are owners of the land on which we stand.

"Let's thank them for sharing this site with us," Marnie says, clapping.

The normally reserved group suddenly breaks into hoot-and-hollering applause. The couple looks embarrassed, too shy to speak. They lower their heads for a minute as the crowd showers them with gratitude. Maybe I'm just emotional from this whole bearing-witness-to-the-three-dimensional-universe thing—or maybe it's some lingering effect of those anecdotal shadow bands' unproven infrasound—but I start to tear up at the sight of them.

These ranchers spend their days running gold prospectors off this property. For generations, they have resisted the extraction of material wealth to hold this land together. When Marnie called and asked permission to camp here, they could have said no. They could have chased us away from this precious landscape to which they hold the deed.

Totality will not be visible from this place for more than three hundred years, and they had the legal right to keep its precious diamond ring for themselves. But they didn't. When asked to share their wealth of wonder, they unlocked privacy gates to let us in.

We loiter on the brush-cleared cow paddock for a long time after the cosmic event, as if we're theatergoers in a reception recounting the show.

"Thanks for inviting me," Connor says, embracing his mother.

"Thanks for coming," she says.

When Ray and Cilla wander over, Jennifer tells them, "You know, it doesn't really matter if we find all the answers."

"It matters to me," Ray says.

Jennifer shrugs. "I just like to marvel."

She casually runs a hand through her hair. Unwashed, it stands on end. But she's glamorous without a stitch of makeup, even though her spunky straw touring hat has been left in her tent. She surveys the group and says, "I love being around people who are looking into this kind of stuff. They don't talk about crap."

"Well, we do talk about crap."

"But it's interesting crap."

This seems, to Ray, an invitation to broach aboriginal astronomy again. But Jennifer—maybe concerned that, in the face of all this wonder she's gone soft on rationality and reason—says: "I still don't believe in *pyramid power.*"

This mention of pyramids sparks Connor's imagination, which reaches around the world to Mexico's Teotihuacan, home of the pyramid of the sun and the moon, birthplace of the Aztec god Quetzalcoatl. The feathered serpent was traditionally considered organizer of the cosmos, a creator and a destroyer. He was son of a virgin goddess. Bringer of culture. Patron of both arts and science. God not just of Venus, but also dawn and wind. Quetzalcoatl, symbol of death and resurrection, was—as the story goes—among those who ensured a return of light after a tiger-like paw plunged earth into darkness by abruptly knocking the sun from the sky.

Connor says, "I suppose those guys at Teotihuacan weren't that different from us."

Ray smiles. "They were doing science in their own terms. They conceived of a harmony we don't see now."

But maybe we could.

According to the late anthropologist Loren Eiseley, "Man was a reader before he became a writer, a reader of what Coleridge once called the mighty alphabet of the universe. There is an instruction hidden in the storm or dancing in auroral fires. The future can be invoked by the pictures impressed on a cave wall or in the cracks interpreted by a shaman on the incinerated shoulder blade of a hare. The very flight of birds is a writing waiting to be read. Thoreau strove for its interpretation on his pond, as Darwin, in his way, sought equally to read the messages written in the beaks of Galapagos finches. But the messages, like all the messages in the universe, are elusive."

Still, we hunger for them. We bear witness to what the universe brings. And our interpretations of its messages become our mythologies.

Eggs sizzle under the camp's mess tent. I take up residence in a folding chair across from Ray, who has told me that, among the Yolngu, the moon is often referred to as Ngalindi, or Moon-man, a characteristically fat and lazy character. As we break bread, Ray recalls a trip he took a few years back to Arnhem Land to view a lunar eclipse. While he was there, a group of children came upon him strolling a red-dirt road. To his delight, they began to shout: "Ngalindi! Ngalindi!"

He thought to himself: *Fantastic that they are so excited about astronomy!*

"But then," he says, "I realized they were pointing at *me*!"

Some people might take offense at being taunted this way, but Ray laughs joyfully when he tells the story. It serves as proof that the astronomical stories of the Yolngu are thriving. They are being passed on not just to curious visitors, but to children who will develop their worldview with these stories as part of them.

Not long after he became known as the Moon-man, Ray was holding a lecture for local elementary students when he noticed a little girl in the back of the group shifting in her chair. Ray flops around and rolls his eyes, mimicking her actions. He recalls: "I was saying the sun is just a star."

Finally, the girl spoke up: "It is *not* a star. It's huge! You have no idea what you're talking about!"

Patiently, he told her, "If the sun was a long way away, it would look like any other star. But it's really close so it looks much bigger."

For the rest of the lecture, she was on the edge of her seat, actually gripping her chair. She had grown up with mythology. Her community was functioning as a hunter-gatherer society. Its nature-based stories were remembered because they were still used as paths of survival. She knew the stars as her ancestors, and she was connected to the sky as my Hawaiian friends are connected to the earth by Pele-reinforced *pikos*.

Now, standing before her, was a Moon-man who—despite his own skepticism—valued the mythology of her culture. And he was asking her to value his abstract, scientific ideas. He was encouraging her to trust his word until she could go far enough to discover, for herself, value in what he was saying.

In that moment, in her young mind, she began to reconcile the rational with the visceral. The practical with the spiritual. She began to embody the sort of harmony we've just witnessed via a three-dimensional universe. She understood that his slide images were just symbols, stand-ins for the mysterious, immeasurable cosmos. Through them, she'd learned that the sun was important because of earth's perspective. That the cosmos were grander than she could even dream. And, by extension, so was she.

Because if the sun was a star, it didn't have to be *just* a star. It could also be—as traditional stories relay—a woman shaking ornamental ochre from her skin to color the clouds. This new perspective didn't make the sun smaller, it only served to make the universe bigger. It was suddenly full of sun sisters—brighter, wiser ancestors of unknowable numbers.

Ray revels in the memory. "I love teaching. There's nothing like it. You get the conversion experience."

The conversion he's talking about has nothing to do with science or religion. It exists outside of dogma and rules and culture, and—depending on how it's delivered—even language itself. It is the transformation from cynicism to wonder. Ray—as someone tenuously straddling the line between mythology and science—had offered that little girl an abstract idea as a way of expanding, not belittling, her direct experience.

She was—in that very moment—starting a new, personal relationship to mystery. The not knowing. The joy of seeking. Because wonder isn't about finding answers; it's about becoming more comfortable with questions.

Though we live in the information age, I've come to believe that it's how we deal with mystery—as cultures, institutions, and individuals—that ultimately dictates how we live out our lives. We are animals with the capacity for abstract thought, but we are still animals. So, we continually grope for ways to make the mystery real. Phenomenal. Directly observable through our senses.

In the face of natural phenomena, we sometimes let them speak. But when it comes time to share knowledge, we cannot explore complex abstractions without using metaphors from the phenomenal world. So, with limited language and rituals, we mix them to get at what we mean. We mash them. We fight over and about them. And the symbolic stories we trust and the way we tell them guide our hands as they shape the earth; as we are shaped by it.

Kate has found that witnessing an eclipse tends to inspire a sense of connectivity to "the universe, God, or nature." To me, Universe, God, and Nature are all words that can stand in as symbols for the same thing: *Mystery.* And to experience an eclipse—or any of the phenomena I have explored—is to be granted an audience with it.

"Awe," Schneider writes, "is our relationship to mystery."

And it is something we each have to recognize and reclaim for ourselves.

Emotions of awe and wonder have been found to make people less impatient, less materialistic, more willing to help others, and more satisfied with life. They are feelings most often and most strongly born of direct, phenomenal experience. But they can also be inspired by story, ritual, image, metaphor, or meaningful coincidence. Sometimes, they're found in all, simultaneously.

Take, for instance, my morning.

I've been viscerally dazzled by the greatest phenomenon known to man. And the overwhelming awe of that experience has been compounded by the synchronicity of this: *I just stared directly into The Eye of God with a bunch of atheists.*

So what, pray tell, do I make of all this?

It's a question recently posed to me by a friend who was present at Archer's birth. She asked if I'd come to any conclusions about life's larger questions as I wound down my travels. I didn't know how to answer. I couldn't gather my thoughts well enough to say that I have had a personal metamorphosis since I saw those swirling monarchs in Mexico. That I have died and been resurrected in the light of lightning and lava since she saw me through labor. That I, someone nervous even to hear someone utter the word God, have been transformed by wind and wildebeest into the sort of person who brings up faith in conversation with atheists.

But if I were to run into her today, I would offer this: There is no conclusion. There never will be. Because I have faith in ever-living mystery. Because I believe in the power of stories. Because I have felt, with my eyes and ears and hands, the inspired words of storyteller Brian Andreas: *The sound of what cannot be seen sings within everything that can.*

I have begun to better trust my senses and intuition, my many ways of knowing. Nature's ongoing creation song affects me in ways my intellect cannot fully conceive, and it connects us all on a scale too large to imagine. But, even so, clues to its grandeur are everywhere—in the formation of fast-moving clouds, the weaving of a migratory bird's nest. Awe-inspiring phenomena have been swirling around me all my life—antidotes to anxiety and other ills—but I've only just discovered how to fully drink them in.

Ray pushes a yellow, yolk-smeared plate to the center of the table. Then, the Moon-man tells me that he still thinks about that little Sunstar girl sometimes. He says, when he looked at her that day, he thought to himself: *Now, there's a kid who's seen the light.*

As soon as I get home from Australia, I take Archer on my knee to tell him that he is made of stardust. He immediately lifts his shirt to stare at his stomach. He instinctively puts a finger to his navel. Overwhelmed with the good—if somewhat abstract—news that the glory of the night sky is also within him, he proceeds to spread the word.

It isn't long before Archer and his best friend are regularly taunting: "You're stardust!"

"No, you are!"

Given this, I shouldn't be surprised when he strips to his underwear—in preparation for a bath—and slaps his stomach, shouting with open lungs: "I'm stardust!"

He pauses and points toward me.

"Yep," I say, "I'm stardust, too. So is Daddy. Everything on earth . . ."

He shakes his head. He's heard all this before. "No, look!" he says, waving his index finger at something behind me. I turn to see the small window above the bathtub. "It's dark!" he exclaims. "Let's go see the stars!"

It's taken twenty minutes of wrangling to get him to this stage of our nightly ritual. And that's not counting the extended family hug that commenced when bath time was announced—six arms intertwined, tight as vines, until Matt set Archer down and guided him into the bathroom, hand on back.

Now, bedtime is closing in.

Had I never seen a volcano dance, if I'd not just stared into The Eye of God, I would protest Archer's inconvenient request. But even here in the trenches of day-to-day life, especially here, I have to be willing to act as a vigilant witness. Because—though I'm confident my traveling days are not done—I've honed a sense of wonder that will thrive wherever I am, as long as I exercise it.

And Archer is showing me how.

I'm moved that all this stardust talk has reminded him that he is connected to a world beyond these walls, over this roof. Is this not what personal stories of monarchs and lightning and solar winds have done—and will continue to do—for me? Is Archer's inspiration not part of their legacy?

"Where are my clothes?" he says, searching the tiled bathroom floor.

I want to encourage this outdoor expedition, but I also want him to get to sleep at a decent hour. So, I run into the living room and grab a velveteen blanket. I wrap it around his shoulders.

"Where are my shoes?" he says, worried.

Dramatically, I scoop him off his bare feet and into my arms. He is getting big. His skinny legs dangle all the way down to my knees. I will not be able to carry him for much longer. But tonight I heave him upward with all of my strength, so that I'm cradling him like a baby. I cocoon him until only his face is exposed. He is giggling.

Outside, the air is dry, freezing. The moon is only a memory, hidden in our shadow. But the sky is full of stars, silver glitter spilled on a charcoal slate.

I point out the Big Dipper. Then I go quiet, instructing Archer to pay attention, but not to me. Phenomena are, in this very moment, all around us, speaking. Above, the stars flicker. Below, the river rises and falls like the soft vulnerable flesh of our chests.

The back door of the house is slightly ajar. I turn my gaze from the heavens to study my son in the honeyed light that's leaking from the doorway. His eyes are focused upward, growing wider. He wiggles his arms out of the blanket and throws them around my neck. Then—in the presence of this shimmering, living night—he leans in to whisper, with reverence, "We're stardust." And the radiance of his awestruck face is something truly magnificent to behold.

ACKNOWLEDGMENTS

My parents, Randall and Carolyn Henion, empower me by being involved, yarn-spinning grandparents—a practice influenced by the memory of mine: Daynese, Herman, Lois, and Richard. This book belongs to them, as it belongs to Matt and Archer, my partners in everyday adventure.

To me, taking three children under the age of four grocery shopping is more intimidating than swimming with sharks, but Cassie Koerber-Pennington has done it with ease. Archer's seat in her cart has given me writing time, and Landon, Maya, and Everett Pennington have made my entire family feel part of their own. I'm also thankful for the Hrenaks.

Sunny Townes Stewart read this manuscript before anyone else, as she has much of my writing over the years. She claims to have a poor sense of direction, but she's never led me astray. The same goes for Aaron Beck-Schachter, who challenges my worldview and unfailingly walks beside me. David Rowell, my editor at *The Washington Post Magazine*, has become a trusted friend and mentor over the years. The first two chapters of this book began as articles under his guidance at the *Post*, and they were all improved by his generous suggestions, off the clock.

When my agent, Molly Friedrich—a flesh-and-bone woman with the creative power of Pele—first heard my far-reaching book idea, she didn't make any promises. But I knew my life was about to change. And, well, this is the story of what happened next! Thanks to Lucy Carson, Molly Schulman, Nichole LeFebvre, and Maggie Riggs for making me feel so well taken care of by the Friedrich Agency, personally and professionally.

When Ann Godoff acquired this project, she gave me a piece of field advice: *Pay attention*. She seemed to know, even before I did, what this book was really about. I will always be thankful she had the instinct to invest in me. At The Penguin Press, I appreciate the work of Lindsay Whalen, Ginny Smith Younce, Ben Platt, Sofia Ergas Groopman, and everyone else who touched this project.

For years, I've enthusiastically cornered friends at grocery stores and toddler parties to talk phenomena. Some people—I'm looking at you, Andy Miller, John and Erin Peters, Kathy Henson, Jamie Goodman, Rebecca Gummere, Betsy Carr, Natalie Cooper—were targeted more hardily than others. But many patient friends have helped this project along—too many to mention—and that's not counting the poor souls trapped with me on airplanes as I tried to make sense of it all. I remain appreciative of their saintly willingness to listen and offer wisdom.

My sage confidante Bethany Jewell advised against packing jeans for the jungle. Many professionals supported her suggestion: Jo Salamon at Arc'teryx; Lee Weinstein and Deborah Pleva at ICEBREAKER; Dave Simpson at Outdoor Research; Dave Campbell and Jess Clayton at Patagonia; Deanna Rakowsky at The North Face. Without them, I would have been soaked, melted, and frozen in turn.

Paula Franklin at &Beyond gave me indispensable help with the Tanzanian leg of my journey, and the staff of Hotel Arctic Eden went out of their way to be helpful when I was in Sweden, as did Johanna Sandström of Abisko Turiststation. I'm indebted to Judy Marshall and Michael Healy at Quicksilver,

Maryanne Jacques at Adventure North, and Willie Gordon and Judy Bennett at Guurrbi for their assistance in Australia. The Big Island Visitors Bureau, Jessica Ferracane, Catherine Tarleton, Noreen Kam, and Roger Dubin, helped me find my way in Hawai'i.

This project was supported by the North Carolina Arts Council, a division of the Department of Cultural Resources, with funding from the National Endowment for the Arts, in the form of an Artist Fellowship. The Watauga, Avery, and Ashe County Arts Councils also assisted. I'm grateful to magazine editors Elizabeth Hudson and Mike Graff for offering freelance flexibility during the writing of this book, and to my old friend Wiley Cash for encouragement and advice.

My colleagues at Appalachian State University have been exceptionally supportive. A special nod to the incomparable Betty Conway—who has the ability to stave off wolves, four-legged and metaphorical—as well as Joseph Bathanti, Sandra Ballard, Tony Calamai, Mike Mayfield, David Huntley, and Dave Haney. Also, my students, who inspire and accept me, year after year, for the wildly animated speaker I am. My teaching style is, as a pupil once pointed out, a form of interpretive dance. I will no longer play this down.

I'm grateful to my own teachers—formal and otherwise—who have emboldened me over the years, especially Dean Hedley, Larry White, Heidi Kelly, John Wood, Neal Menschel, Kate Philbrick, Donna Galluzzo, Judith Bevan, and Crystal Kelly. I also appreciate the influence of everyone I studied under and with at the University of North Carolina at Asheville, Queens University of Charlotte, and the Salt Institute for Documentary Studies.

Serengeti scholar Tom Morrison gave me an understanding of what it's like to research elusive wildebeest, and Anton Seimon, Kenneth Pickering, and Rachel Albrecht were particularly helpful when it came to probing the Catatumbo lightning. I've taken great pains to relay research that was current during my time on the ground with each phenomenon. But the story of science is ever evolving.

I'll refrain from repeating the names of everyone in these pages, but I would like to acknowledge their generosity of story and spirit. Over the past few years, I have witnessed some of the most awe-inspiring natural phenomena on earth. But it was the individuals encountered who ultimately made the journey meaningful.

And then, there is you, dear reader. Countless people took a chance on me based on the promise that, someday, you would hold this book. I lift a hand to my heart and offer you all, loud as a lion's roar: *Gracias. Mahalo. Tack. Giitu. Asante. Thank you.*